Press,
Party, and
Presidency

Press,
Party, and
Presidency

Richard L. Rubin

SWARTHMORE COLLEGE

W · W · Norton & Company

New York   London

Copyright © 1981 by W. W. Norton & Company, Inc.

Published simultaneously in Canada
by George J. McLeod Limited, Toronto.
Printed in the United States of America
ALL RIGHTS RESERVED
FIRST EDITION

Library of Congress Cataloging in Publication Data

Rubin, Richard L.
  Press, party, and presidency.
  Includes index.
  1. United States—Politics and government—
1945–   2. Press and politics—United States.
3. Presidents—United States—Election. I. Title.
E839.5.R82 1981   320.973   81-14108
ISBN 0-393-01497-5   AACR2
ISBN 0-393-95206-1 (pbk.)

W. W. Norton & Company, Inc. 500 Fifth Avenue, New York, N.Y. 10110
W. W. Norton & Company Ltd. 37 Great Russell Square, London WC1B 3NU

1 2 3 4 5 6 7 8 9 0

To the memory of my mother and father

Contents

Preface

How have major changes in mass communications affected the American electoral system, and how have such changes affected, in turn, presidential leadership? Seeking answers to these questions is the motivating force that propels this book.

To get at such questions requires not only an examination of crucial electoral institutions such as the presidency and the political parties, but a sense of perspective about change itself. How can we know how serious the influence of recent changes in mass communications may be on our electoral institutions if we do not know what the effects of earlier changes in mass communications were on the very same institutions? How can we distinguish the temporary political effects of the mass media from the durable ones, the short-run responses of particular candidates and issues from the long-term changes in the political system itself, if we have no benchmarks by which to judge? This book hopes to provide that very perspective by analyzing the changing relationship of mass communication to the political parties and the presidency through crucial historic periods from the country's beginnings to the present.

Above all this book is about elections, mass communications, and the key institutions—the press, the parties, and the presidency—that shape, structure, and translate political information in our political system. One central theme that is followed throughout the book is how changes in the velocity, range, and depth of penetration of mass communications have affected presidential leadership, the political parties, and the structure and content of politics itself.

In looking back over the last three years of effort culminating in this book I fully realize the debts I have to others.

Special recognition must be given to two former students and colleagues of mine, Steven Howard and Douglas Rivers, who helped me develop the research and the critical arguments for this manuscript. Their help and enthusiasm is deeply appreciated. On the technical end thanks is also due to Dan Traister for editorial assistance and to Pauline Chapman for typing and retyping the manuscript.

Other scholars and friends have helped improve this manuscript at various stages of its development. The criticism of Richard Pious of Columbia University aided me significantly in sharpening the analytic focus of the book. My colleagues at Swarthmore College, Charles Gilbert, Roland Pennock, David Smith, and James Kurth, Stephen Hess of the Brookings Institution and Lee Benson of the University of Pennsylvania, all offered constructive criticism involving various parts of the book.

Thanks is due also to Everett C. Ladd, Jr., University of Connecticut, who served as reader for the original manuscript. His counsel and encouragement are deeply appreciated. Thanks are also due to Richard Neustadt of the Kennedy School of Government, Harvard University, for his helpful suggestions. Finally, the efforts of Donald Lamm of W. W. Norton should be acknowledged for his help in revising the original manuscript and in making the arguments clearer and the book more cohesive and readable than it might otherwise be. To all who helped, my thanks are offered, though I accept, of course, responsibility for the ultimate substance and form of the book.

Swarthmore, Pennsylvania
February 1981

1

Introduction

Sweeping changes in the nature of presidential elections, together with the heightened difficulties of exercising presidential leadership, have markedly affected the political life expectancy of the contemporary chief executive. Besides the increasingly intractable economic, social, and foreign problems, thirty-five state presidential primaries, as well as an intense general election battle, currently confront incumbent presidents who seek reelection—as well as those aspiring challengers who seek to take the job away. The extraordinary increase in electoral activity, now involving more than a full year of intense presidential campaigning before a final decision is made, is at least partly responsible for the fact that three of our last four presidents have been denied renomination or reelection.

Overall, challenges to presidential tenure from one source or another have increased, and one-term presidencies, with accompanying instabilities resulting from frequent turnover and shifting public policies, have also become increasingly characteristic of contemporary American politics. A central theme of this book is that the present state of the presidency is directly linked to major changes in both the mass media and the political parties, and that knowledge about the interrelationship of these institutions with the presidency is crucial to understanding politics as a whole.

Almost all observers and practicing politicians who have

assessed the new configurations of power in American politics assign a prominent position to the press. They frequently charge that the press "makes" or "breaks" presidents or presidential hopefuls. The actual effects of the print and electronic "press" on American politics are, however, difficult to assess, and cannot be explained by looking only at a snapshot of contemporary American politics. A genuine understanding of the interrelationship between mass communications and electoral institutions requires a historical dimension, one that will help us define what changes have actually occurred, how durable they are likely to be, and how they are likely to affect the political system in the future. An analysis focusing specifically on the changing relationships of mass communication institutions to political parties and the presidency—through critical historic periods—becomes the means toward that end.

What do we mean by the press and how shall we examine it? As used here the term "the press" includes managers, editors, and reporters who are personnel of the print media and comparable television and radio organizations: in short, all who shape and transmit our political news through mass channels. Many specific journalists were—and are—colorful and important political personages in their own right, holding vastly differing opinions, approaches, and values; but the particular concern of this book is not with individuals but with a free and privately owned press that is a major institution of political influence.

Although the changing structure and range of political conflict can be best understood by examining institutional interrelationships between the press, the parties, and the presidency over time, this book is not a chronological history of any of these institutions alone. It is, rather, a study of critical changes in the relationships of key American political institutions in different mass communications contexts. Within each stage, changes by one or another of these institutions has affected the relative strength and impact of the others—each institution being partly autonomous of and partly dependent on the others—and, as a result, altered the nature, style, and content of American politics.

These stages in the relationship between political and communications institutions begin with the press's initial economic instability during the nation's first half century and its consequent dependence on the political parties and the president for both economic subsidy and political direction. The growth of the first mass communications "networks," newspapers tied to and actually sponsored by the national government and the political parties in the early decades of the nation, is traced, and an evaluation is made of the impact of a press, then lacking financial and political autonomy, on the development of rudimentary American political institutions. Particular attention is given to the joint role of early party leaders and their newspapers in changing the style of American politics, first, by undermining the deferential attitudes of the people that prompted the selection of high status individuals as political leaders; and, second, by reinforcing party efforts to base American politics on numbers rather than status.

In the next stage, the rapid development of the telegraph, the press's growing market orientation, and the growth of newspapers' financial and political autonomy all gradually separated the press from the partisan political ties characteristic of the politics-dominated first period. The extraordinary expansion of newspaper circulation and advertising revenues in just over three decades following the Civil War effectively broke the press's organizational links to party institutions and established a new relationship between mass media and electoral institutions. The impact of the growing commercial strength of the press on its relationship to political reform movements—populism, progressivism, and the New Deal—is then examined and an assessment is made of an independent press's ability, in the pretelevision era, to influence the agenda of American politics.

The great range and power of television journalism, together with other technological and social forces, significantly changed the balance between the press, the party, and the presidency, ushering in the contemporary stage of relationships between mass communications and electoral institutions. These new relationships make a decisive though not complete break with earlier stages. The contemporary stage is marked by the electorate's increased demand for political information and an increasingly rapid increase in the penetration of political journalism into the electoral system as a whole. The influence of mass media journalism during this stage has, among other things, accelerated the decline in the power of the political party, deepened significantly the political separation of the president from his party's organizational apparatus, and simultaneously elevated and weakened the presidency.

An important concept guiding the analysis that follows is *electoral circuitry,* a metaphor that suggests a new way of thinking about mass communications and electoral institutions. This metaphor directs our attention to the interaction between the velocity, range, and penetration of mass information transmitted by the press, on the one hand, and those specific electoral institutions that respond to, structure, and translate that political information, on the other. The press, as the prime instrument of mass communications, conducts the downward flow of political information from political leaders and institutions to the mass of voters. But the press also plays an important role in the upward flow of messages sent from the people to the political leadership, particularly during elections. The channels of mass communications are thus intimately linked to electoral institutions, such as the presidency and the political parties.

The responsiveness (or lack of responsiveness) of these electoral institutions plays a critical role in determining the velocity of the flow of mass communications through the system as a whole. In certain periods messages flow from voters to institutional leaders and back very quickly, while at other times these messages travel slowly or, perhaps, not at all. What will become clear during the course of this discussion is that *the very structures of key electoral institutions both respond to and are transformed by the intensity and velocity of mass communications.* As a result, the changes in the circuitry—the interplay among political leadership institutions, the means of mass communications, and the mass public—profoundly shape American politics.

Until recently, few political scientists have demonstrated any continuing interest in mass media effects. We have tended to accept the preliminary findings of early studies that the mass media primarily "reinforce" existing attitudes rather than change them. This acceptance permitted most of us to put the question of mass media effects comfortably on the back burner, where it remained until a growing body of contrary findings, largely from outside the field, precipitated new interest. The subsequent analysis will, in fact, incorporate an assessment of these recent studies, indicating both readily identifiable and more varied mass media effects on individual perceptions of issues and specific voting responses, i.e., "micro-effects." But the crucial thrust of the research that follows focuses primarily on media effects on key political institutions, i.e., the "macro-effects" of changes in mass communications. This investigation seeks to define with some precision the dimensions of the influence of the press by examining the impact of substantive changes in mass communications on crucial electoral institutions and the impact of institutional changes, in turn, on the public's political awareness and ultimate choices.

Some political analysts find both the tremendous increase in the reach of the press and its increasingly competitive relationship to other institutions vital to American democracy. The enormous growth in the power of the presidency, some say, requires a countervailing opposition force to keep a president from controlling politics for his own purposes. The Watergate-related crimes of Richard Nixon's administration, for example, are instances of important misdeeds revealed not by partisan or governmental efforts but by vigorous independent political journalism. Certainly, in this case, the press served democracy well as a counterweight against undemocratic attempts to control politics.

These kinds of benefits, derived from power checking

power, have long been lauded, most notably in the Federalist Papers' praise of the political stability derived from numerous fragmented, competing, and decentralized forces in American politics. But the founders planned for a society characterized by a slow-moving, conserving tendency toward equilibrium—a relative stability—produced by numerous small pockets of power. What has, in fact, developed, instead, are extraordinary large-scale institutions—the presidency, the parties, and the press—whose size, organized power, and mode of interaction in no way conform to the 18th-century political model used by the Founding Fathers.

Where have the tremendous changes in the size and in the relationship of these institutions left us? Do we really have a rough political balance on a new scale, and, if so, what kind is it and what price have we paid for it? What is the cost to an electoral system when, for example, the centralizing thrust of the mass media increases enormously, but the party, the traditional tool for organizing and structuring political interests, remains largely decentralized and unable to function adequately? What, for example, has been the press's role in the rapid development of a major electoral system of presidential primaries, and how do these new crucial "preliminaries" affect the electoral circuitry as a whole? Finally, how will the combination of growing influence of the press and diminishing influence of the political parties affect the nature of presidential leadership and the ultimate product of the American electoral system?

These, then, are only some of the questions this book addresses, seeking a glimpse of our political future by 'a better understanding of the structuring of political conflict in our past and present. We need to know more about the impact of an enlarged and increasingly centralized political information process on our electoral institutions from a systematic perspective, and to know how and why such changes in the electoral circuitry have affected American politics as a whole.

2

The Dependent Partnership

Any attempt to understand the developing relationship of the press, the party, and the presidency during the course of American political history requires a hard reassessment of the myth that, from its birth, the press was truly "independent." Clearly the press was meant to be "free," and its protection by the Bill of Rights was unique for an institution both private and profit making. However, *freedom of the press* was—as it still remains—a matter of *legal right*. *Independence*—the practical and operational capability of the press to withstand external control—is something else.

Genuine independence for an institution depends, at least in part, on financial and economic security. A newspaper, for instance, must be able to withstand any customer's withdrawal of advertising. The resources to withstand external pressure—either economic or (in some cases) political—remain the essential ingredient for genuine press independence. Institutional independence, then, is a function of economic security, while freedom of the press is a matter of political and legal right.

But the resources of early American newspapers were very limited, since their economic base was extremely narrow in the first decades of the nation's existence. Costs for printing materials—most particularly, for paper—were high, and only a few cities (such as Philadelphia, Boston, New York, and Baltimore) had populations sufficiently numerous and prosperous to support more than a single weekly. Papers could not be sold economically by the copy but only by annual subscription. At an average price of eight dollars for a yearly subscription to a daily paper and three dollars for a weekly newspaper, only people with strong commercial interests or members of the advantaged classes could regularly afford to buy their own newspapers. While the demand for news was great, the number of copies that could be *sold* (compared to those actually read, but at second or third hand) was small. That a yearly subscription of over a thousand newspapers was considered a solid circulation achievement is one indication of the problems of developing prepaid circulation at the close of the 18th century.[1]

The most significant factors in the development of the early American press were, first, its rapid transition from a primarily commercial press to a heavily political press; and, second, the chronic financial weakness of the expanding number of political papers. Those newspapers that grew rapidly at the turn of the 18th century were edited by individuals who, unlike pre-Revolutionary printers, were concerned primarily with politics rather than commerce. Stimulated to publish by provocative political decision-makers rather than by primarily trade or commercial concerns, these editors and their new papers appealed increasingly to audiences both wider and more politically oriented than the audiences of the trade papers. In 1800, daily newspapers amounted to only about 10 percent of all papers, and approximately 80 percent of these dailies were primarily commercial. But by 1810, only 50 percent of the daily newspapers were trade-oriented journals, the rest political.[2]

Commercial journals reported the arrival and departure of ships, the availability of merchandise, and other news that affected business. A relatively small amount of political argument appeared in occasional articles and editorials,

[1] Frank Luther Mott, *American Journalism: A History, 1690–1960*, 3rd ed. (New York: Macmillan, 1962), p. 159.

[2] Alfred McClung Lee, *The Daily Newspaper in America: The Evolution of a Social Instrument* (New York: Macmillan, 1937), p. 59.

their content inevitably related to commerce. However, the developing "new" journalism focused on politics, openly proclaimed its political support for one governmental faction or another, and made no effort either to relate its perspective to business or to present a dispassionate view.

Newspaper mortality rates indicate most clearly the hazardous nature of publishing. Many newspapers did not survive their first year of existence while, of the approximately five hundred newspapers that had begun publishing between 1780 and 1800, almost three hundred failed to continue into the 19th century.[3] Overall, the new nation's press operated in an extremely limited financial position. Thus it was not surprising that the new brand of politicized editor would turn to national factional leaders for financial help in sustaining existing sympathetic newspapers or in starting new ones. In the early years of the republic, newspapers could not generate on their own the resources they required for institutional independence. By willingly subordinating themselves to rising national and local leaders and their parties, they maintained a free, protected, but dependent voice.

As newspapers became the prime source of political communications and the most suitable means for spreading the fame of leaders to the population at large, efforts by contesting political leaders to assure themselves a means of disseminating information became, in turn, a natural development. The basis for the rapid linkage between conflict, political organization, and the press in the new democratic nation was incisively defined in midcentury by Alexis de Tocqueville:

When men are no longer reunited among themselves by firm and lasting ties, it is impossible to obtain the cooperation of any great number of them unless you can persuade every man whose help you need that his private interest obliges him voluntarily to unite his exertions to the exertions of all the others. This can be habitually and conveniently effected only by means of the newspaper;

---

[3] Mott, *American Journalism*, p. 113; and Lee, *Daily Newspaper*, p. 30.

nothing but a newspaper can drop the same thought into a thousand minds at the same moment.[4]

The role of the press in the developing democracy had become more than just protection of free expression. The press had become a vital part of the practical organization of political conflict. Writing of early press-politics relationships, de Tocqueville continued,

The effect of a newspaper is not only to suggest the same purpose to a great number of persons, but to furnish means for executing in common the designs which they may have singly conceived. . . . If there were no newspapers, there would be no common activity.[5]

Factions or incipient parties had formed within Congress and the administration shortly after the ratification of the Constitution. But they lacked systematic connections with the mass population. These first governmental groupings were really the beginnings of what Maurice Duverger has described as parliamentary, or "interior," parties—clusters of contesting elected and appointed officials *within* the government, with few formal and specific linkages between themselves and like-minded followers outside.[6] Newspapers formed around leadership blocs furnished the first instruments linking political leaders to their mass constituencies. They thus helped to expand the scope of popular political interest and provoked new forms of political organization.

Rapidly transformed from a commercial to a predominantly political organ in the early decades of the nation, and prompted and directed by the efforts of contesting national leaders, the press became the initial focal point for the first mass political parties. The linkages established by the press between political leadership and the people,

---

[4] Alexis de Tocqueville, *Democracy in America*, trans. Henry Reeve, 2 vols. (New York: Knopf, 1945), 2: 119–20.

[5] *Ibid.*

[6] Maurice Duverger, *Political Parties, Their Organization and Activity in the Modern State* (New York: John Wiley and Sons, 1954), pp. xxiii–xxxvii.

between partisans in the national government and their potential copartisans outside, served not only as a means of mass communication but also as a catalyst and functioning part of the new nationwide political party organizations.

Sponsoring the Political Press

The ratification of the Constitution and George Washington's election as the first president brought only a brief period of agreement among politicians in the new nation. Natural differences in the outlook and concerns of the nation's leaders quickly destroyed the short-lived political consensus and created the beginnings of public opposition. Lacking partisan structures from which to spread factional points of view, major governmental leaders—whether they supported or opposed the first administration's policies— turned to the press. Where they could find willing like-minded editors they utilized them; where they could not, they created and subsidized new journalistic organs to articulate and coordinate the publication of their faction's point of view.

One example of the politician-as-patron was Alexander Hamilton, the first secretary of the treasury and a leading proponent of Federalist policies. When the new government established its capital in New York it found, oddly enough, no strong "political" paper there. A number of mercantile papers incidentally supported the Federalists, but no reliable political organ existed to further the interests of Federalist leaders at the seat of the national government.[7] This state of affairs was remedied quickly when Hamilton and other Federalist leaders set up John Fenno, its first editor, to begin publishing the Federalist *Gazette of the United States* in New York. A polemicist rather than a printer, Fenno moved directly into his new position on the recommendation of the Boston Federalists, who

---

[7] Mott, *American Journalism*, p. 122, and Edwin Emery, *The Press and America: An Interpretative History of the Mass Media*, 3rd ed. (Englewood, Cliffs, N.J.: Prentice-Hall, 1972), p. 105.

assured their New York allies of his abilities as a writer and defender of the Federalist cause.

Hamilton, Adams, and other Federalists contributed editorially as well as financially to the paper, which quickly established itself as the voice of the developing Federalists party. Although the Federalists had previously engaged in little concerted mass communications activity, they soon effectively employed the *Gazette* to articulate and coordinate Federalist policies and themes. Federalist newspapers and Federalist supporters in other cities and states paid particular attention to the *Gazette*. In a sense, it became under Fenno the "court journal," an officially sanctioned organ of incumbent political opinion that sharply criticized the Federalist's opponents and was, in turn, sharply attacked by them. When, after a few years, the seat of the national government moved to Philadelphia, Fenno and his paper moved with it.

The relationship between the developing Federalist party and a press, dependent on and subordinate to active politicians, is indicated by the *Gazette*'s economic basis. Hamilton had arranged official patronage for the *Gazette*—printing orders from the treasury and Senate—to help it keep publishing. Despite this aid, Fenno faced imminent insolvency by 1793, only four years after he began publishing. A loan from Hamilton and his associates helped sustain the *Gazette* while, simultaneously, a group of ten notable Federalists (including John Jay, Rufus King, and Alexander Hamilton) granted a "temporary loan" to Noah Webster, a respected journalist of strong anti-Republican sentiments later better-known for his spellers and dictionaries, to begin publishing the *Minerva* in New York.

Growing tensions between the Federalist party and its Republican opposition—Hamilton's debt plan, questions of the proper concentration or dispersion of political power, and, particularly, America's relationship with France and England—soon forced a major breach within the government. As a result, the Republicans, led by Madison and Jefferson, found that they, too, needed a news organ to help carry on their fight. Their response to Hamilton's

Gazette was to bring Philip Freneau, a well-known poet
and writer, to Philadelphia to publish a Republican newspaper, the *National Gazette*. Jefferson, as secretary of
state, secured a job for Freneau as a translator in his own
department, a position that required little work and provided a modest salary. Like Hamilton, who utilized the
patronage resources of the Treasury Department, Jefferson
used his own considerable departmental resources to
establish a strong press voice for the growing Republican
opposition. Freneau, who perceived himself as a crusader
against Federalist domination, stridently attacked Hamilton, Adams, and eventually President Washington. These
attacks helped to polarize groupings and organize conflict
among the nation's top leadership and an increasingly
attentive public.

Although readers quickly accepted the *National Gazette*
as the key Republican organ of opposition, Jefferson did
not publicly acknowledge his general direction of its policy
declarations or his close connections to its editor, Freneau.
His public position of detachment was probably, at least in
part, a response to the fact that, unlike Hamilton, he was
opposing his own president on issues of foreign relations
and domestic economic policies. The *National Gazette*'s
vitriolic attacks were ultimately considered attacks on the
president himself, and Jefferson's response to demands by
Washington to clarify his relationship with Freneau were
evasive and disingenuous.[8]

The lively battle between the *Gazette of the United
States* and the *National Gazette* raged until 1793. In 1793
Jefferson resigned as secretary of state and Freneau was
forced to give up his clerkship. Shortly after, the *National
Gazette* closed permanently, victim not of partisan attack
or governmental interference but, rather, of economic mal-
nutrition. By then, another paper, the Philadelphia
Aurora, was sufficiently established to take over the

---

[8] Frank Luther Mott, *Jefferson and the Press* (Baton Rouge: Louisiana
State University Press, 1943), pp. 23–26. See also Jefferson's letter to
Thomas Randolph (May 15, 1791), quoted in Robert A. Hendrickson,
Hamilton, 2 vols. (New York: Mason Charter, 1976), 2: 112.

Republicans' voice in the nation's capital and continue their fight. In their battles, Fenno's *Gazette* and Freneau's *National Gazette* had acted as national spokesmen of opposing syndicates of newspapers that reached into most of the states. They helped establish a new pattern linking distant newspapers directly to governmental controversy, thus preparing the political terrain for local party organizational efforts and, as a result, extending the potential scope of political conflict.

The Nature of Press Power

How to assess the actual impact of the press on the citizenry is hard. But political leaders went to such pains to gain advantage from the press that they must surely have *believed* its impact to be great. Throughout the history of American political journalism, perceptions by political leaders of the efficaciousness of the press have been—as they remain—a most important dimension in an assessment of press power.

The Sedition Act of 1798—*inter alia,* a blatant attempt to limit Republican newspaper outcries against the Federalist pressure for war with France—clearly demonstrated the Federalists' concern with the potential power of the press. The vague language of the Sedition Act made criminally libel virtually any criticism of the government or its leaders. Any attempts to organize or combine for such criticism were specifically prohibited by the act, so that the courts could punish *opinion* even in the absence of any overt act. The Federalists considered their legal justification for limiting the press to be sufficient, as Richard Hofstadter has noted:

If we may judge by the reaction of leading Federalists to the Alien and Sedition Acts, few of them would have made so bold as to claim a categorical right to do away with opposition. Yet none of them doubted the right of the government, in their particular circumstances, to silence newspaper opposition or to police the expression of political opinion by statute (though one, John Marshall, doubted the *expediency* of it).[9]

The Federalists' actual ability to control the opposition press was much less certain than their claimed legal basis for doing so. Not only was the populace as a whole used to relatively free and uninhibited expression by the press but also, at the time of the Acts, almost a hundred papers were either strongly Republican or leaned in that direction. The most zealous of Federalists counted on a declaration of war—one that never came—to fan anti-Republican feeling and permit effective operation of the Federalist strategy to control the opposition press under the Sedition Act. Lacking any declaration of war, fearful of Republican political strength, and increasingly aware of potential large-scale disruption by local Republican sympathizers following large-scale suppression of the press, the Federalists had eventually to moderate the harshness of their original aims.[10]

The Federalists sought to control the Republican press by striking directly at its leading journals in Philadelphia, New York, Baltimore, Boston, and Richmond. These journals not only originated the political cues for other papers in the partisan syndicate but they also supplied much of the copy eventually printed in their allies' papers. The Federalist campaign, executed by Timothy Pickering, Jefferson's successor as secretary of state, consisted of a series of prosecutions (under both the Sedition Act and common law) for seditious libel, bringing over a dozen indictments and resulting in several jail sentences. Most of the cases actually came to trial just prior to the presidential campaign of 1800 and were doubtless meant to intimidate the press as a whole and prevent its expression of opposition sentiment.[11]

---

[9] Richard Hofstadter, *The Idea of a Party System: The Rise of Legitimate Opposition in the United States* (Berkeley: University of California Press, 1969), p. 103.

[10] *Ibid.*

[11] For an account of Jefferson's role in opposing Federalist efforts of suppression, see Dumas Malone, *Jefferson and the Ordeal of Liberty,*

In fact, Federalist political strength was far less secure than its technical legal position, for during the life of the act the opposition press by no means stood along. The Republicans serving in Congress were by this time at least as numerous as the Federalists, better organized, and beset by no such factionalism as that which divided Hamilton and Adams in their own party. In addition, the Republican opposition had strong support among large masses of the population and, in a thoroughly decentralized society, the potential support of strong local military forces.

Significantly, the opposition press continued in its freedom largely because of the backup power of its elected partisans. The segment of the press which the Federalists threatened was still extremely vulnerable economically and far too weak politically to defend itself without the support of political leaders both in and out of government. In fact, legal expenses for defending themselves in court ended the career of several journals that lacked adequate financial resources with which to continue publishing.[12]

The attempt to silence and intimidate the press during the three years of the life of the Sedition Act covered two elections of the entire House, part of the Senate, and a crucial presidential election. It was, in a sense, a flattering act of suppression by a government against its opposition press. To think that the press *could* play a role in the election of governing leaders important enough to warrant suppression made the developing parties increasingly susceptible to the notion of "the power of the press" and the press's power as a political force.

After his election, President Jefferson released those serving sentences under the Sedition Act (the act itself had already expired), and a brief but important era had passed. The national government had abandoned its first and most

Jefferson and His Time, vol. 3. (Boston: Little, Brown, 1962), pp. 359–406. An interesting analysis of the legal and political aspects of the Alien and Sedition Acts appears in Leonard Williams Levy, *Legacy of Suppression: Freedom of Speech and Press in Early American History* (New York: Harper and Row, 1963), pp. 258–92.

[12] Mott, *American Journalism*, pp. 147–52.

strident effort to legislate out of existence political criticism and dissent. When, as president, Jefferson was himself pounded in print, he did reach the point where he suggested that a few prosecutions "would have a wholesome effect in restoring the integrity of the presses." And though he did not actually seek to deny newspapers the right of publication as the Federalists had done, he did encourage others to pursue several prosecutions under state libel laws.[13] Although Jefferson held firmly to the theoretical notion of an unrestricted press, his actions as president showed far less indulgent adherence to such liberal ideas.

Overall, the press in the first decade of the 19th century was in a unique position as an American political institution. Accepted as a potentially powerful political influence by both people and government, the newspaper business as a private enterprise remained economically weak and, in many cases, dependent on party and government subsidies of one kind or another to sustain its health. Its special position as an institution of mass communications—free, heavily valued, but economically dependent—explains much about the very development of certain major American political institutions. Within a few decades, the political leadership of the new nation would shape a unique role for the press in American politics, a role defined by presidents and their challengers for office, and linked tightly to a new and fast-growing vehicle of political mobilization, the American political party.

Expanding the Presidential Voice

American journalism during the approximately three decades from President Jefferson to President Jackson experienced enormous growth. The era began with somewhat over two hundred newspapers publishing simultaneously and ended with over twelve hundred. Writing about this period, a noted historian of the American press, Frank

---

[13] Levy, *Legacy of Suppression*, pp. 299–307.

L. Mott, describes journalism's early development in typical terms:

The whole period . . . was in many respects disgraceful—a kind of "Dark Ages" of American journalism. Few papers were ably edited; they reflected the crassness of the American society of the time. Scurrility, assaults, corruption, blatancy were commonplace.[14]

Blatant and extravagant partisanship ruled out objective reporting. Editors acted, instead, in accordance with contemporary press standards: their opposition, after all, stated their case in equally harsh and personal terms. Yet such fierce and one-sided partisanship was probably a necessary catalyst for the rapid formation of mass political organizations. At once extravagant in criticism, politically biased, and unafraid to declare their partisan sponsors, newspapers wore their close relationship to a president or opposition party leaders like a coat of arms. By sharply politicizing and polarizing political elites and rank and file, the partisan press deepened political cleavages and provided a key stimulant for mass mobilization.

It is, of course, difficult to assess motivations, particularly at great historical and psychological distance, and whether important Republican editors followed the orders of Jefferson and his two Virginia successors or were merely in "active" agreement with them on most political matters cannot now be easily determined. The fact is, however, that the key papers Jefferson established in Washington were continued by the Virginia dynasty as the party's "official" news organs, and they remained faithful, not to say servile, supporters of their patrons. Despite the independent spirit of some of the early political editors, little if any evidence survives to suggest that the political interests of the president and his leadership cadre were ever subordinated to any professional, merely journalistic concerns.[15] While press "freedom" was acknowledged as an important

---

[14] Mott, *American Journalism,* p. 169.
[15] James Edward Pollard, *Presidents and the Press* (New York: Macmillan, 1947), p. 71.

professional concern, press "independence" was not. The editors, it seems clear, were politicians first.[16]

During this era of political journalism, the economic viability of newspapers continued to be a significant problem for editors and political promoters. Various sources of patronage were needed to sustain the operation of most newspapers. In fact, press dependence upon governmental patronage was actually built into the nation's system of political communication prior to this "Dark Age." The seeds of a national communications and organizational network had been planted by the very first Congress when it gave the responsibility for informing the public of governmental actions to the executive branch. Nowadays, wire services and television spread news of national legislation almost instantaneously. At the end of the 18th century, however, the only broad-based method of publicizing new legislation was the newspaper. Responsibility for such publicizing of the laws was specifically given to the State Department. The Department of State was authorized to use "at least three" public newspapers printed within the United States to spread the language and substance of the new laws. Both the choice of newspapers to print the laws and the rates of pay were left to the judgment of the secretary—providing him with a powerful source of patronage. This early act of Congress, together with later modifications, formed the political framework for a media network that was to prove greatly influential in the development of critical linkages between national political leaders and their distant local sympathizers.

The original act designated three papers to spread word of national legislation. It was quickly found inadequate. Just before the turn of the 18th century a new public information act required the secretary of state to select one newspaper in each state to publish federal laws. Should one newspaper have less than adequate coverage of a state, the secretary of state, *at his discretion*, could choose up to

---

[16]Culver H. Smith, *Press, Politics, and Patronage: The American Government's Use of Newspapers, 1789–1875* (Athens: University of Georgia Press, 1977), pp. 24–48.

three newspapers in each state to publish new federal legislation "By Authority" of the national government. Thus his patronage potential rose quickly from a total of three newspapers to forty-eight at the time of Jefferson's election and the numbers increased as new states joined the Union.[17] These public information laws enhanced the potential for important national party linkages available to future administrations. As the population continued to move West, press patronage enabled presidential administrations to establish an ever-strengthening web of political communications and a group of sympathetic press-politicos over vast regions.

Special privileges or indirect subsudies accorded newspapers of all kinds attest to governmental responsiveness to the appetite for news of the eager but scattered citizens of the new nation. By an act of the Second Congress, newspapers were considered mail for purposes of distribution. The same law fixed the charge for newspaper mail delivery at exceptionally low levels, thus ensuring cheap and wide dissemination of the news. Letter rates varied during this period by weight and distance; a four-page letter mailed over four hundred and fifty miles cost *one dollar* for the trip—a particularly large sum of money at 1800 prices. Newspapers, in marked contrast, could be sent anywhere in the country for a maximum of *one and a half cents per newspaper*.[18]

Another special benefit, free delivery of newspapers between publishers, was in one sense an even more important benefit than low postal charges, particularly to editors in distant, less populated areas. Before telegraphy and news-gathering agencies, free exchange was the prime source for editors of news from other parts of the country. The official "Washington Press," the Republican *National Intelligencer*, was able, as a result of free exchange, both to spread knowledge of new legislation and other political

[17]*Ibid.* As Smith points out, the doubling of the number of post offices from 453 to 903 by 1800 markedly increased the feasibility of using newspapers to circulate the laws.

[18]*Ibid.*, pp. 6–9.

news, and simultaneously to establish a group of political organizers at local levels from corresponding editors across the nation.[19]

The political utilization of postal privileges and governmental patronage developed quickly, providing a steadily growing set of economic and political incentives to each president. Although the printing of congressional documents was the largest single printing order available for political patronage, constant congressional bickering limited its political impact. Presidential patronage, dispensed through the executive agencies, provided a much more focused and flexible weapon for political organization.

Those newspapers the Republicans considered most important to Jefferson's rise to the presidency, for example, received valuable contracts for publishing the laws. Secretary of State James Madison made vigorous use of press patronage in building the foundation of a national party structure. The use of the press as a base for local activist support was expertly refined by Jackson in the 1820s and '30s, but he was building on techniques actually established in the early Republican administration. In Virginia, for example, Madison assigned the *Examiner* and the *Virginia Argus* the valued "By Authority" publishing links to the government. The editors of these papers, not coincidentally, were members of Jefferson's Central Party Committee in Virginia, charged with coordinating the efforts of the county committees and communicating Jefferson's ideas to the people at large.[20] Jefferson's cultivation of local opinion through coordinated press and party organizational activities strengthened both the partisan press and the party, and in addition gave a decided presidential thrust to party politics at a relatively early stage in the development of organizational structures.

The selection as "By Authority" publishers of federal legislation of pro-Republican newspapers by Republican pres-

---

[19]*Ibid.*, pp. 39–55.

[20]Noble Cunningham, Jr., *The Jeffersonian Republicans in Power: Party Operations, 1801–1809* (Chapel Hill: University of North Carolina Press, 1963), p. 238.

idents became an established organizational procedure,
although pursued with somewhat less zeal after the Jefferson and Madison administrations. This de facto nationalization of a political information network helped establish
valuable links between local and national politicians. Jefferson and his secretary of state, by rewarding acknowledged
partisan journalists, encouraged editors and printers from
outside the ranks of known supporters zealously to offer up
their dedicated services. In volunteering themselves as
worthy choices for the printing contracts, editors sought to
assure the administration of their political reliability.

Editors, for example, quickly learned how to make use
of their representatives in Congress to help them secure
these journalistic plums. The interlocking network of newspapers, party organizations, and political representatives
was much in evidence when the entire South Carolina
congressional delegation jointly proposed three newspapers as "By Authority" printers for their home state—
which was accepted by the secretary of state.[21] Thus partisans in Congress, in the press, and in the executive branch
found common cause in patronage decisions, fostering, as
a result, some of the first centralizing steps of party organization.

While the subsidies for printing the laws helped a number of papers survive, particularly those in hostile political
regions, the several hundred dollars a year received on
average by most newspapers was not sufficient by itself to
sustain a partisan editor. Newspapers geographically close
to Washington did get other types of general printing contracts, but those away from the center of government
received their prime economic support indirectly, as a subsidiary benefit of being recognized as a politically "connected" newspaper. Their ability to print "By Authority"
enabled selected papers to present themselves as presidential representatives to their localities; conversely, each
became the national administration's local eyes. In short,
official status enlarged the importance (and the number of

---

[21] Smith, *Press, Politics, and Patronage,* pp. 48–50.

subscriptions) of a selected paper, making its words and opinions somehow more important than those of other newspapers.

To a nation hungry for political news, the Washington press and its network became more of a political provocateur than merely a simple business enterprise; it also became the key centralizing link in early efforts to build a national party organization reaching out from the leadership core in Washington to sympathetic local leaders and rank and file. The range and penetration of mass communications thus became intimately linked—as it would be repeatedly in the future—to the structure and strength of mass political organization; and, as a result, the potential influence of the presidency—our only national elective office—vastly increased.

Essential to the president's ability to organize his supporters nationally, the Washington press and its followers played a critical role during the first four decades of the 19th century. Without the special privileges enjoyed by the press, without the power of patronage, and without presidential initiative, the basic framework for a national partisan network of political organizations ordering the terms of political controversy would not have been established. As it was, the Washington press network began a long and symbiotic relationship with the political parties. Before that relationship ended half a century later, it would massively extend the voice of the president and help shape new democratizing structures in American electoral politics.

The Politics of Competition

The national government's press-party network continued to grow after Jefferson's tenure. Despite the fact that linkages between national, state, and local parties were slowly building, party linkages within the central government—i.e., between the branches of national government—were, in fact, disintegrating. Jefferson's initial efforts to promote legislative cohesiveness at the national level might be accurately described as an early attempt at presidentially led party government.[22] However, the defections of Republicans in Congress over the embargo policy effectively ended Jefferson's leadership and brought a major decline in the influence of the presidency that lasted for two decades. With this decline in presidential power and initiative, the party, as an incipient instrument of policy cohesion, collapsed.[23]

The party disintegrated not only as a link between the president and Congress, but within Congress as well. James S. Young's analysis of Congress between the last year of Jefferson's administration and the first year of Jackson's presidency shows that, as a means of conflict resolution and policy leadership, the party was exceptionally weak. Boardinghouse fraternities in Washington—congressional dormitories with primarily regional constituencies— were often better indicators of voting patterns than party affiliations, indicative of the decline in party power after some promise in the early years of Jefferson's administration.[24]

The peaceful succession of the Virginia dynasty of Jefferson, Madison, and Monroe had experienced no genuine competition for the presidency. But the campaign of 1824 not only reopened the question of presidential succession but also provoked new public interest in the national government. The Congressional Caucus had served for roughly two decades as a rudimentary mechanism for party decisions. But by 1824, it had lost its practical effectiveness in nominating a party candidate for president. Despite William H. Crawford's nomination by the caucus, other eager

---

[22] Cunningham, *Jeffersonian Republicans in Power*, offers an analysis in chapters 4 and 9 of party efforts in Congress during this period. See also William N. Chambers, *Political Parties in a New Nation: The American Experience 1776–1809* (New York: Oxford University Press, 1963).

[23] Leonard Dupee White, *The Jeffersonians: A Study of Administrative History 1801–1829* (New York: Macmillan, 1961), pp. 34–35.

[24] James S. Young, *The Washington Community 1800–1828* (New York: Columbia University Press, 1966), p. 147.

candidates, ignoring the caucus choice, began anew the competiton for the presidency. With no successor named by President Monroe, and the caucus in disrepute, competing candidates sought evidence of the "people's will" in endorsements of all kinds. They both solicited and bought press support, while the endorsements of state committees, conventions, and other legislative endorsements were all highly valued as signs of popularity at or near the "grass roots."[25]

Candidates appealing to various levels of public acclaim of course viewed press influence as important. Consequently, the use of patronage to ensure press support was very much a part of the competition for the presidency in the 1824 election. Crawford relied on the *Washington Gazette*, a paper to which, as secretary of the treasury, he had awarded treasury printing contracts. John Quincy Adams's press connection in Washington was the *National Journal*, recipient of State Department printing contracts controlled by Secretary Adams himself. The third presidential candidate, John C. Calhoun, served as secretary of war; his "special relationship" was with a Washington news organ edited by an employee of his own department.[26] Outside Washington, Adams and Crawford had the most substantial press support, particularly in the East, probably because, of the five candidates, they were most closely connected to powerful government—and patronage producing—agencies.

Two other presidential candidates, House Speaker Henry Clay and Senator Andrew Jackson, had no connections to Washington papers. Newspapers that supported Clay were concentrated primarily in Kentucky, Indiana, and Ohio. In some major cities, such as Philadelphia and New York, Clay had no press support whatsoever. Although Jackson had solid newspaper support in Philadelphia as well as some additional support in parts of Ohio and the Middle States, his first run for presidential office lacked

---

[25] Smith, *Press, Politics, and Patronage*, pp. 56–58.
[26] *Ibid.*, p. 57.

influential press support even where he had some, while in certain regions, like New England, he had little support at all.

Possibly because they were confronting their first widespread intra-party presidential battle, newspapers generally were quite restrained in their treatment of the candidates. The candidates were, of course, all Republicans, and generally maintained a sort of "clubby" style of competition—clubby by comparison with some earlier Federalist-Republican battles and, certainly, with presidential battles to follow. Overall, Adams had a press advantage in 1824 since, as secretary of state, he selected the newspapers in the "official" network. His patronage potential did not require support for his candidacy, but it must certainly have weakened opposition from those who benefited from it. The press would not bite hard on the hand feeding it.

Adams might actually have pursued a much more aggressive campaign in the public arena outside of Washington than he did, for as secretary of state he had control over an "official" newspaper network of seventy-six journals. But the potential to use political power for one's own purpose and the will to do so are, of course, quite different. As secretary of state, Adams did occasionally deny the "By Authority" designation to newspapers noted for their "steady devotion to the fame of General Jackson." But he lacked both the strong partisan sensibility and the organizational perspective necessary to maximize his political resources.[27]

In the multicandidate presidential election of 1824, Jackson won the largest share of the popular vote. But because no candidate received a majority in the electoral college, the decision was shifted to the House of Representatives. There "negotiations" resulted in Adams's election as president. This decision was made, as Federalist No. 27 had feared, by a "government continually at a distance and out

---

[27] See Pollard, *Presidents and the Press*, pp. 126–43 for an assessment of John Quincy Adams's relations with the partisan press.

of sight," and provided a political entrepreneur like Jackson with an issue in his next presidential bid that capitalized on the citizenry's feelings of remoteness from its national government.

In effect, the 1824 conflict for succession triggered a new kind of conflict for the presidency in the following election, one that would firmly establish the linkage of the people to their national government by expanding the political arena. With Jackson, the presidency became the objective of a new kind of fiercely partisan candidate, a political entrepreneur who sought the support not only of political elites but also of the mass electorate in the individual states as well. In organizing and developing a political network combining press and party to help him win office, Jackson and the political elites behind him initiated a new era of political organization and partisan management. Eventually, through reinforcing both party and press, they created a highly developed partisan network, a new kind of popular psychological identification with a political party, and a new institutional framework for a two-party system.

Without the stabilizing pressures of an active and interested citizenry, Jefferson's tentative organizational connections between populace and politicians could not be sustained. The weakening of the rudimentary links between leaders in Washington and their supporters elsewhere was, in fact, almost proportionate to the decline of the Federalists' ability to contest for the presidency. Without the pressure of political competition, embryonic party mechanisms that might reach out to the mass electorate were left to atrophy, and energies used earlier to promote the Republican party were spent in fragmented, internecine struggles. Without popular, externally initiated pressure forcing leaders to transcend the fragmentation of governmental power structured by the Constitution itself, those leaders could establish no stable electoral connection to the general populace, either.

The Congressional Caucus had clearly limited the scope of political conflict, confining the battle for the presidential designation to congressional elites. The expanded contest for presidential leadership served to broaden the range of conflict and introduce new forces into the political arena. In effect, strong competiton for the presidency moved conflict beyond the narrow confines of national legislative leaders, incorporating local leadership cadres and rank-and-file voters in a new decision-making process dependent upon mass electoral mobilization. Failing in the narrow confines of the national legislature, Jackson's determined quest for the presidency sought to increase the scope of political conflict by enlarging the numbers of the politically relevant citizenry beyond Washington and thus to change the balance of electoral power controlling the presidency. His new electoral connection combined presidential competition, political mobilization, and a systematically organized partisan press to bring about more than an election victory alone. It triggered, as we shall see, new activity by vast untapped popular forces in American political life, a new mania for political organization, a radical transformation in the political thinking of aspiring political leaders, and a greatly expanded and mobilized national electorate.

3

The Electoral Connection

Jackson's second, 1828, campaign for the presidency firmly established popular election as the political basis for presidential choice. Taking the decision to the people, even if, technically, their decision was mediated by the electoral college, became firmly entrenched as the "American way" to select the president. This campaign, and the dynamics released by it, also framed a broad principle of American politics that would be frequently reaffirmed: competition by politicians for the highest office would stimulate new electoral structures, new styles of campaigning, and new modes and levels of mass participation. Political ambition became, then, a critical catalyst in creating a broad popular base in American politics, institutionalizing a two-party system within a dozen years, and establishing a vital electoral connection between the leadership and the led. By the end of Jackson's successful campaigns, "remoteness" and "distance" no longer seemed to characterize the relationship of the government in Washington to its widely dispersed people.

Jackson's strategy, to shift the presidential choice away from the Washington elites who had rejected him earlier, undoubtedly reflected his awareness of his own popularity with the public at large. At the same time, Jackson and his supporters realized that a new and different political environment had developed between 1800 and 1828 making mass popularity a viable route to the presidency.[1] Jackson based his successful strategy of organizing large numbers of voters on what proved to be a valid assumption: the mode of selecting delegates to the electoral college was changing. In 1800 presidential electors had been chosen by state legislatures in a large majority of the states. But by 1824 only six states made presidential selection a matter of legislative rather than popular choice; by 1832 only South Carolina did not choose its electors by statewide popular vote. As Richard McCormick has noted:

The significance of this change in the method of conducting presidential elections has been too little appreciated. The general adoption of the popular, statewide voting procedure gave a popular dimension to the presidential contest, created or enhanced the need for state party machinery, weakened the political authority of legislative caucuses, occasioned the development of national party conventions, and made the presidential election the dramatic focal point of American politics.[2]

To gain the popular support necessary to win a state's presidential electors and a subsequent majority in the electoral college, Jackson and his supporters developed an extraordinarily intense and systematically organized partisan apparatus. His campaigns for popular support in 1828 and again in 1832 prompted political organization and counterorganization in almost all states, and rapidly brought about by 1840 a full-blown two-party system.[3]

This new party system itself brought about a new organizational synthesis between the press and the party apparatus. Jackson and his leadership cadre combined political communications and political organization in an extraordinary way. While they effectively decentralized campaign

---

[1] Richard Patrick McCormick, *The Second American Party System: Party Formation in the Jacksonian Era* (Chapel Hill: University of North Carolina Press, 1966), pp. 28–31.

[2] *Ibid.*, p. 29.

[3] See *The American Party Systems; Stages of Political Development*, ed. William Nisbet Chambers and Walter Dean Burnham, 2nd ed. (New York: Oxford University Press, 1975), for further development of the idea of distinct party systems.

activities and objectives, granting considerable autonomy to eager activists outside Washington in each state and local community, they simultaneously centralized the flow of political information and the direction of the campaign as a whole by using Jackson's press in Washington as a critical organizational base. Jackson's "party line" was, in fact, sent from Washington, and his press and party leaders there became the central clearinghouse of all political communications.

Only with difficulty can contemporary observers of the press place earlier press-party relationships in perspective. We are, at present, so used to newspapers and magazines limiting their direct involvement with partisan organizations (with television and radio even more circumspect in this regard than the print media) that it is difficult to perceive accurately how differently the press operated during this stage of political development. Today many news organs ultimately endorse one or another candidate or party in an election (except television networks), and some media maintain a surreptitious bias in their "selective" reporting. But the professional standard of news reporting—the ideal—is of nonpartisan reporting of events, positions, and candidacies. Despite preelection editorial endorsements, it is rare, indeed, that a modern news organ admits to premature support of a candidate or his party and publicly states its intention to give only a single partisan side of a story in its columns. Even more rare is a news organ openly functioning as part of a party organization, coordinating, by its own volition, its political opinions with other national, state, and local partisan positions. But all these partisan activities were pursued by many newspapers both for and against Jackson.

Jackson's supporters sought to extend the size of the political marketplace, sensing their own advantage to nest in superiority of numbers. They perceived the already widened use of political parties as vehicles of communicating with a mass audience. They also recognized the press, the principal means of mass political communications, as an increasingly important political weapon as the size of the electorate increased. Not surprisingly, therefore, Jackson's cadre of political entrepreneurs sought to link these two structuring sources of political communications tightly together in the service of their candidate. As a result of their efforts to coordinate election publicity and local party organization, the distinction between the press and the party nearly vanished. It is fair to say that the most important editors in this period were actually politicians wielding newspapers. Since few, if any, pressure groups possessed countervailing political organizations of their own, these politician-editors became disproportionately influential in the political process as a whole.[4]

During this important era of American politics, newspapers that supported Jackson or his opponents provided an instrument of political organization and "furnished means for executing in common" the party's political strategies. Although Jackson's forces brought to the campaign of 1828 an approach to party organizations and press supporters that was rather more systematic and polished than their opponents exhibited, both sides bound their party organizations and press supporters tightly together. Sharing organizational functions between Jackson editors and local party leaders was directly related to Jackson's attempt to mobilize masses of supporters, and typified the merging of press and party interests at this stage of American political development.[5] Jackson's forces well understood the role of the press in organizing the political environment. They made the news media a disciplined arm of their overall campaign structure. At this stage of its development, the press—small in scale, and still substantially dependent on external political support for resources and prestige— became an eager part of the political organizations that linked elected leaders to the public at large.

Both press and party share many common functions—

<hr />

[4] Culver Smith, *Press, Politics, and Patronage* (Athens: University of Georgia Press, 1977), p. 69.

[5] For a discussion of the overlapping press and party functions, see James Edward Pollard, *Presidents and the Press* (New York: Macmillan, 1947), pp. 147–66.

political communications, mobilization, and organization—that serve to link the masses of voters to potential office-holders. However, it required the charismatic appeal of Andrew Jackson and a skilled cadre of assertive politicians to bring together these two important tools of political campaigning, the party and the press. Jackson had been a loser in his 1824 presidential battle with Adams, when the arena was the House of Representatives. To win, he had to find a larger arena with a bigger audience, find a more advantageous set of political forces, enlarge the scope of conflict, and make presidential politics the politics of numbers.[6] The combination of his personal appeal, his espousal of such ideas as equalitarianism, superior organizational leadership, and improved mass political communications techniques, all these allowed Jackson's forces to initiate new public attitudes toward political parties, a new way of seeking public office in American politics, and a new set of relationships among the presidency, the people, and governance.

Organizing Partisan Press Power

What changed during the Jacksonian period was not the press but the uses politicians made of the press. Politicized reporting of events was common before Jackson, and even during the so-called Era of Good Feelings newspapers had close links with various political leaders and their factions. What was new was the extent to which journalists became regular functioning parts of Jackson's political organization and, to a less significant degree, his opponent's. As noted earlier, Jackson had lacked a Washington newspaper in 1824. To remedy this want, his supporters purchased a failing Washington daily and renamed it the *United States Telegraph*. Duff Green, a politically astute editor and quintessence of the politician-journalist-promoter, came in

[6]This concept is fully developed in Elmer Eric Schattschneider, *The Semi-Sovereign People* (New York: Holt, Rinehart and Winston, 1960), p. 2 *et passim.*

to run the paper and laid the groundwork for Jackson's second presidential bid by corresponding with sympathetic editors throughout the country, uniting them with politicians into a systematic national organization.[7]

Both Jackson's and Adams's supporters clearly manifested their belief in the press's ability to sway public opinion in 1828. Many newspapers sprang to life simply in order to take part in the first genuinely popular campaign in the country's history. As Culver H. Smith notes:

Many of these lasted but for the season, having found sustenance only in the excitement engendered by the campaign. Prospectuses were issued of many more newspapers that never came into being. Established papers entered into the campaign with a vigor that suggested either abundant patriotism or concrete encouragement. The political leaders of each side were interested in giving aid to editors who needed it, and whose services were considered important.[8]

Adams's most supportive political organ, the *National Journal*, charged that the Jackson forces had raised a substantial fund of $50,000 to establish new Jackson papers. Ample evidence suggests that Clay and Webster also raised large amounts of money to subsidize opposition news organs.[9] New forms of political journalism appeared as the election neared. The special weekly or "extra," for instance, confined itself strictly to political news, the doings of newly established correspondence committees, and campaign arguments. These news organs were, by and large, the more competitive and scurrilous mudslingers of the campaign.

Partisan newspapers highlighted the contents of many political pamphlets. Particularly able was the Jackson campaign organization's synchronization of its network of newspaper publicity. The *United States Telegraph* claimed to

[7] Smith, *Press, Politics, and Patronage*, pp. 66–68.

[8] Culver H. Smith, "Propaganda Technique in the Jackson Campaign of 1828," *East Tennessee Historical Society Publication*, no. 6 (1934), p. 45.

[9] *Ibid.* See *National Journal*, March 22, 1877, quoted in Smith, "Propaganda Technique."

distribute forty thousand copies per issue; at least half of these were probably given away rather than sold. Congressional Jacksonians, for instance, mailed numerous copies under their postal franking privileges, using such available resources as this one far more aggressively than the competing Adams forces.[10]

Despite possessing the power of incumbency, Adams used only a small fraction of his patronage power. He had some newspapers considered friendly to Jackson removed from the list of those who could print federal laws "By Authority," although even this small dose of partisan politics ironically prompted a Congress no longer supportive of Adams to investigate patronage abuses. Basically, Adams's "above-the-battle" attitude prevented his exploitation of his direct and indirect appointive powers and precluded his building a press-party combination to rival Jackson's.

Adams's reluctance to exploit his advantages did not stop Jackson's *United States Telegraph* from claiming a political foul when it detected presidential patronage directed, however sparingly, toward a few editors favoring Adams:

It is in vain to talk of a free press, when the favor of power is essential to the support of editors, and the money of the people, by passing through the hands of the Executive, is made to operate as a bribe against liberty. It is a most solemn truth, and should be deeply impressed on every mind, that if liberty shall ever expire in our country, it will die of the poisonous draught of corrupt patronage.[11]

It was, of course, not patronage as such but "corrupt patronage" that became Jackson's antiadministration war cry. It became a critical issue in the campaign, successfully alarming and mobilizing support from voters. Corruption by the "ins" was a key theme of the "outs," an election strategy enhanced by the bargain allegedly made between Adams and Clay in 1824 to give Adams the presidency. Green never documented the *United States Telegraph*'s initial claim of a "corrupt bargain" in the House presiden-

---

[10]*Ibid.*, p. 50.
[11]*Ibid.*, p. 53.

tial election, but the mystery in which he shrouded the subject harmed Adams's campaign, accentuating once again Adams's lack of a popular base.

While Adams was reluctant to use fully his press patronage for purposes of political organization, his supporters were not similarly loathe to use their news organs to defame Jackson. Adams's press shared responsibility for bringing the level of campaigning to a new low, spiritedly attacking Jackson's family, scandalizing his wife, condemning his sanction of military executions as "murder," and accusing him of slave trading and semi-illiteracy. All these charges were assembled and printed in the closing weeks of the campaign in *Truth's Advocate and Monthly Anti-Jackson Expositor*. It concluded a typically uninhibited evaluation of the vulgar, animallike presidential challenger by commenting,

You know that he is no jurist, no statesman, no politician; that he is destitute of historical, political, or statistical knowledge: that he is unacquainted with the orthography, concord and government of his language. You know that he is a man of no labour, no patience, no investigation, in short, that his whole recommendation is animal fierceness and organic energy. He is wholly unqualified by education, habit and temper, for the station of President.[12]

Jackson's strategy called for the candidate personally to answer none of the vilification meted out by the Adams press. But if Jackson's lips were sealed, his friends were under no such limitation. Jackson vigorously protested his supporters' unproven insinuations against women; Duff Green was less squeamish. After printing a ten-column refutation of attacks on Mrs. Jackson, Green warned the Adams press to desist from personal attacks on her. When they did not, he concocted a story that Mrs. Adams and the president had been "guilty" of premarital sexual relations and printed it.[13]

During the 1828 campaign, newspaper support was fairly

[12]*Ibid.*, p. 56.
[13]James Pollard, *Presidents and the Press*, p. 150.

evenly divided between Jackson and Adams. Although each side accused the other of trying to control the press through patronage or money, evidence suggests a slight advantage for Jackson in total numbers of newspapers. But Jackson also possessed a much greater "professional" edge over Adams in the kind of political editors required for an aggressive campaign. The important variable, it seems, was not strictly numbers but rather the quality and penetration of the editor-politicians supporting one candidate or the other.[14]

The Press in Spoils Politics

It was only logical that those journalist-politicians who had played a major role in Jackson's successful quest for office would want to benefit from their support. Many editors, expecting to share the spoils of victory, joined the multitudes of office seekers that petitioned the president before and after his inaugural. Jackson had already declared his decision to establish the principle of "rotation in office," arguing that all intelligent men of all classes should serve in office. "In a country where offices are created solely for the benefit of the people no one man has any more intrinsic right to official station than another." Arguing that long tenure invited inefficiency and corruption, he strongly supported replacing the "ins" with the new and fresh blood of the "outs," his loyal supporters.[15]

New modes linking official appointments to prior election efforts on his behalf were necessary to open fresh opportunities for the growing numbers of party workers

[14] For example, when the *New York Evening Post* declared for Jackson it gave a great boost to his campaign in the Northeast. Long the voice of the Federalist party, that paper represented an important and aristocratic element of the party. See Smith, *Press, Politics, and Patronage,* p. 67; and Lee Benson, *The Concept of Jacksonian Democracy: New York as a Test Case* (Princeton: Princeton University Press, 1961), pp. 21–43.

[15] Andrew Jackson, "First Annual Message," *The Age of Jackson,* ed. Robert Remini (Columbia: University of South Carolina Press, 1972), p. 44.

who had mobilized large numbers of newly enfranchised voters. Ambitious political leaders sought to replace their rivals in government by using patronage to reward accomplishment of the hard chore of organizing a campaign. Although Jackson's support for rotation in office, or "the spoils system," brought harsh criticism from his opponents, at least part of the antispoils, anti-Jackson criticism—concern for the "proper qualifications" for office and the need of bureaucratic protection—could be seen as a struggle for official power by different sets of leaders competing for the rewards of office.[16]

In the rotation that followed, numerous members of the press were rewarded with office for the first time. At the beginning of the century, Jefferson had assigned printing contracts and the privilege of printing laws "By Authority" to favored printers. But he had not actually appointed journalists to government positions. While Jackson himself appointed no editors to high office (although there is some evidence that he offered at least one cabinet position to a journalist), he made numerous appointments of his press politicos to valued offices. Postmasterships were the greatest in number, the customs service next, and the list included all kinds of positions, from librarian of Congress to a clerkship in the treasury office.[17] At least fifty-nine journalists were appointed early in Jackson's administration; in all likelihood the figure was higher. Of the total number of nominations sent for confirmation to the Senate in Jackson's first six months in office, journalists represented at least 10 percent—making the press a visible recipient of the benefits of rotation.[18]

A historian of patronage and the civil service, Carl R. Fish, has remarked that "newspaper men were the most important single class of party workers." In fact, their prominence in party politics really came of age with Jack-

---

[16] Martin Shefter, "Parties, Patronage, and Political Change," delivered at the 1976 American Political Science Association annual meeting, Chicago, Illinois, p. 12.

[17] James Pollard, *Presidents and the Press*, p. 161.

[18] Smith, *Press, Politics, and Patronage*, p. 90.

son.[19] Never had so many members of the press been appointed to public office. As leaders of an awakened "public opinion," the press-politicos became a recognized class of officeholders named by Jackson to serve his administration. Most of Jackson's journalist nominations were confirmed, but four very prominent editors were rejected (one was later renominated and approved by one vote). Those rejected were defeated decisively, whereas those finally approved were approved by very narrow margins. Daniel Webster reported that closed debates on the approval of the journalists were very heated. With careful appreciation of the popular electoral connection linking Jackson and the public, he noted: "were it not for the fear of the *out-door popularity* of General Jackson, the Senate would have negatived more than half his nominations."[20]

Jackson's approach to patronage and the press was distinctively characterized by a coherent overall approach to new political realities. His official recognition of journalists served quite obviously to strengthen the Jackson party by rewarding a vital part of its campaign organization. In another sense, it provided symbolic (and tangible) recognition of the importance of a dominant electoral factor—public opinion—and of a valued instrument, the press, useful in its manipulation. Jackson had staked his career on popular esteem. In power as in his campaign, he sought to reinforce his popularity by maximizing his use of both party and press in support of that end.

In office, the tough-minded Jackson elites moved to utilize the existing "By Authority" network of newspapers, rapidly substituting pro-Jackson papers for those that had supported his opponent. By the end of the administration's first year, over three-quarters of the seventy-eight official publishers of the laws had been replaced. Those retained had become pro-Jackson or were considered politically inoffensive.[21] Particularly by comparison to his much more

---

[19] Carl Russell Fish, *The Civil Service and the Patronage* (New York: Russell and Russell, 1967), pp. 123, 148–49.

[20] Smith, *Press, Politics, and Patronage*, p. 97 (italics mine).

[21] *Ibid.*, p. 100.

modest turnover of regular officeholders, Jackson's rotations in the sensitive area of political communications appear very extensive and deliberate. Both Jackson and Van Buren, his party campaign manager and secretary of state, were quick to respond to the opportunities that incumbency afforded, demonstrating that their earlier fight against press patronage was not essentially against the system of patronage but only against the opposition's use of it.

The new administration's actions not only aided efforts to bulwark decentralized local party organizations but also served imaginatively to centralize political communications by linking national and local party politicians. Commenting on the advantages of such partisan linkages between national and local politicians, the Massachusetts Central Committee wrote that "the pecuniary benefit arising from this patronage was altogether of trifling importance. It is the moral influence, which the selection has, by indicating the confidence of the government in those papers friendly to *correct principles*, which we value." Interestingly, three of the eleven signers of this petition were affiliated with newspapers recommended by the committee.[22]

The principle of intense partisanship in assigning the privilege of publishing federal laws "By Authority" was firmly carried out by the Jackson leadership, first under Green and subsequently under Francis P. Blair. It continued, with the exception of one brief period, until the Civil War. "By Authority" appointments, departmental newspaper advertising contracts, and other forms of printing patronage were all carefully organized by the Jackson administration, seeking to build advantages for its supporters in the mass media, coordinate partisan political positions, and build a new kind of loyalty to a political party.

The Party and a Party System

It would be hard to overestimate the importance of the drama of presidential elections in establishing the modern

---

[22]*Ibid.*, p. 106 (italics mine).

American political party. Jackson's popular quest for the presidency initiated a new brand of politics which changed significantly both the political institutions and environment of American politics. In the Jacksonian era the drama of the presidential election firmly established the basic structure of a new American two-party system, which, with only a few modifications, has endured until the present.

The spectacles generated by these national campaigns apparently served certain psychological needs of the American people. Mass rallies, mile-long processions, songs, and hoopla became parts of the presidential battle which brought the American public the thrill of involvement in a major national event. In a period of limited opportunities for diversion, the presidential campaign provided a responsive electorate with theater, spectacle, and the excitement of individual participation.

On the one hand, this new style of politics seemed to lack political substance. It promoted loyalty and support for one side or another in the electoral arena, but lacked much relationship to specific issues of public policy.[23] On the other hand, these campaign extravaganzas built into American election processes a new political dimension: the intense participation by large numbers of ordinary people. Seeking to build popular support for a candidate, party leaders sought, in effect, to convert large numbers of previously uninvolved people into voters. As a result, they institutionalized a new organized way of selecting leaders. By stimulating and structuring the ordinary person's participation in the political process, by linking his participation to centrally articulated sets of values and preferences, by tying the presidency to the voting choices of the masses of citizens, partisan political leaders introduced changes in political form that led in brief order, to changes in political substance.

Large-scale increases in the numbers of citizens who

---

[23] For an interesting contrast between the constituent functions of the parties and their policy functions, see Theodore J. Lowi, "Party, Policy, and Constitution in America," *The American Party Systems*, ed. Chambers and Burnham, pp. 238–76.

voted in presidential contests were not simply a response to Jackson's own campaign. His efforts to organize a popular campaign in 1828 did, in fact, raise the national voting average from approximately 26 percent of the eligible voters in the preceding election to 56 percent. But the 1824 voting average was an abnormally low benchmark from which to judge. In earlier elections, voter participation in certain states had been even more substantial than in 1828. Thus, the surge in voter participation cannot simply be attributed to Jackson's arousal of the "common man."[24]

A large increase in voter participation followed Jackson, when intense competition between two strong parties characterized electoral contests in almost all states. Whereas the 1828 and 1832 campaigns were one-sidedly for or against Jackson in many states, in following elections candidates of both parties, the Democrats and Whigs, were involved in closely competitive contests across the country. As a result, voter participation reached extraordinarily high levels, as when, in 1840, approximately 80 percent of the eligible voters cast ballots. McCormick suggests that we find in these facts an important feature promoting the development of parties and the establishment of a party system: high levels of voter turnout require not only mobilization by one party but countermobilization by the opposition to stimulate publicity and other organizational efforts, arouse the people, and make the individual's vote appear meaningful.

The Whig countermobilization copied many of the Jacksonian Democrats' campaign innovations, furthering a powerful nationalization of political form, style, and identity in the political process: in 1840 a military hero from the West, William Henry Harrison, as the presidential candidate, a vice-presidential candidate from the South, identification of the Whig party symbols with the common people, strong local organizational efforts, and, of course, immense publicity coordinated by the party press. In addi-

---

[24] Richard Patrick McCormick, "New Perspectives on Jacksonian Politics," *American Historical Review* 65 (January 1960): 106.

tion, the Whigs developed some new campaign features of their own: singing party songs, mass meetings with bands, banners, "spirits," and miniature "log cabins" as symbols of the party and its candidate.[25]

The most significant innovation, from the point of view of future presidential campaigning, was the participation of noted political figures as speakers on the campaign trail. Commenting on this development, former president John Quincy Adams noted that "one of the most remarkable peculiarities [of the campaign] is that the principal leaders of the political parties are traveling about the country from State to State, and holding forth like Methodist preachers, hour after hour, to assembled multitudes under the broad canopy of Heaven." Clay, Webster, Tyler, and many other prominent politicians traveled around the country. Even General Harrison, the Whig candidate himself, hit the campaign trail—the first time a presidential candidate actually went on a speaking tour to greet ordinary voters.[26]

The enormous increase in the involvement of the mass electorate in this period no doubt owes much both to the readiness of the people to participate in political activities and to the vast combative flow of political information generated by the party presses. However, no explanation of the major transformation in American politics made by the development of the political party and the two-party system can rely exclusively on changes in the public and its response to the flow of political information. More than a shift in the state of mind of the electorate at large, this transformation found its major catalyst in the equally radical transformation of the ideas and attitudes of the political leadership in the country.

With Jackson, a new generation of political leaders had entered the political arena. The first of the professional party politicians, their ideas, attitudes, and organizational skills played the most critical role in changing how the electoral game was played. These new organizers of elections

[25] Smith, *Press, Politics, and Patronage*, p. 147.
[26] Letter from John Quincy Adams quoted in Smith, *Press, Politics, and Patronage*, p. 148.

were not generally men of wealth or aristocratic background. No political positions had been offered them out of
deference to their high economic or social positions. They
were not "notables" in their local communities to whom
opportunities for office flowed as a normal result of the deferential attitudes ordinary people directed at political leadership. New men, political leaders like Van Buren and
Marcy, were party men, builders of a new political institution. They found in the party itself both a means and an
end. Not only a vehicle to mobilize large numbers of voters, it served also as an organization that provided its members with a vocation with tangible rewards, an institutional
symbol, a sense of social community and standing within
that community.[27] As Richard Hofstadter noted, party
principles served other purposes as well:

Party unity was the democrat's answer to the aristocrat's wealth,
prestige, and connections. In these they could never match him,
but by presenting a united front in party affairs, they could give
democracy a more than compensating foundation of strength.[28]

Full-time professionals, these new party leaders altered
the forms of political decision-making. They considered
negotiation, bargaining, and "management" of mass opinion better than mere deference to their political "betters."
Unlike the notables, often deferred to in the first generation of political leaders, they found the ceremonies that
enlisted the support of common voters not at all distasteful.
Of great importance, they no longer held the belief—common even among earlier Republicans like Jefferson—that a
quest for unity among the parties was either useful or productive for American politics as a whole. Van Buren and
his fellow party leaders wanted none of Monroe's fusion
policy, believing that a permanent opposition party was a
necessary development of positive social value. Competition between two parties would inform the people, period-

---

[27] Richard Hofstadter, *The Idea of a Party System: The Rise of Legitimate Opposition in the United States* (Berkeley: University of California
Press, 1969), p. 242.
[28] *Ibid.*, p. 246.

ically throw the corrupt from office, and serve to preserve the larger social peace.[29]

To bring about such a significant and durable change in American politics, various elements in the political environment had to be ready to respond to these new organizational leaders and their popular modes of politics. Growing feelings of respect and admiration for "the people" were already evident, institutionalized (as noted earlier) in the popular election of presidential electors in most states. A rising democratic spirit helped form a new and different public opinion, one less respectful of prominent leaders, less anchored in deferential patterns of the past, and more vigorous and assertive in tone than what had preceded it. Such public opinion would aid the new party professionals in their transformation of the political parties into mass movements.

But important questions persist. Even if we admit that the new party professionals possessed exceptional organizational abilities, how could public opinion shift so dramatically and in such a brief period of time to permit party politicians such an easy victory over the semiaristocrats, the notables of status? How could an earlier consensus, one that had converted respect for higher status into political leadership, yield so rapidly to mere personal popularity, the politics of quantity rather than of supposed quality? And finally, what role did the press play in creating this new environment of popular opinion, this latent consensus that could be activated by the new professional party leaders?

The Party Press: The Great Leveler

Accompanying the significant changes in mid-19th-century electoral politics, an equally important but perhaps

[29] See James W. Caeser, *Presidential Selection: Theory and Development* (Princeton: Princeton University Press, 1979), pp. 123–64; and Robert Vincent Remini, *Martin Van Buren and the Making of the Democratic Party* (New York: Columbia University Press, 1959), p. 24. Theodore Lowi, "Party, Policy, and Constitution in America," pp. 238–41,

undiscerned change affected the style and content of political journalism. Intimately linked to the politics of mass mobilization, this change contributed substantially to the transformation of popular attitudes about political leadership and political involvement. In the first third of the 19th century, the so-called dark ages of journalism, the press served as a significant political leveler, "vulgarizing" and popularizing public argument, and setting the stage for major political changes.

Specifically, changes in style and tone—greater explicitness in personally directed criticism, decreasing civility— did much to erode earlier attitudes of deference; even more revered leaders were subject to mounting barrages of often scurrilous personal criticism. Highly politicized editor-politicians made the press serve as an important instrument of social and political leveling, bringing patrician leaders into the intense and often disrespectful "heat" of partisan warfare—and treating them with harsh indifference. These changes in the language of political criticism did not by themselves bring about changes in methods of political organization. The stimuli for most political criticism in the press came from partisan leaders. But these changes in journalistic style helped diminish respect for "position" and made the organization of large numbers of ordinary people a viable leadership alternative to smaller groupings of notables. The partisan press of the Dark Ages served, in essence, to desanctify public office and public leaders, thus opening the possibility of office, leadership, and political activity generally to the "unsanctified" ordinary man.

The press, then, served several functions in changing the political environment. First it helped puncture the posture of "above-the-battle" respectability that the first generation of American leaders had felt was the appropriate political stance for individuals of education and social status—in one sense, an arrogant vestige of *noblesse oblige*. The mud of

uses the concept of constituent function to emphasize the maintenance role of the American parties, i.e., their stability oriented service for the political system.

American politics was to hit *all* participants, regardless of position or background. Second, the press pitched the tone of politics in the mass media at a level where most people, not just the relatively well educated, could understand, participate, and enjoy the political dialogue. For the aristocrat's rapier, the press supplied instead the cannon and grapeshot.

This increased vulgarity—the style of the common or ordinary—admittedly built upon a tradition of personal and vindictive political criticism already a feature of the American press as early as the latter part of the 18th century. Washington himself had been accused of "traitorous ideas" and criticized (by the *Aurora,* for example) as "treacherous," "inefficient," and "full of ostentatious professions of piety" and "pusillanimous neglect." Beyond that he was often denounced, under such classical pseudonyms such as "Atticus," "Pittachus," and "Valerius," as a despot and would-be monarch.[30] However, despite the harsh personal attacks of certain editors, much of the political dialogue, particularly between opposing politicians, was still carried on in a fairly cultivated style, usually veiling direct personal attacks with a veneer of literary reference.

Differences between Hamilton and Jefferson, for example, produced a series of newspaper attacks and rejoinders frequently clothed in scholarly metaphor and sophisticated indirection. Answering charges made against him by "Aristides" (Madison and Monroe), "Catullus" (Hamilton) alluded snidely to Jefferson's sexual habits, pointing out that Jefferson's real character would be revealed "when the visor of Stoicism is plucked from the brow of the epicurean; when the plain garb of Quaker simplicity is stripped from the concealed voluptuary; when Caesar coyly refusing the proferred diadem, is seen to be Caesar rejecting the trappings by grasping the substance of imperial domination."[31]

This style of political argument clearly demonstrates the tendency of the first generation of American political lead-

---

[30] James Pollard, *Presidents and the Press,* pp. 19–23.

[31] From the *Gazette of the United States,* quoted in Robert A. Hendrickson, *Hamilton,* 2 vols. (New York: Mason Charter, 1976), 2: 185.

ers to clothe their scurrilous attacks on one another's personal character and political positions in educated verbiage, perhaps in a style of scholarly discourse typical of the 18th century rather than the 19th. Unless a man were well schooled in classical literature, much of the flavor—and, probably, much of the meaning—of these attacks would be hidden from him, effectively disbarring him from knowledgeable participation in the political process. Leaders were writing more for other leaders and an attentive, small, relatively homogeneous, and educated segment of the population than for a mass audience. Since the voting electorate at this time was less than 10 percent of the population as a whole, interpretation of their behavior in this way does not seem unreasonable.[32]

It would not be accurate to suggest a clean break between the press style of the earlier Federalist-Republican conflicts and that of the Democratic-Whig struggles three decades later. But despite some continuities and cumulative effects, certain stylistic changes did occur between one period and the other that furthered the development of a new style of campaigning and political mobilization. For example, in 1828 Adams was accused by the opposition press of detesting popular government, fostering corruption, and, while ambassador to Russia, prostituting an American girl "to the carnal desires of Czar Alexander the First."[33] Adams's supporters had themselves struck at least as hard and even more often at Jackson, charging him with crudity, adultery, and murder. Not much sophistication is necessary to appreciate the point of such attacks. On a few occasions, the Adams press allowed a tone of upper-class contempt for Jackson to creep into its

---

[32] In the election of 1800, only five of sixteen states had a popular vote. New York, Pennsylvania, New Jersey, and Massachusetts all held elections for electors in their state legislatures. Ten percent would be the highest estimate of popular participation, See *Guide to U.S. Elections* (Washington, D.C.: Congressional Quarterly, Inc., 1975), pp. 202–4.

[33] Glyndon Garlock Van Deusen, *The Jacksonian Era, 1828–1848* (New York: Harper and Row, 1963), p. 22.

attacks on him—as when it criticized the vulgar places where Jackson attacked Adams, "in stages, steamboats and bar-rooms . . . places in which no man whose manners had not been formed with such men as figure at race grounds, cockpits, and gambling tables would ever have thought of venting his spleen."[34] However, Adams's editors did not frequently permit such civility to get in their way. They adapted the "broadside" for use as a special election hand-bill to pummel their opponents with crude, often slander-ous accusations. The campaign broadside symbolizes, in fact, the new way in which press battles were fought: no Greek quotations, none but the most obvious metaphors, little intricate sword play, and much pounding by cannon—firing, as it were, broadside.

The best-known campaign broadside put out by either camp was the "coffin handbill," entitled in bold letters "SOME ACCOUNT OF SOME OF THE BLOODY DEEDS OF GENERAL JACKSON." Blackened coffins representing Jackson's various alleged murders and atroci-ties led the viewer naturally to a belief that all the deaths were due entirely to Jackson himself rather than to court-martials and other military activities carried out under his overall command. Variations of the "coffin theme" were widely distributed. One handbill which began by boldly claiming to be the "Official Record from The War Depart-ment of The Proceedings" proved to be nothing more than a variation of the coffin theme, a misleading forgery distrib-uted by the Adams party organization and by congressmen using their franking privileges.[35] Variations of this theme alone were printed in editions of up to ten thousand copies each. Effective material from these broadsides and other campaign pamphlets received repeated circulation by the partisan newspapers which reprinted it as "news."

During the 1828 Jackson campaign, a breakthrough in print technology helped escalate emphasis on the personal characteristics of the candidate. The new technical devel-

---

[34]*We, the People*, April 12, 1828, quoted in Smith, "Propaganda Technique," p. 62.

[35]*Ibid.*, p. 62.

opment was lithography, the new weapon of press criticism the political cartoon. Writing of this development, Stephen Hess and Milton Kaplan observe:

For political cartoons to have mass appeal required two developments: a process that would cut the cost of production and a subject colorful enough to inspire broad interest and controversy. The election of 1828 produced both—lithography and Andrew Jackson.[36]

Until 1828 the political caricature was a rare item in American printing. Less than a hundred separate images can be identified from both the colonial period and the early years of the Republic. The laborious task of making a cartoon by engraving on copper or cutting in wood was very expensive, and early images usually portrayed major events or some grand statement of enduring principle rather than normal, short-term, social or political activities. High costs of production thus prevented already financially undernourished newspaper publishers from using cartoons for partisan purposes until the technological breakthrough of lithography drastically reduced the cost of producing printed personal images. In 1829 the first lithographed political cartoon appeared in America.

This inexpensive method of reproducing a pictorial image quickly made the cartoon—a new visual method of meting out punishment and shaping public opinion—a regular feature of the political press. While the first newspaper cartoons portrayed rather stiff figures issuing balloons of text from their mouths, they nevertheless offered editors a sharp instrument of expression which, in effect, could accentuate the personal aspect of political attack. Illustrators might, for example, place public figures in incongruous and ridiculous positions, reducing them to objects of derision and laughter. The leveling effect of the political cartoon, consistently bringing down those in high public office, helped markedly in diminishing deferential atti-

---

[36] *The Ungentlemanly Art: A History of American Political Cartoons,* ed. Stephen Hess and Milton Kaplan (New York: Macmillan, 1975), p. 67.

tudes that underpinned leadership choices. The cartoon, together with the other changes in the political style of the press, clearly helped to deflate surviving reverence for public office and public leaders.[37]

Journalism helped to shape changes in the political environment extending beyond style, beyond the manner in which political attack was made. Multiplying the impact of stylistic change was the extraordinary increase during this period in the sheer *quantity* of political communications, brought about primarily by increased numbers of papers rather than by the circulation gains for individual papers. The rapid increase in the number of newspapers and other journals in a span of only three or four decades dramatically facilitated the penetration of the politicized press, which now reached a much larger share of the total population than only a generation earlier. Whereas some 234 newspapers were published in 1800, by 1833 about 1,200 newspapers were being printed—a large share of them dailies—representing almost a fivefold increase in the number of newspapers by the midpoint of Jackson's presidency, not including over 200 assorted other periodicals.[38]

This expansion of mass communications continued unabated. By the end of the closely contested Democratic-Whig battles only two decades later, the number of newspapers had once again doubled, while the number of papers printing on a daily basis had tripled. The young nation was virtually flooded by small politicized newspapers. As the partisan press penetrated most American homes, the press became an increasingly vital and powerful part of the organizations created by the two mass parties.

---

[37] *Ibid.*, p. 73.

[38] Data derived from Donald H. Stewart, "Jeffersonian Journalism: Newspaper Propaganda and the Development of the Democratic-Republican Party 1789–1801." Unpublished Ph.D. dissertation, Columbia University, 1950. From Noble Cunningham, Jr., *The Jeffersonian Republicans in Power: Party Operations, 1801–1809* (Chapel Hill: University of North Carolina Press, 1963), p. 236; Frank Luther Mott, *American Journalism* 3rd ed. (New York: Macmillan, 1962) p. 216; and, Alfred McClung Lee, *The Daily Newspaper in America; The Evolution of a Social Instrument* (New York: Macmillan, 1937), p. 64.

"Neutrality in this country and this age," a prominent paper noted "is an anomaly—it is a hybrid state." Midway through the century, the United States census reaffirmed the intensity of press partisanship developed during the Jacksonian era, listing only 5 percent of all newspapers as "neutral" or "independent."[39]

The organizational synthesis of the press, party, and president during this period of American politics had culminated, then, in a unique relationship between mass communications and major political institutions. Common ties between the press and key institutions of political mobilization created an unusual electoral circuitry—directly linking the sources of political information and the actions of electoral institutions in a way that would never again be duplicated. The press was, at this point, largely devoid of any independent political content, loyally supporting or opposing one or the other of the two major political parties and serving, in the main, as important parts of the party organizations themselves. Conflict was, in effect, structured around two warring camps. Unlike the situation of present-day politics, both of the chief instruments of mass mobilization and communications, the party and the press, served to increase partisan organizational activity and reinforce lines of electoral cleavage. More effectively than substantive issue differences alone, the extensiveness of the press's political coverage, the penetrating partisanship of its new journalistic style, and the press's tight organizational links to the parties, all helped make possible a new and tumultuous era of American politics—the politics of mass mobilization in a firmly entrenched two-party system.

The expanded scope of political conflict which the second generation of American political leaders stimulated served to distinguish them from the first generation. The founding generation, distrusting parties, sought to protect public and private rights against what they considered the tyranny of a majority party, fearing as Federalist No. 51 warned, that if "a majority be united by a common interest,

---

[39] Frank Mott, *American Journalism,* p. 216.

the rights of the minority will be insecure." The second
generation not only did not fear the evils that might
develop from a majority but also believed, instead, that the
formation of popular majorities was a valuable means of
promoting the stability and security of the political system.
They regarded the uniting of the "common interest" by the
political parties, the building of majorities behind popular
leaders, as the best means of ensuring the safety of democracy.

As Schattschneider has observed, the outcome of political conflict in a democracy is largely determined by the
extent to which the audience becomes involved. Jacksonian
strategy was clear: expand the decision-making arena from
the narrow band of governmental elites, the Congressional
Caucus, to voters in the states, thus defeating those who
sought to retain their own power by constricting the scope
of conflict to a small, decisive audience, themselves. By
increasing the scale of battle, seeking a new and better balance of forces to help his drive for the presidency, Jackson
and his supporters had extended the political arena to a
fully national dimension.[40] A critical factor in the development of this strategy was public visibility. To enhance Jackson's popular standing, his supporters had to organize
instruments of mass communications to provide him with
the necessary publicity. The press, the prime mass communications tool for creating public visibility, became,
along with the party, critical in reaching, focusing, and
solidifying a new and expanded electorate.

The overall extension of newspaper distribution, the
evolution of a new style of political journalism, and the
tight organizational links between press and party, all
served to expand the potential reach of the president by
permitting broad mobilization of relatively inert citizens
into partisan voters. The symbiotic relationship of press,
party, and president activated the American population at
large, filtering an aroused public opinion through two
mediating parties, and firmly institutionalizing popular

---

[40] Schattschneider, *The Semi-Sovereign People, passim.*

democracy for the first time in any nation. A newly
enlarged decisive public was mobilized, a new scale of
political conflict was established, and a new kind of electoral connection was made.

4

Refragmenting the National Arena

The carnage of civil war was followed by a period unique in American politics, one in which the universe of political debate was sharply narrowed. In contrast to the dramatic growth of industry and the rapid centralizing development of the American economic system in the last third of the 19th century, the national political system devolved rather than developed. Without any commanding political issues, such as slavery or secession, or any post-Reconstruction national legislative program, or any articulate presidential voices, national political debate was for the most part submerged beneath local and regional antagonisms. What debate did continue—predominantly Northern recrimination against the South over the war—cast a thin but concealing veil over those deep-rooted, unreconciled industrial tensions which required new governmental initiatives.

To a large extent, the power and authority that had so quickly accrued to the presidency and the national government during the Civil War shifted back to the states and localities. Localized, narrowly based conflicts dominated the political agenda, and patronage, rather than the articulation of any national program, became the principal output of politics.[1] All of the major political institutions contributed to this uniquely mute period in American political history. The presidency, the parties, and the press—and other political institutions, as well—all played important roles in limiting the scope of political conflict, dulling the articulation of social and political discontent, and, generally, fragmenting the political arena.

Accompanying this relative quiescence, the later 19th century experienced a marked reduction in the scope of presidential activity by the unassertive and limited men who held the office and the growth and refinement of local party "machines." It also witnessed the weakening of important links between the nation's political leadership and channels of political communications. Perhaps as the result of stunned reaction to past events or fearful anticipation of the future, this period saw the political disengagement of the three institutions most capable of enlarging the arena of politics, organizing decisive national majorities, and defining the issues and agenda for action confronting the nation and its leadership.

Departisanization of the Press

Although the partisanship of the press during the last three decades of the 19th century is much emphasized in historical literature, in fact the tight links earlier forged between press, party, and president were weakening by the end of Reconstruction. Even though many papers retained an official partisan affiliation between 1870 and 1900, and were often uninhibited in support of their favored candidates, the loosening of the ties between party organizations and the press was an important feature of this period, and significant in its ultimate impact. No such sudden shift toward an independent or nonpartisan press, as was thought to occur during the later Progressive era,

[1] James L. Sundquist, *Dynamics of the Party System: Alignment and Realignment of Political Parties in the United States* (Washington, D.C.: Brookings Institution, 1973), p. 93.

actually happened. In fact, the harbingers of a press genuinely independent of the parties are found in major changes
in the political economy of newspaper publishing that had
begun even before the Civil War—changes which, after
Reconstruction, steadily loosened the links between party
and press and between national and local party politicians.

Critical in reshaping the symbiotic relationship of press
and party was a major change in the *marketing* of newspapers. Starting with the first tentative manifestations of the
"penny press" in the late 1830s—newspapers that sold at
one cent per issue rather than the traditional six cents—the
mass marketing of "news," human interest, scandals,
sports, in addition to politics, came to displace political
editorials as the dominant mode of American newspapers.[2]
This change steadily improved the economic strength of
the newspaper and opened the way for the development of
newspapers as large-scale and powerful business organizations.

Just as politically oriented newspapers had replaced
commercial journals at the turn of the century, so political
papers now began to lose ground to new journals focusing
on "news" of all kinds. News with a strong, human-inter-
est, narrative line—"stories"—rather than editorial brilli-
ance became the key to the success of most newspapers.
The driving force behind the altered style of successful
newspapers was their appeal to the general public. As "selling" the people replaced "telling" the people, the marketplace rather than the editor-politician became the
dominant force in the life of most newspapers.

What began as a successful attempt by the penny press
to reach the ordinary and poorer urban classes a few

[2] For an interesting analysis of marketing changes during this period
see Michael Schudson, *Discovering the News: A Social History of American Newspapers* (New York: Basic, 1978), pp. 14–60. For discussions of
the impact of technological changes on the press see Frank Mott, *American Journalism,* 3rd ed. (New York: Macmillan, 1962), pp. 495–503;
Alfred McClung Lee, *The Daily Newspaper in America* (New York: Macmillan, 1937), pp. 119–25; and Edwin Emery, *The Press and America,
An Interpretative History of Journalism,* 3rd ed. (Englewood Cliffs:
Prentice Hall, 1972), pp. 402–6.

decades before the Civil War became, in the postwar period, a rising tide of change in American journalism. The strident and serious tone of the political journals had, on balance, dominated the press before the Civil War. But after the war, lively, spicy organs aiming "news" at the broadest readership began to crowd out political journals that did not adapt their format to the marketplace. Certain "quality" papers still retained a segment of their readership with a more "serious," less sensationalized approach to "news." But in general, personalized, human interest, events-oriented news came to dominate the popular dailies in the last half of the 19th century.[3]

The new market orientation of the popular press did not mean a drastic decline in overall political coverage. Rather, political news now had competition—vigorous competition—from other kinds of news for the attention of the public at large. A recent content analysis of the most prominent stories featured in daily newspapers during the 1880s and 1890s demonstrates just how successful this competition was. Of the major front-page stories appearing in the papers surveyed from this period, approximately 80 percent were nonpolitical, only about 20 percent political. The prominence of political news on the overall news agenda had clearly diminished.[4]

Publishers who controlled the successful penny presses, and their successful imitators in the post–Civil War period, themselves differed from earlier press-politicians in at least two respects. First, they operated large-scale businesses unlike the small-circulation political journals of the earlier period. A circulation rate of four thousand in 1833 was very healthy for the higher-priced journals that appealed to the

---

[3] Mass-oriented newspapers also brought about changes in the focus of advertising communications. Advertising directed to business was gradually replaced by what was previously considered "offensive" consumer advertising for products of health (patent medicines) and entertainment. See Schudson, *Discovering the News*, pp. 17–18.

[4] See Richard L. Rubin and R. Douglas Rivers, "The Mass Media and Critical Elections: A First Report," a paper delivered at the Northeastern Political Science Association, 1978, pp. 18–19.

"more important" people. By contrast, in New York just prior to the Civil War, Horace Greeley's *Tribune* reached forty-five thousand copies and James Bennett's *Herald* more than sixty thousand. Second, the editors of this new generation were likely to be publishers first and professional politicians second, unlike many of the politician-editors who dominated the newspaper field in the Jacksonian era.[5] By 1870 a new ideology of "independence" had begun to influence certain successful editors and publishers. In consequence, the solid and dependable channels of mass political communications that press-party coordination had previously provided now began to fragment.

The trend among leading publishers to editorial independence was self-propelling. As mass marketing strategies diverted the press from a partisan to a news function, the more the party's voice in shaping news diminished. As the party's voice diminished, the greater freedom the press had to criticize party policy, further depoliticizing the press-party relationship. As the decade of the 1870s began, the idea of independence from the parties was in the air among editors of leadership journals. For example, shortly before taking over the editorship of the *New York Tribune*, Whitelaw Reid exclaimed, "Independent journalism! That is the watchword of the future in the profession. An end of concealment because it would hurt the party; an end of one-sided expositions."[6]

Reid and the growing band of independent journalists were not, in fact, political neutralists. In most cases, they sided with the candidate of their party. But their claim of independence meant "freedom from party discipline," permitting criticism of policies and leaders from within the party. Such a posture was not long in provoking splits within party ranks. When a number of well-known Republican editors refused to support Grant's bid for reelection in 1872, they were derisively branded "mugwumps," i.e., bolters or renegades. In 1884 an even greater number of

[5] See Mott, *American Journalism*, pp. 411–13, for a discussion of this transition.

[6] *Ibid.*, p. 412.

Republican papers bolted from Blaine to the Democrat Cleveland, a defection further undermining the principle of party loyalty. Although the majority of papers continued strongly to support their party's candidate and color political news in partisan fashion where they could, a number of the larger, more renowned, and most financially successful papers were able to flout partisan control, report political stories as they liked, and still grow stronger.[7]

Journalist-entrepreneurs such as Joseph Pulitzer tended to treat both national and local politics in the same style as they treated publishing—a style characterized by excitement, provocation, and independence. Pulitzer helped build up Cleveland for nomination and election in 1884, for example, but turned on him shortly thereafter and attacked him mercilessly. Local party corruption similarly became the frequent object of crusades by Pulitzer and his imitators. As small communities exploded into large-scale cities, public utilities—water, transportation, and power—offered many opportunities for bribery and "honest graft" to petitioners for special privileges and politicians with the granting power. Political scandals became regular circulation-building features of local newspapers, which focused repeatedly on the corruption of the dominant political party and its leadership. Readership-building news for the daily press was often "bad news" for the local party.

Also weakening their partisan ties was the very growth of the number of daily newspapers in the same area. Only 65 dailies published in 1830. By 1870, 574 newspapers printed daily, and fast-growing cities supported several different dailies of various quality, appeal, and political perspective. By 1880 the number of daily newspapers had increased to 971, by 1890 to 1,610, and, by the turn of the century, over 2,200 newspapers printed every day.[8] Even papers supporting the same party in the same community required diverse approaches to politics in order to attract and hold readership. Without such diversity, they could neither justify nor sustain their own existence.

---

[7] Emery, *The Press and America*, p. 265.

[8] Lee, *The Daily Newspaper*, pp. 64–65.

The development of the evening daily and the Sunday newspaper also helped to increase the number and kinds of papers published in the first three decades following the Civil War. Major circulation increases, particularly by large-city newspapers, helped to establish many newspapers as large-scale, profitable enterprises; by 1880, at least three papers had surpassed the hundred thousand circulation mark. At the same time as circulation rates of urban papers began to explode, low-circulation rural papers (weeklies and dailies) also began to multiply rapidly. The tremendous growth of newspapers in the major population centers was paralleled by the rapid proliferation, in number and variety, of small newspapers in almost all the remote parts of the country. The establishment of newspapers in most communities of over three hundred population gave a strong local character to the American press as a whole, a feature of mass communication in sharp contrast to the primarily urban newspapers of France and England in the same period.[9]

Technological developments reduced the cost of printing and paper and permitted the quick printing of large editions even before the development of the linotype in the 1880s. But the most important stimulant to the growth of the dailies came from critical changes in the marketing approach of urban newspapers. By catering to the popular preferences of the masses of new immigrants, by focusing on human interest stories, sensationalism, and attention-getting pictures, the major urban dailies broadened extensively the potential for new newspaper readers (and new advertisers) in the rapidly growing marketplace.

Probably the most important technological advance contributing to the growth of newspapers, one that critically augmented journalistic independence from the parties, was the telegraph, a development of major political importance. Following its first use in 1844, a "wire communica-

---

[9] See S. D. North, "The Newspaper and the Periodical Press," published in *American Industry and Manufactures in the 19th Century*, vol. 8 (Washington, D.C.: Bureau of the Census, 1880), p. 73f.

tions" network spread rapidly throughout the country, speeded by the requirements of the Civil War. It quickly became a valuable tool for journalists in the transmission of news to places at great distances from the source of the news itself. "Feeder" news agencies, such as the New York Associated Press, placed a vast number and variety of national and international reporters indirectly at the disposal of a newspaper for a relatively small fixed fee. Most importantly, national political news became quickly accessible to many papers far removed from events. The heavy influence of national party leaders and their papers over the flow and treatment of political information was thus broken.

The use of the telegraph by newspapers after the Civil War was rapidly increased by a number of factors. The major expansion of telegraphic facilities was accompanied by a significant reduction in the cost of wire service, increasing demands by the reading public for more timely news, and the enlargement and refinement of the feeder news services provided by contract from press associations.[10] This drastic change in the nature of the channels of national political communication brought about major changes in the relationship between the press and the party.

In order to maximize use of telegraph and wire service reporters, much of the partisan bias still prevalent in the reporting of national political stories had to be muted or replaced by standardized, less opinionated, or "neutral" descriptions, a change with far-reaching effects. The logic behind neutral wire service reporting was fundamentally economic. Wire associations prospered by selling their reports to as many papers as possible. But different papers supported different parties and different political creeds. Hoping to maximize sales of their services, news agencies such as the Associated Press could hardly expect to sell strongly Democratic papers political news slanted against

---

[10] See Donald L. Shaw, "News Bias and the Telegraph: A Study of Historical Change," *Journalism Quarterly*, Spring 1967, pp. 7–10.

Democrats. Thus, the agencies adopted a detached, uncontentious style of reporting nonlocal news, increasing the objectivity of political reporting, and making their services more attractive to varied partisan newspapers.[11]

Donald L. Shaw, in a case study of news bias, has demonstrated this "neutralization" of political reporting. Shaw defined a biased news story as "any which contained value statements in such a way that the overall impression created a positive or negative feeling toward the referent."[12] He found, over time, a strong relationship between increased use of wire service stories and a sharp drop in biased reporting. For example, in Wisconsin, where wire service stories doubled between the presidential campaigns of 1880 and 1884, stories adjudged biased dropped during the same period from 42 percent to 3 percent. Comparing wire and non-wire stories over the period from 1852 to 1916, Shaw judged nonwire stories to exhibit bias approximately fifteen times as frequently as wire stories. In addition, Shaw found a remarkable change in the originating source of stories on presidential campaigns. Whereas, in 1856, no presidential campaign wire stories were carried in the Wisconsin newspapers, approximately half of their campaign stories came from the wire services in 1880, and three-quarters in 1890.[13]

Standardization and neutralization of nonlocal political news by the wire services strongly reinforced trends toward more independent reporting of political communications. The wire services thus weakened the simultaneously partisan and national slant characteristic of political

---

[11] See Fred Siebert, Theodore Peterson, and Wilbur Schramm, *Four Theories of the Press: The Authoritarian, Libertarian, Social Responsibility and Soviet Communist Concepts of What the Press Should Be and Do.* (Urbana: University of Illinois Press, 1963), p. 60, For a history of development of wire services see A. M. Lee, *The Daily Newspaper,* pp. 476–575. For a discussion on the age of standardization and the effects of syndications see Martin Mayes, *An Historical-Sociological Inquiry into Certain Phases of the Development of the Press in the United States* (Richmond, Missouri: Missourian Press, 1935), chapters 3 and 4.

[12] D. Shaw, "News Bias and the Telegraph," p. 5.

[13] *Ibid.,* p. 6.

news since the Jacksonian era. In combination with the shift, during the three decades following the Civil War, to relatively more varied, human interest news, the national partisan linkages of press and party, supported in the past by party newspaper networks, were gradually eroded.

The rise of large-circulation dailies in the cities and the increased penetration by new weekly newspapers of smaller communities was accompanied, then, by the steady decline of direct presidential influence over the press and political communications channels as a whole. Even before its official demise in January of 1861, the presidential newspaper, the keynote paper of the earlier era, had lost much of its importance politically, most probably because it no longer served the same broadly based informational needs it had served earlier. The telegraph had eliminated much of the need for an "official" communications network ready to print the laws of the land "By Authority." It also reduced the dependence of various outlying newspapers on the "By Authority" journals for national political information. Since all newspapers could receive the laws and other news, from Washington and everywhere else, simultaneously from the wire services, exclusivity and the special patronage apparatus that went with it were lost.[14]

The decline of direct presidential influence over the press after the Civil War contributed to weakening national influence over the party system as a whole. The presidential press network had hitherto played a key role in developing local organizational structures linked to the president and the national party leadership. Following the Civil War, presidential patronage resources once necessary to organize and structure local political communications were obsolete. Newspapers, now connected to national news sources by telegraph and other agencies, were no longer dependent on a centralized presidential party news network.

A substantial amount of natural partisanship still characterized the news system during this period, particularly

---

[14] After 1861 all federal statutes were published by the Government Printing Office, thus obviating the need for publication in designated papers.

outside the highly urbanized East. But the trend toward an "independent" press was unmistakable. Many new and improved channels of political information reached directly to the mass public in the last half of the 19th century, dislodging the president from his prominent position at the central and creative point in a limited network of political communications. The center-periphery press system developed during the Jacksonian era broke down when presidential resources declined at its center while the newspapers' own resources and motivations underwent significant changes at the periphery. Not only was there a vast increase in the amount of news of all kinds (with which the president had to compete), but also the president had increasingly to assert himself in his relationship with the press in order to mobilize mass opinion for political purposes.

Combined departisanization of the press and loss of presidential influence over the flow of national political communications heightened the difficulties of presidential leadership. The independence of the press deprived the president and national leaders of an important tool for structuring and mobilizing popular opinion and votes. But other changes in the presidency and the parties—the "demobilization" of the presidency and the increased localization of party politics—also advanced the fragmentation of the national political arena and the growing constriction of the range of political controversy.

Presidential Demobilization

The designers of the federal Constitution kept firmly in mind two desiderata: dispersion of power and restraint of majoritarian actions. These considerations were institutionalized by firm assignments of power to diverse localities away from the center of the federal government. The many elective offices and the numerous political functions regularly carried out by governments in towns, cities, counties, and states, provided substantial bases for political organizations built and operated at a distance from the national seat of government. In addition, the sharply defined local basis of election to national office heavily weighted the system against decisive national action by ensuring that local considerations could divide the unity of national governmental institutions themselves. In fact, the centrifugal tendencies deliberately built into the system became so strong that only forceful leadership at the system's center could initiate and make effective major national policies.

Such was still the case during the Civil War. President Lincoln greatly expanded the centralizing powers of his office, above and beyond his constitutional prerogatives. He increased his power still further by adroit use of political organization, patronage, and the manipulation of political communications.[15] Lincoln's expert grasp of party politics enabled him to control national politics even under severe pressure from the radical wing of his own party.[16] Overall, the Republican party provided Lincoln and the Union a sturdy vehicle of political communication and organization during the war, a means by which commitment to "the cause" could be defined and affirmed through the electoral process. Partisan elections in the North, for example, were a critical step in nationalizing the war, as party and electoral activity extended local and state loyalties into national loyalties.[17]

However, while a party system led by a strong and adept president facing a major crisis could nationalize the bases

---

[15] See Harry J. Carman and Reinhart H. Luthin, *Lincoln and the Patronage*, 2nd ed. (Gloucester, Mass.: Peter Smith, 1964), chapter 5; David M. Potter, *Lincoln and His Party in the Secession Crisis*, 3rd ed. (New Haven, Conn.: Yale University Press, 1962); Stephen B. Oates, *With Malice Towards None* (New York: Harper and Row, 1977), p. 405; and Robert S. Harper, *Lincoln and the Press* (New York: McGraw Hill, 1954).

[16] Potter, *Lincoln and His Party*, p. 32; Eric McKittrick, "Political Parties and the Union and Confederate War Efforts," in *The American Party Systems: Stages of Political Development* ed. William Nisbet Chambers and Walter Dean Burnham, 2nd ed. (New York: Oxford University Press, 1975), p. 148.

[17] Eric McKittrick, "Political Parties," p. 151.

of its support from those removed from the center of the system, that same party system, lacking assertive presidents, facing no emergency conditions, and enmeshed in strong sectional biases, could through simple inertia permit decentralization of political power and its dispersal out toward the periphery of the system. No doubt, the initial weakening of the presidency following the Civil War owed much to Andrew Johnson's inept, contradictory role in Reconstruction policy. The numerous scandals of the Grant administration provoked widespread investigations and kept the presidency under attack by Congress, the press, and its partisan opposition. The deterioration in the stature of the presidency continued through the Hayes, Garfield, and Arthur administrations, as well.[18]

This deterioration was not exclusively a result of unassertive presidents with limited talents and perspectives. Several electoral and institutional factors during the last three decades of the 19th century contributed to the restriction of presidential range and the blunting of presidential impact, and limited the success of attempts to recoup the office's stature and power. First, in circumstances unique to this period, every president elected from 1876 to 1892 lacked the support of a simple majority of votes cast for all presidential candidates.[19] Second, thin and fluctuating party majorities in the two Houses of Congress precluded unified presidential and congressional party-building activity and forestalled any durable policy thrust to politics.[20] Third, the strength of sectionalism forced aspiring presidential candidates to adopt political strategies that tended

---

[18] John Arthur Garraty, *The New Commonwealth 1877–1890* (New York: Harper and Row, 1968), p. 229; E. B. Andrews, *History of the Last Quarter Century in the United States*, 2 vols. (New York: Scribners, 1897), 1:32.

[19] See Richard Pious, *The American Presidency* (New York: Basic Books, 1979), p. 103.

[20] Morton Keller, *Affairs of State: Public Life in 19th Century America* (Cambridge, Mass.: Harvard University Press, 1977), p. 545; also, *Historical Statistics*, vol. 2 (Washington, D.C.: Department of Commerce, Bureau of the Census, 1957), p. 691; and Garraty, *The New Commonwealth*, p. 223.

to produce segmented, noncongruent majorities. For example, the Democrats of the rural South provided 135 of the 185 electoral votes necessary to win the election. A Democratic candidate could thus win the presidency by supplementing that base with the votes of only a few large urban states. When, for example, Cleveland added to the solid Democratic South the four states of New York, New Jersey, Connecticut, and Indiana, he became the sole Democrat successfully to penetrate the Republican bastions in the North. However, although he gained the presidency, he inherited along with it the mutually opposing policy positions of Northern urban Democrats and Southern rural Democrats.[21]

In other words, during the post-Reconstruction decades both parties were essentially evenly matched at the national level but could not be broadly policy-directed and policy-consistent. Political combat was based less upon the policies and positions of nationally oriented statesmen than upon religious, cultural, and other regionally oriented factors.[22] The prevailing tone of political activity was essentially localistic and sectional. Lacking the centralizing, organizing counterbalance of strong presidents, the fragmenting, decentralizing tendencies built into the electoral structure tended to reassert themselves and dominate the political system. Neither the president nor the Congress could easily produce major legislation since both were subordinated to sectional policy interests and the particularistic patronage needs of local party organizations. When major legislation occasionally overcame the formidable layers of resistance to successful passage, the tentative balance of power between the different sides almost always ensured a subsequent challenge to, and often a reversal of, the new policies.

Though it is not a principal focus of the present analysis,

---

[21] Sundquist, *Dynamics of the Party System*, pp. 128–35.

[22] Paul Kleppner, *The Cross of Culture: A Social Analysis of Midwestern Politics, 1850–1900* (New York: The Free Press, 1970); and Richard Joseph Jensen, *The Winning of the Midwest: Social and Political Conflict, 1888–1896* (Chicago: University of Chicago Press, 1971).

the Supreme Court, it should be noted, added its influence in restricting the scope of national political activity. Its domination of critical economic decision-making processes denied much of their potential political influence to farmer and labor groups that sought economic redress through traditional, popular-based electoral processes. Legislative initiatives to regulate aspects of the economy, whether at national or state levels, were often vitiated by Court decisions, limiting and confounding those mass electoral efforts to bring about change.[23]

For example, the Court denied the constitutionality of national income tax legislation; found that the Sherman Act could not be applied to the sugar trust but could be applied against labor unions; and permitted judicial intervention based on "property rights" in labor disputes on the side of the corporation, and in railroad disputes on the side of railroad companies against rural municipalities. Thus the Court raised still higher an already high threshold for popular policy making and narrowed the reach of electoral politics. While a powerful, activist Court, in the least representative branch of the federal government, limited the range of existing legislation, and a weakened presidency presided timidly at the center of the political system, unrestrained decentralizing tendencies inherent in the sys-

[23] See Alan Westin, "The Supreme Court, the Populist Movement, and the Campaign of 1896," *Journal of Politics* 15 (1953): 3–41. Two articles that challenge the position that the Supreme Court was either conservative or unrestrained in its exertion of judicial power, see Charles Warren, "A Bulwark to the State Police Power—The United States Supreme Court," *Columbia Law Review* 13 (1913): 667–95; and "The Progressiveness of the United States Supreme Court," *Columbia Law Review* 13 (1913): 294–313. For an approach to Supreme Court decisions from the perspective of whether they advance or retard states rights see Charles Collins, *The Fourteenth Amendment and the States* (rpt. New York: Da Capo Press, 1974). See also Loren Beth, *The Development of the American Constitution 1877–1917* (New York: Harper and Row, 1971), chapter 5: "The Supreme Court and National Business Regulation," and chapter 6: "The Supreme Court and State Regulation of Business." For a more ideological perspective see Arthur Selwyn Miller, *The Supreme Court and American Capitalism* (New York: The Free Press, 1967), chapters 2 and 3.

tem encouraged a shift of political energy away from attempts to build a national agenda and toward the further development of specialized and localized politics.

The Localization and Segmentation of Politics

The demobilization of the presidential voice in American politics was accompanied by a powerful resurgence of localism encouraged by the electoral framework of the Constitution itself. The post-Reconstruction period witnessed the further development and refinement of organizational structures that substantially enlarged and accentuated these tendencies toward decentralization. Within Congress, for example, operating structures that controlled the flow and substance of legislation were rapidly institutionalized, abstracting power from congressional action as a whole and vesting it increasingly in leaders, committees, and sectional blocs. Back in the localities, powerful "machines" organized to capture elective offices and the growing resources attached to those offices were transforming local party structures. In general, politics during this era was oriented toward "extractions" and "benefits" rather than broad issues. Patronage rather than policy was the central focus of political organization.[24]

Political localization and segmentation were perhaps most apparent in the organizational changes that Congress developed in response to the rapid growth of legislation. Over twenty-three standing committees were added to the organizational structure of the House of Representatives between 1860 and 1901, effectively dispersing power within the House. Tenure and seniority became primary considerations for leadership positions. While only two of thirty-nine House committee chairmen were "senior" members in 1881, twenty-five of the forty-nine chairmen

---

[24] Sundquist, *Dynamics of the Party System*, p. 92.

in 1893 were "senior."[25] Their relatively secure power bases insulated chairmen from all but their local constituencies. Such insulation was particularly significant in an era that specialized in large volumes of patronage-oriented bills and few nationally oriented pieces of policy legislation.[26] A gradually decreasing rate in the turnover of committee memberships heightened the importance of seniority, while a simultaneously decreasing turnover rate for the House as a whole augmented the insulation of power.[27]

A local congressional district could most effectively advance its own interests by continually reelecting its representative. In an era of presidential demobilization, the possibilities for a national perspective thus became increasingly unlikely. Long-service but only locally accountable congressmen, protected by their insulated power bases, became almost impervious to broader public interests.

Together, these developments advanced the denationalization of politics and facilitated the assertion of particularistic interests in the House of Representatives.

[25] Nelson W. Polsby, "The Institutionalization of the U.S. House of Representatives," *American Political Science Review* 62 (1968): 145–49. See also Polsby, *et al.*, "The Growth of Seniority in the House of Representatives," *American Political Science Review* 63 (1969): pp. 78–87; see also George B. Galloway, *History of the House of Representatives*, 2nd ed. (New York: Thomas Y. Crowell, 1976); and Ralph da Costa Nunes, "Patterns of Congressional Change: Critical Realignment, Policy Clusters and Party Voting in the House of Representatives," unpublished doctoral dissertation, Columbia University, 1977.

[26] See Benjamin Ginsberg, "Critical Elections and the Substance of Party Conflict," *Midwest Journal of Political Science* 16 (1972): 603–25; and "Elections and Public Policy," *American Political Science Review* 80 (1976): 41–50. In these two articles, Ginsberg offers empirical evidence that discrete policy agendas developed in the late 19th century. For a critique of his work see Barbara Deckard Sinclair, "Party Realignment and the Transformation of the Political Agenda," *American Political Science Review* 71 (1977). Sundquist occasionally makes reference to the rise of partisan issues; see *Dynamics of the Party System*, pp. 111–13 and 134–35. However, his main thrust is a description of parties as antiprogram and antipolicy. In any case, the agenda proposed in the House did not become legislated and enacted.

[27] Nunes, "Patterns of Congressional Change," pp. 94, 96, 100.

Decentralization of power among committees and chairmen yielded other, antimajoritarian consequences. Action
desired by a majority was often stymied by procedural constraints. Strategic blocking points, often controlled by
minority-interest representatives whose seniority had
given them influence and power, could retard the flow of
legislation thought to be threatening to the institutional
stability of the House or to the parochial interests of the
minority. Frequent resort to dilatory motions or quorums
evaporated by disappearing minorities could at any given
moment frustrate the will of the majority of representatives.[28]

Much more than the House, the Senate between 1870
and 1895 reflected the insulated nature of politics. Unlike
members of the House, Senators were not elected by popular vote but by their state legislatures. They were thus
particularly immune from presidential, electoral, or other
popular pressures. Senators such as Conkling, Aldrich,
Sherman, and Platt were all deeply immersed in the organizational politics of their home states; indeed, their very
presence in the Senate attested to their local organizational
acceptability, reliability, and importance. Confronting no
such requirement of mass popularity as faces contemporary
senators, the senators of this earlier era operated under
rules that forged unusually tight links between them and
their local organizational leaders. Although the Senate took
an active legislative role during this period, particularly on
certain economic and foreign policy issues, its interests
were grounded, on balance, in localistic and particularistic
concerns. It neither reflected nor developed any "national"
consensus. As David J. Rothman has noted, "since senators
came from very secure state organizations, they could act
freely in the Capitol without fear of reprisals from the
national party."[29] State and local party organizational
power was, therefore, the source of a unique kind of political immunity for senators: immunity from much national

[28] Galloway, *History of the House of Representatives*, p. 164.
[29] David J. Rothman, *Politics and Power; The United States Senate,
1869–1901* (Cambridge, Mass.: Harvard University Press, 1966), p. 178.

party politics, from presidential coattails, and from rank-and-file voters in their home states.

In linking elected officials of the national government to their local organizational roots, one important point needs to be underscored. Before the advent of regularized primary elections, no aspiring candidate could run for office under a particular party label without the endorsement and official designation of local or state organizational leadership cadres.[30] What this meant in practical terms was that a party's candidate, if successful in the general election, was expected to conform to party direction on those matters that concerned organizational leaders. To deny the organization's demands meant that an officeholder would lose future nomination support. Thus, members of Congress in both the Senate and House had obligations that were of far greater practical significance to them than the needs of their electoral constituents (particularly in one-party areas) or of the nation (at least, when it faced no real or evident crisis). Without the support of their organizational constituents for nomination, they would be forced to run under a different party label. The organization's monopoly over the nomination required members of Congress to keep a careful eye on the needs of the local and state "machine," an appartus needing fuel that could in part be provided by favorable decisions on federal patronage-oriented issues.

The great growth in sources of patronage at the state and local levels itself came to provide party organizational machinery with substantial political resources essentially independent of the national party. Local organizations still sought to gain what they could from their representatives in the national government. But the tremendous explosion of urban life in the post-Reconstruction decades provided large-scale and diverse sources of patronage, kickbacks,

---

[30] While certain state and local machines held incipient organizational primaries, popular primaries had not become a significant political factor. See Martin Shefter, "Parties, Patronage, and Political Change," a paper delivered at 1976 annual meeting of the American Political Science Association, Chicago, Illinois.

preferments, and "honest graft" at the local level. In New York City alone, for example, over twelve thousand full-time locally controlled patronage jobs made up the foundation of the Democratic party machine in the late 1870s.[31] The elaboration and refinement of local party machinery resulted in the funneling of vast amounts of money—legal and illegal—directly into the party's hands. Together with their rapidly growing lists of discretionary job appointments, these funds made the local parties "independently wealthy."

Thus the period from Reconstruction to the end of the 19th century was marked by a growing disparity between a decentralized political system and a rapidly centralizing industrial system. On one hand, the growth in congressional power vis-à-vis the president combined with the narrow, particularistic nature of congressional activities to undermine concern with and the articulation of national issues. On the other hand, weakened by a combination of post-Reconstruction reaction, ineffective and unimaginative presidents, and narrow and essentially noncongruent electoral contests, the presidency also could not muster popular majorities for particular programs.

Adding to the fragmentation of the national arena was the significant change in the character of the press and the resultant change in the relationship of mass communications to the president and the party. Major marketing changes, as well as such technological innovations as the telegraph, combined to weaken significantly the national partisan content of political communications. An autonomous press, no longer linked organizationally to political institutions, was markedly immune to presidential input in the channels of political information. Unable any longer to structure mass communications nationally, and unwilling

---

[31] Keller, *Affairs of State*, pp. 310ff; *Appleton's Annual Cyclopedia and Register of Important Events, 1977*, n.s. 11 (New York: 1978), p. 563; Ernest S. Griffith, *A History of American City Government: The Conspicuous Failure, 1870–1900* 2 vols. (New York: Oxford University Press, 1976), 2: 76ff.

to find new ways to "use" an independent press, presidents found their influence sharply limited as an integrating, nationalizing force of government.

Presidents continued to court and manipulate editors and reporters for their own advantage during election campaigns. But they made little coordinated effort during the last decades of the 19th century to use their office to build popular esteem through the mass media and then convert favorable public opinion into political power. Efforts to mold public opinion by manipulating the press were generally distasteful to the personal sensibilities of late-19th-century presidents. They were in any case unnecessary to their limited policy and administrative purposes.[32]

Using the news-creating potential of the presidential office actually to shape or "create" public opinion, and then using that support as a major political resource, depended upon a changed conception of the presidency and a new understanding of the relationship of the president, an independent press, and the force of public opinion. The first modern "media president," Theodore Roosevelt, made such a new attempt to guide mass communications. His efforts began the process of creating a new centrality to the presidency in the political system, and began a new relationship between the press, party, and presidency.

---

[32] James Pollard, *Presidents and the Press* (New York: Macmillan, 1947), p. 532.

5

The Politics of Reorganization

During the decades just before and after the turn of the 20th century, America's economy, its means of political communications and transportation, and its traditions of political mobilization underwent an extraordinary transformation and reorganization. For the nation's industry, this was a period of unparalleled expansion, rapid corporate consolidation, and massive centralization of economic forces. For the press, affected by the same processes of consolidation and institutional specialization, the growth of numerous large-scale corporate publishing enterprises broke its remaining organizational links with the political parties. This political independence, an outgrowth of the press's newly developed economic power, necessitated the formation of new kinds of linkage between political institutions, aspiring leaders, and the channels of political communications.

The major changes of this period were reflected in a significant redefinition of the presidency as well. Activist presidents, Theodore Roosevelt and Woodrow Wilson, ended a period of presidential passivity and vastly expanded the range and intensity of presidential involvement in the political system as a whole. Their expansion of presidential power and their emphasis on presidential initiative in forming new policies and programs were part of the growing centralization of political and economic forces that moved the presidency to center stage.[1] In reaching for new sources of power and in seeking broad-based popular affirmation for their new initiatives, both presidents sought to mold mass opinion. Thus they were to help reshape the relationship between the presidency, the existing channels of political communications, and the press.

Unlike the press and the presidency, however, the political parties were significantly weakened rather than strengthened in the period before World War I. Following the final decades of the 19th century, when organizational resources and structural solidity of local parties reached a height, the first decades of the 20th century launched successive waves of Progressive reforms that, intentionally or not, curtailed party organizational strength. By their end, such reforms as party primaries, direct election of senators, and referenda and recall procedures had been broadly instituted. While some reformers aimed their efforts at eliminating bad party leaders rather than at the party as an institution, the net *results* of the Progressive attacks were to weaken party organizations as mediating links between governmental leaders and voters. While the presidency and the press were building political resources and extending their potential powers of political mobilization, the party was, in fact, losing them. Fearful of concentrated political power in a party "machine," resentful of extensive partisan corruption, and insistent on more direct, less mediated connections between the leaders and the led, Progressive reformers brought about a significant transformation of party structure and its powers of mass mobilization.

---

[1] Arthur M. Schlesinger, Jr., *The Imperial Presidency* (New York: Popular Library, 1974), pp. 89–105. This chapter was researched and written with Steven Robert Howard of the Department of Political Science of Columbia University.

The Politics of Differentiation

While political activity in post–Civil War America had gravitated toward local centers of power, economic forces had worked toward a consolidation and centralization of economic power. Never before had a nation undergone as rapid and pervasive an economic transformation as America experienced from the end of the Civil War to the start of World War I. For example, in spite of the fact that the population had more than doubled between 1869 and 1903, gross national product expanded from $147 per capita to $234 per capita. Steel, oil, railroad, telegraph, and telephone all emerged as major industries in this era, gaining dominant positions in the American economy by the turn of the century. Capitalizations from mergers and combinations, for example, rose from $41 million in 1895 to $2,263 million in 1899; and, the number of companies absorbed by these corporate consolidations jumped from 43 to 1,208 in just the same four-year period. Clearly, the rapid industrialization of the nation's economy translated into the significant concentration and the centralization of private economic power.[2]

In this period, the "visible hand" of managerial capitalism was adroitly defining corporate relations and implementing the consolidation of hierarchical corporate structures. Values of efficiency, stability, security, and financial accountability were achieved by nationalization of both the corporation and the economy. Functional specialization and professionalization become recurring themes of American business.[3] But these processes were not confined

---

[2] Robert Higgs, *The Transformation of the American Economy 1865–1914: An Essay in Interpretation* (New York: Wiley, 1971), p. 19; *Historical Statistics of the U.S.: From Colonial Times to 1957* (Washington, D.C.: U.S. Census Bureau, 1966); Gabriel Kolko, *The Triumph of Conservatism: A Reinterpretation of American History 1900–1916* (New York: Quandrangle, 1963), pp. 18–19; Ralph L. Nelson, *Merger Movements in American Industry, 1895–1956* (Princeton, N.J.: Princeton University Press, 1959), pp. 33–38.

[3] Alfred D. Chandler, *The Visible Hand: The Managerial Revolution In American Business* (Cambridge, Mass.: Harvard University Press, 1977).

to corporations, for similar institutional differentiation, specialization, and professionalization came to characterize the entire fabric of American society. In medical and legal practices, engineering, merchandising, academe, the trades, and even sports, appropriate training, certification, official credentials, and membership in occupational associations began to define careers and set them apart from other activities.

One scholar has argued that these underlying processes of professional differentiation were expressions of deeply rooted psychological needs of the American middle class that would eventually define what he termed a powerful "culture of professionalism."[4] Other scholars have considered these functional and social processes as arising from the need generated by industrialism to link smaller and larger contexts of life in an emerging "organizational society."[5] Most historical perceptions, however, underscore the importance of the increasing complexity of American society as businesses, professions, and public institutions all promoted their institutional differentiation and autonomy and the rationalization of their activities.

The press, too, fits a similar pattern of development, self-consciousness, and reorganization, and is best understood within the framework of the broader communications and transportation revolutions of this period. Something of the dimensions of these revolutions can be grasped from the following facts. Daily newspaper circulation increased sevenfold between 1870 and 1900. The number of post offices increased nearly three times, and the sale of ordinary postage stamps by eight times. Miles of telegraph wire increased nine times, and the volume of telegraph mes-

---

[4] Burton Bledstein, *The Culture of Professionalism* (New York: W. W. Norton, 1976); and William R. Johnson, *Schooled Lawyers: A Study in the Clash of Professional Cultures* (New York: New York University Press, 1978).

[5] Samuel P. Hays, *Building the Organization Society*, ed. Jerry Israel (New York: The Free Press, 1972), pp. 1–17; see also Hays, *The Response to Industrialism* (Chicago: University of Chicago Press, 1957); Robert H. Wiebe, *The Search for Order, 1877–1920* (New York: Hill and Wang, 1967), pp. 11–43, 52–66.

sages seven times. The number of telephones increased from 3,000 in 1876, shortly after the initial manufacture of Alexander Graham Bell's invention, to 1.3 million in 1900.[6] At the same time the extraordinary expansion of railroads across the nation revolutionized transportation in America. The number of miles of railroad track increased from 47,000 in 1879 to 190,000 in 1899; during the 1880s alone, 75,000 miles of track were laid—by far the greatest amount of railroad mileage ever built in any decade in any part of the world. Telegraph lines followed the newly constructed railroad tracks, bridging distances and constantly expanding the range of mass communications.

Developments in print technology and steadily improving communications support from the telegraph and telephone provided the press with means and incentives to expand news sources economically and to establish itself as an important corporate enterprise. As a result, the newspaper industry followed some of the same tendencies toward greater concentration and consolidation that the great industries—steel, oil, the railroads—were pioneering, though at a slower pace and on a smaller scale. For example, newspaper chains, press syndicates, and publishers' associations were organized by the late 1880s. By the 1890s, three chains had gained national prominence under the entrepreneurial management of E. W. Scripps, William Randolph Hearst, and Frank Munsey.

Several different factors facilitated the beginning of newspaper consolidations: combining a morning paper with an evening paper could promote the more economic twenty-four-hour operation of a single plant; advertisers would find it cheaper to buy space in one paper with a general, nonoverlapping circulation; the restrictive rules adopted by the Associated Press in regard to new members would make it virtually impossible to obtain a franchise except by purchasing an AP paper. By 1900 eight chains controlled twenty-seven papers and perhaps 10 percent of

[6] Robert G. Albion, "The Communications Revolution," *American Historical Review* 37 (1932): 718–20; Chandler, *The Visible Hand*, part 2: "The Revolution in Transportation and Communication," pp. 79–206.

national daily circulation; but by 1920 about sixty chains owned three hundred dailies and accounted for over one-third of the daily circulation in America, equivalent to over twelve million papers a day.[7]

Frank Munsey, nicknamed "The Great Executioner of Newspapers," was perhaps the archetypal newspaper consolidationist. He acquired seven papers in New York alone, and by 1918 Munsey could observe "the same law of economics applies in the newspaper business that operates in all important business today. Small units in any line are no longer competitive factors."[8] The reorganization of the press was a clear consequence of technological and marketing transformations. Except in remote, rural areas or in cases of specialized audiences, small units of production had become obsolete.

Although the press's economic strength freed it of party influence, the major urban newspapers had in a certain sense become hostages of a different kind—to their own commercial needs to continually expand their daily circulation and advertising base. The result, an almost continuous series of circulation wars in major cities, not only led inexorably to further newspaper consolidations as victors absorbed losers in these wars, but also markedly lowered the quality of journalism as a whole. The battles of the press giants for circulation ushered in the era of "yellow journalism," a period of unrivaled sensationalism before and just after the turn of century, where the prime object seemed to be to sell newspapers by any means, however sensational.

Hearst's *New York Journal* and Pulitzer's *New York World*, for example, engaged regularly in circulation wars: stories of scandals, disasters, and sex, scare headlines, and lurid illustrations typified their sensationalist appeals. The Hearst-Pulitzer circulation war paralleled the beginnings of

---

[7] Frank Luther Mott, *American Journalism: A History, 1690–1960* 3rd ed. (New York: Macmillan, 1962), pp. 635, 648; Alfred M. Lee, *The Daily Newspaper in America* (New York: Macmillan, 1937), p. 168.

[8] Mott, *American Journalism*, pp. 637, 648; Lee, *The Daily Newspaper*, p. 726 (Table XIII).

the Spanish-American War, which it helped initiate, and represents the peak of this style of journalism. "Spanish atrocities," fabricated stories of innocent victims in Cuba, were accompanied by repulsive illustrations meant to incite U.S. intervention in Cuba. The day following the sinking of the U.S. battleship *Maine* in Havana harbor, the circulation of each paper passed a million. The ensuing Spanish-American War subsequently provided an array of subject matter—military battles, reconnaissance missions, and massacres—that not only sustained but also even increased already enormous circulations; at one point in 1898 the *Journal* was issuing forty editions a day. Not until after the conclusion of the war and the assassination of President McKinley in 1901 did a reaction set in against the Hearst papers and this type of squalid American journalism.[9]

During this period of both rapacious sensationalism and extraordinary corporate growth the press was, with exceptions such as the presidential election in 1896, remarkably detached and disinterested in domestic national politics, focusing its news headlines instead on nonpolitical "human interest" affairs or on foreign events. Recent historical evidence of the period underscores the fact that the major urban newspapers, while growing independent of party concerns, were also growing politically disinterested.[10] Equally noteworthy, however, is the fact that despite a massive increase in the channels of communications—a sevenfold increase in newspaper circulation, the expansion of telegraphic services, and the development of the telephone—only Mark Hanna's efforts for the Republicans during and after 1896 attempted systematically to turn these new and expanded means of mass communications to political advantage.

A pattern of presidential passivity was abruptly ended with the succession of Theodore Roosevelt to the presi-

[9] For a full discussion of the news coverage of Spanish-American War see Mott, *American Journalism*, pp. 527–44.

[10] Richard L. Rubin and Douglas Rivers, "The Mass Media and Critical Elections: A First Report," a paper delivered at the 1978 annual meeting of the Northeastern Political Science Association, Figure 1.

dency, following McKinley's assassination. With Roosevelt as chief executive, the style, structure, and substance of political communications emanating from the White House was significantly transformed. Whereas McKinley's personal style typified the mode of presidential-press relationships in the late 19th century, Roosevelt initiated a new presidential style of the 20th, actively interposing his office in the news process in an attempt to shape and use the news for political purposes. McKinley saw the president-press relationship from a primarily defensive posture, relying on party organizational activities to politicize and mobilize his partisans: Roosevelt used the relationship in an offensive manner. What could he, as president, gain by selecting and structuring newsworthy political information? How could he build new political leverage, and how could he use the vastly expanded channels of communications to increase the scope of his office and the power of the presidency?

The Presidency and the News Process

The presidency of Theodore Roosevelt initiated a major transformation in the role of the president in the news process, one that was linked to his own understanding of the nature of executive leadership, his personal assertiveness, and a new view of public opinion and political power. Roosevelt himself wrote, "I have a definite philosophy about the presidency. I think it should be a very powerful office, and I think the president should be a very strong man who uses without hesitation *every* power that the position yields."[11] Roosevelt meant what he said, and by wielding presidential influence over the channels of political communications he greatly increased the potential powers of the office.

Roosevelt's major political strength had not come through traditional sources in party politics, and his selec-

[11] Matthew Josephson, *The President Makers: The Culture of Politics and Leadership in the Age of Enlightenment 1896–1919* (New York: Harcourt, Brace, 1940), p. 139 (italics mine); see also pp. 106–74.

tion as McKinley's vice-presidential running mate was apparently a move by the New York State Republican organization to "kick upstairs" an individualistic, troublesome, and disruptive politician.[12] Roosevelt's prime political strength was, in fact, his own personality and character, which had made him a popular though unorthodox local candidate; and as president, Roosevelt maintained his preference for personal rather than organizational politics.

Given the tenuous relationship between Roosevelt and regular party leaders, exacerbated by his own activist, reformist predilections, it seems likely that he could have neither maintained his political viability nor advanced his own programs without resort to a kind of appeal different from partisan loyalties. For Roosevelt, whose actions in such instances as the Northern Securities case and the anthracite coal strike often went counter to party leadership opinion, broad emphasis on the "public interest" rather than partisan interest became a strategic political theme.[13] Perhaps because of his own weakness in party politics, or possibly because of his own strength in making broad popular appeals, Roosevelt sought new channels of political communications through which to build his own personal power and the power of his office. To do so required a new relationship with the press, one which, unlike the relationship of late-19th-century presidents, understood the necessary prominence of the president's public image and accommodated—and thus used—the press's professional interest in the nation's chief executive. Unlike his immediate predecessors, Roosevelt not only welcomed pervasive public exposure but also sought to deploy it for planned political advantage, hoping to instigate broad electoral support for himself and his politics *across* party lines.

Roosevelt's direct cultivation of public opinion outside usual partisan channels seems to mark the beginnings of a partial but important *disengagement* of the president from

[12] *Ibid.*

[13] Richard Pious, *The American Presidency* (New York: Basic Books, 1978), p. 123; Schlesinger, *The Imperial Presidency*, pp. 95–100.

the party, a separation of the candidate from the party organization that would later be confirmed institutionally in the establishment and proliferation of primary elections. The loosening of the link between president and party was in part the result of broad Progressive reforms that sought the emphasis of such qualities as candidate character and specific issues rather than party loyalty as the key to voter choice—and Roosevelt typified the Progressive mentality in his political style and approach.[14] Reaching for strength and power beyond that which the regular party leaders would provide, Roosevelt needed a link to the public that would, in effect, serve as a counterforce against party organizational power and as a new tool for his own presidential ambitions.

Such a linkage, however, could not be forged independently, since the press played a crucial "gatekeeper" role in the formulation and dissemination of political news. Thus Roosevelt had to find a way to interpose himself in the news process and gain significant influence on the creation and interpretation of political information. The development of a new relationship with the press was a necessary step toward that end.

In the decade before he took office, all the major newspapers had established bureaus in Washington and the hundred and fifty to two hundred Washington correspondents had looked primarily to important leaders in Congress for political news. Within the first year of his presidency, however, the combination of Roosevelt's political assertiveness and his ability to dramatize himself and his office to the press and public alike had moved the central focus of national political news from Congress to the presidency.[15] Sensing the interest of people and press in the country's singularly symbolic office, Roosevelt rigorously exerted executive powers in pursuit of "bad trusts," labor settle-

---

[14] Josephson, *The President Makers*, pp. 111–74, Austin Ranney, *Curing the Mischiefs of Faction: Party Reform in America* (Berkley: University of California Press, 1975), p. 110.

[15] Richard L. Rubin and Douglas Rivers, "The Mass Media and Critical Elections."

ments, political reform, and overseas expansion, and rapidly made the presidency the focal point of the political news system.

Roosevelt had maintained a friendly, warm, and mutually profitable relationship with news correspondents throughout his career, and his stature with journalists only increased when he initiated the first presidential press conferences and then set aside an office in the White House for journalists to use as a permanent news room.[16a] With the possible exception of Lincoln in wartime, no other president was as continually pursued both as a source of information and as a creator of newsworthy activity. If there was no news, reporters expected Roosevelt to make some, and he rarely disappointed the press by failing to create some newsworthy story of either his personal or public life. Thus Roosevelt changed the expectations of the press and public alike, establishing a new sense of what a president should be like and how he should relate to both press and public.[16b] After Theodore Roosevelt, a weak president was likely to be identified as an unassertive man with poor press and public relations, a strong president as a maker of news with good press relations, able to control the flow and timing of news. Most importantly, a strong president would be able to incorporate the press in his efforts to push through Congress his legislative intentions and programs.

Unable to count upon an assured communications channel as in the earlier days of the party press, Roosevelt needed new techniques and strategies for dealing with a now independent, news-hungry press, and thus shape public opinion. One example of those techniques was his perfection of the "trial balloon" by which he himself sought, before the era of polls and surveys, to pretest popular reac-

---

[16a]James Pollard, *Presidents and the Press* (New York: Macmillan, 1947), p. 574.

[16b]For a seminal study linking the modern presidency to mass communications and public opinion see Elmer E. Cornwell, *Presidential Leadership of Public Opinion* (Bloomington: Indiana University Press, 1965).

tion by leaking (without attribution) news of a possible presidential action.[17] Because of his close relationship with the press, the correspondents became part of a presidential sounding board, which Roosevelt would use to test the substance and volatility of public opinion on a particular issue or political initiative. Unlike many of his 19th-century predecessors, Roosevelt understood the needs of the press, courted the press, and actively sought to enhance his public image through the press. In short, he was the first modern media president.

Roosevelt's interest in public opinion and the press's intricate role in the process itself was not shared by his successor, William Howard Taft, whose posture more resembled that of the late-19th-century presidents. But Taft's successor, Woodrow Wilson, shared Roosevelt's interest in presidential centrality, in presidential initiative, and in the value of public opinion. He firmly imbedded the presidency and press relationship in the structure of the political process. For example, shortly after entering the presidency in 1913, Wilson made the presidential press conference—sporadically held by Roosevelt—into a formal and regularly scheduled part of the president's responsibilities. He thus elevated what had been an innovative, informal relationship under Theodore Roosevelt to an institutionalized channel of political information for both the press and the mass public.[18] In response to Wilson's actions, Washington journalists established the White House Correspondents Association, an attempt by the press corps to professionalize and regulate itself so as to prevent the abuse of their new "official" privileges. Throughout Wilson's first term and until America's entry into World War I, president and press met regularly twice each week.

The establishment of regular press conferences was important for two different reasons. First, the decision to

[17] Melvyn H. Bloom, *Public Relations and Presidential Campaigns: A Crisis in Democracy* (New York: Thomas Y. Crowell, 1973), p. 12.

[18] See Leo C. Rosten, *The Washington Correspondents* (New York: Harcourt, Brace and Co., 1937), p. 24.

establish them set the tone of Wilson's first administration, which, he declared, would be clear, candid, and subject to "pitiless publicity." Wilson was unable to maintain such standards in the general deterioration of his press relations during his second term. He had, however, by his actions, again raised the level of expectations among press and public alike for presidential openness to scrutiny.[19] Second, and more important, the press conference formalized the emerging relationship between the president and the press. The press now felt entitled to access to the president and expected regular and timely official political information from the chief executive. The president, in turn, had established an institutionalized forum and vantage point from which to influence the flow of news to a diverse audience that included the Congress, the bureaucracy, pressure groups, foreign governments, and the nation as a whole.

Thus the White House press conference increased the potential power of presidential efforts at popular mobilization—during elections, in support of legislative programs, or in prosecuting wars—while encouraging the national press to center around the president. Because press conferences reached many audiences at once, they provided a new and convenient mechanism for a president seeking to offer innovative policy approaches that might overcome the stalemate produced by the fragmentation of governmental power. Wilson, a longtime admirer of the British cabinet government in which ministers were subject to regular questioning by Parliament members, was, in effect, partially duplicating that system when he instituted regular, formal presidential news conferences.[20] The establishment of press conferences was, in part, an attempt at political reform, an effort to foster greater cohesion and unity in governmental activities by enhancing the presidential voice.

[19] Pollard, *Presidents and the Press*, p. 630; and H. C. F. Bell, *Woodrow Wilson and the People* (rpt. Hamden, Conn.: Archon, 1968), p. 115.

[20] Barry Dean Karl, *Executive Reorganization and Reform in the New Deal: The Genesis of Administrative Management, 1900–1939* (Cambridge, Mass.: Harvard University Press, 1963), pp. 186–87.

The establishment of the press conference was clearly an outgrowth of a new conception of the presidency shared by Roosevelt and Wilson, both of whom saw themselves as Progressive activists attempting the reform of "old politics." Although each represented somewhat different strains of reform, both differed markedly from those presidents immediately preceding them. Both believed that good government was promoted by public exposure and citizen participation. Both believed in change, in new programs, in an assertive presidency, and in their own conception of America's role in world politics. Importantly, both sought to address directly the vast number of Americans at large—those outside the government—in an effort to affect the actions of the political leadership *inside* the government. With varying success, each sought to utilize the convertibility of public esteem (or "presidential prestige," as Richard Neustadt described it) into presidential influence in the governmental process.[21] Although it took a later president, Franklin Delano Roosevelt, to really maximize the conversion of public support for policy purposes, each of these modern presidents did view presidential-press relationships as opportunities for "offensive" rather than primarily "defensive" presidential strategies.

The presidency thus came to occupy an important position in the news process, one that could be used in efforts to reform the political process and push through new programs originating with the chief executive. But what was the press's reaction to the actual political reforms themselves? How did it respond to the varying strains of reform that aroused the political system both before and after the turn of the century? Where did the press fit into the formative stages of the political processes that might encourage some reforms and discourage others? Was there, in fact, sufficient diversity in the mass press to articulate fairly the various challenges to the status quo made by the different movements and parties in turn-of-the-century America? What was the overall impact of American journalism on the

---

[21] See Richard Neustadt, *Presidential Leadership* (New York: Wiley, 1960), pp. 33–57.

development of political reform, and what were the ramifications of that influence on the strength of party organization and the level of mass mobilization in electoral
politics?

The Press and Political Reform

Any effort to illuminate the role of the press in political
reform must focus primarily on two broad popular movements of the late 19th and early 20th centuries, populism
and progressivism. Comparison of the movements themselves is beyond the scope of this analysis, but the mass
press's reactions to these movements illustrates certain of
its critical features as a politically influential institution.
The relationship of both movements to the channels of
mass political communications helps to define different
phases of the press's transformation from a partisan press
to a market-oriented press. Examination of that relationship underscores how changes in the press's own economic
and corporate structure affected the substance and flow of
mass communications and, consequently, the penetration
of different kinds of political reform.

POPULISM

The Populist movement actually developed its own press
network, located in the West and South, to articulate its
predominantly agrarian sentiments. This network flour-
ished with the People's party (Populist) insurgency in the
1800s and 1890s, and vanished when the People's party was
absorbed by the Democratic party and Bryan's candidacy
in 1896. The Populist press revived the tight, symbiotic
press-party relationships characteristic of pre–Civil War
politics, in which newspapers not only favored a particular
party organization but were part of the very organization
itself.[22]

---

[22] See above chapter 2: "The Department Partnership."

Paralleling the linkage between party and press in the Jacksonian period, the Populist press constituted a major part of the party's efforts to establish an electoral connection between its leaders and potential supporters. Unlike earlier party papers, however, the Populist press did not successfully penetrate into and become an acknowledged part of the national news system by establishing newspapers in important regions such as the East. Essentially, the Populist press remained for its short life the vehement critic of industrial America, a proponent of agrarian-based reform, but a press whose voice would be heard primarily outside the national commercial communications channels and outside the national power system itself.

As part of the People's party organizational apparatus, papers such as the *Advocate*, the *Farmer's Alliance*, and the *Representative*, and the magazine *National Economist* articulated Populist issues and grievances, proposed political and economic reforms, and attempted to mobilize mass support for candidates in elections scattered throughout the South and West. The organizational vehicle that synthesized and organized the channels of communications for the Populists was an umbrella unit, the National Reform Press Association, which came into existence after 1890 when various southern and western Alliance editors coalesced into a propaganda organ of the People's party. Considering the geographic distances encompassed by the Populist movement, without the National Reform Press Association the People's party would have lacked any organizational centrality and ideological coherence.[23]

The messages sent through the party network were political demands for major change in both the economic and political systems: the nationalization of the railroads, telegraph, telephone, and highways; a graduated income tax; advocacy of the subtreasury plan for the redistribution of money without private banks; a major increase in the money supply through free and unlimited coinage of gold

---

[23] Seymour Lutzky, "The Reform Editors and Their Press" (Unpublished Ph.D. dissertation, University of Iowa, 1951) pp. 200ff.

and silver; reclamation of excess lands held by corporations; direct election of the president and U.S. senators by
the people; institution of the referendum and recall; and
the condemnation of black disenfranchisement in the
South.[24]

This regional and radical-sounding agrarian agenda was
disseminated and defended throughout the states under
the auspices of the National Reform Press Association.
Weekly journals like the *Southern Mercury* with a circulation of thirty thousand, the official Alliance *Advocate* with
eighty thousand, and the magazine *National Economist* distributed to over a hundred thousand readers, enabled the
association to both inform vast numbers of its supporters
and to mobilize them electorally behind the People's platforms of 1892 and 1894.[25]

An alternative means of direct political communication
and mobilization was the carefully organized and extensive
"lecture campaign" of the Alliance. Large numbers of
Populist spokesmen took their message directly to the people, particularly into certain areas in which the local press
was unsympathetic or hostile to the Populist cause. This
method of communication was particularly effective in
exposing large numbers of citizens, particularly in the Midwest, to political information that would have been otherwise unavailable to them. The lecture format itself—direct
person-to-person democracy—symbolized, as Lawrence
Goodwyn noted, the Populist belief in a communalistic politics, reaching back in style to the participatory politics of
a rural rather than an urban America.[26]

The newspapers of the metropolitan East and urbanized
Midwest were rapidly explaining dailies. But the Populist

---

[24] For the most sophisticated explanation of the Populists' proposal for
a Sub-Treasury Land and Loan System see Lawrence Goodwyn, *Democratic Promise: The Populist Moment in America* (New York: Oxford
University Press, 1976), esp. appendices A & B. See also the classic
analysis, John D. Hicks, *The Populist Revolt* (Lincoln: University of
Nebraska, 1961).

[25] Lawrence Goodwyn, *Democratic Promise*, p. 175.

[26] *Ibid.;* see also pp. 354–57.

journals were for the most part weeklies, issued from rural and prairie towns. Unlike consumer-oriented urban dailies, they were politically rather than market-oriented. In sharp contrast to the major eastern papers, Populist weeklies inevitably operated on deficits, very often carried no advertising at all, and, therefore, needed party subsidies to survive. Because of the nature of the movement and the relatively radical quality (at least to urban-industrial ears) of its political demands, the Populist press was compelled to reach back in time for its method of political organization and mass communications.

The National Reform Press Association disbanded immediately following what many leaders perceived to be a betrayal of their cause—the nomination of Democrat William Jennings Bryan as the Populist as well as Democratic presidential candidate for 1896—and with this collapse the People's party lost a critical internal communications and organizational link.[27] The dilution and eventual demise of the People's party are, of course, beyond the scope of this book. But the circumstances surrounding the nation's commercial press response to the fusion candidacy in 1896 of Populist and Democrats remains of critical importance in understanding the role of the press in American politics. No coverage of a presidential election since 1860 had reached the heights of emotional fervor and intensity that enveloped the 1896 contest, an election perceived by some as challenging for the first time the basic principles of a capitalist economy and which was, at the least, a direct challenge to the political hegemony of urban industrial sectors of the economy.[28]

The polarization of the nation along urban-rural lines of cleavage was sharply defined by the nomination of Bryan, and a strident, hysterical response by the larger urban newspapers, J. R. Hollingsworth believes, set the tone of the election. South of the Mason-Dixon Line and west of

[27] Lutzky, "The Reform Editors," p. 118.
[28] J. R. Hollingsworth, *The Whirligig of Politics: The Democracy of Cleveland and Bryan* (Chicago: University of Chicago Press, 1963), pp. 69–75.

the Mississippi, William Jennings Bryan was a "tribune of the people" "fighting a new battle for freedom." But in the Northeast, Bryan was a "Jacobin," an "anarchist," a "lunatic revolutionary," and the "chief of the blatherskites."[29] The largest papers in the nation excoriated Bryan for what eastern opinion leadership perceived him to be: a vital threat to its own political and economic hegemony. Even though the Democratic party platform of 1896 watered down the Populist demands by eliminating the planks for the subtreasury plan, land redistribution, and nationalization of the means of transportation and communications, the fear of masked Populist radicalism permeated the press coverage of Bryan wherever he traveled on his grueling national speaking tour.

While his opponent, Republican William McKinley, conducted a "front porch" campaign from his Ohio residence, Bryan sought to take his message personally to the mass of voters for the first time in presidential election history. Adopting for his campaign the Populist lecture format, Bryan tried to force antagonistic Republican newspapers and the traditionally Democratic papers that had deserted his candidacy to provide him with news coverage by making 570 speeches, 317 in October alone— before audiences of between two and three million people. Although almost the entire eastern and some of the midwestern press omitted and distorted much of his political message, and maligned him personally as well, Bryan succeeded in mounting the broadest and most direct personal campaign ever attempted by a presidential candidate.[30]

In retrospect, Bryan's defeat in the presidential election of 1896 can be understood as a confirmation of urban indus-

---

[29]*Ibid.*, and see also Matthew Josephson, *The Politicos, 1865–1896* (New York: Harcourt, Brace, 1938), pp. 684–85; Stanley L. Jones, *The Presidential Election of 1896* (Madison: University of Wisconsin Press, 1968), pp. 303–5.

[30] For details on campaign styles see Richard Jensen, *The Winning of the Midwest* (Chicago: University of Chicago Press, 1971), pp. 167–69 and 270–308; and Robert Batin, "San Francisco Newspapers' Campaign Coverage: 1895, 1952," *Journalism Quarterly* 31 (1954): 297–303.

trial power and leadership. Bryan's rejection by the cities, whether as a result of intimidation, misinformation, or just plain rational self-interest, was vigorous, absolute, and unmistakable. Only three cities with populations over a hundred thousand supported the Democratic-Populist candidate, none in the East or Midwest.[31] The newspapers of the rising metropolitan populations in the East and the Midwest categorically rejected what they saw as radical and self-interested agrarianism; and in New England the only paper to support Bryan went out of business two weeks before the election after "gold men" had withdrawn all advertising because of its editorial position.[32] Significant commercial enterprises themselves, newspapers in most cities were intimately linked to industrial growth and urbanization and they assumed the role of spokesman for resistance to threatening, rural-based political pressure in American politics. This is not to say that following Bryan's nomination every metropolitan newspaper became Republican and conservative in outlook. Rather, the argument here is simply that large commercial businesses, be they banks, railroads, *or* newspapers, did not look favorably upon movements proposing agrarian-based reforms threatening commercial prosperity, and, that the major newspapers, as part of business hegemony, strongly reflected those sentiments.

With the election of 1896 and the expiration of populism as a major movement, an era of partisan journalism finally ended. Party organizations could no longer strongly influence the metropolitan dailies and, in the case of small local papers, the political returns were not sufficient to warrant the exertion of establishing party news organs. For Democrats and Republicans alike, the party press became a relic of the past. For third-party movements, the Populists pro-

---

[31] William Diamond, "Urban and Rural Voting in 1896," *American Historical Review* 46 (1941): 281–305; see esp. table II on Democratic voting in eighty-two U.S. cities, 297–98. Also Carl N. Degler, "American Political Parties and the Rise of the City: An Interpretation," *Journal of American History* (1964), pp. 48–49.

[32] Hollingsworth, *The Whirligig of Politics*, p. 86.

vided a sobering example of the difficulties of sustaining either a sufficient informational system of one's own or of penetrating existing but resistant channels of commercially controlled mass communications.

To assume from the Populist experience, however, that the press was by its nature antipathetic to all political, social, and economic reform would inaccurately gauge the relationship between the press and political reform. Under certain circumstances the mass press could—and did— embrace political programs that sought to alleviate the social and economic ravages of rapid and unrestrained industrial growth. Particularly with respect to many of the changes sought by the Progressive movement, for example, the press vigorously articulated and generated political interest in many of the fundamental tenets and issues underlying the proposed reforms. How and why this was so for the Progressives, though not for the Populists, tells us much about the popular press, the nature of political reform, and the kind of political organization compatible with the press's interests.

PROGRESSIVISM

In marked contrast to populism, progressivism—a movement with a far less geographically concentrated popular base—aimed at a more limited transformation of American politics, and achieved a national hearing that eluded the Populists of the 1890s. Varying strains of political support for the Progressives have been found by scholars among liberal agrarian reformers, the middle class, as well as urban social welfare reformers who cut across various socioeconomic categories.[33] Significantly, much of the thrust of the movement focused on issues, personalities, and political reforms of greater interest to those in urban-industrial,

[33] See Richard Hofstadter, *The Age of Reform* (New York: Knopf, 1956); Samuel P. Hayes, *The Response to Industrialism;* and James L. Sundquist, *Dynamics of the Party System* (Washington, D.C.: Brookings Institute, 1973), chapters 7 and 8.

rather than rural-agrarian, areas—the mass press's major market. In addition, most Progressive concerns closely fitted two important requirements of the press: first, although Progressives aimed in part against monopolistic concentration of economic political power, they did not, on the whole, call for reforms affecting a significant redistribution of income, wealth, or power, nor, as did some segments of populism, did they make threatening attacks on the values and processes of the capitalist system.[34] Second, Progressive demands to examine the excesses of industrialization, to open closed proceedings to public scrutiny, to investigate and root out corruption, and to expand direct lines of communication between the people and their government, all dovetailed with the press's own professional and corporate objectives: to stimulate the interest of a large number of readers and to occupy for itself a larger role in the political process. The Progressive mentality of exploration and revelation was thus harmoniously linked to that of the journalists, so much so that, as Richard Hofstadter writes:

The fundamental critical achievement of American Progressivism was the business of exposure, and journalism was the chief occupational source of its creative writers. It is hardly an exaggeration to say that the Progressive mind was characteristically a journalistic mind, and that its characteristic contribution was that of the socially responsible reporter-reformer.[35]

---

[34] Sundquist, *Dynamics of the Party System*, pp. 156–62; see also Joseph Huthmacher, "Urban Liberalism and Progressive Reform," *Mississippi Valley Historical Review* (1972); Samuel P. Hays, "Politics of Reform in Municipal Government in the Progressive Era," *Pacific Northwest Quarterly* 55 (1964); David P. Thelen, "Social Tensions and the Origins of Progressivism," *Journal of American History* 56 (1968–1970); C. K. Yearly, *The Money Machines: The Breakdown and Reform of Governmental and Party Finance in the North 1860–1920* (New York: State University of New York Press 1970), esp. pp. 15–30; Martin Shefter, "Politics, Patronage, and Political Change," delivered at the annual APSA meeting 1976; and Martin J. Schiesl, *The Politics of Efficiency: Municipal Administration and Reform in America*, (Berkeley: University of California Press, 1977).

[35] Hofstadter, *The Age of Reform*, p. 185.

Indeed, in actual practice the working relationship between progressivism and the press was close and mutually beneficial. Various Progressive reformers, for example, wanted public attention and a public forum for their attacks on party corruption, undemocratic methods of political choice, and inefficiency in government. These the press enthusiastically provided. The press, on the other hand, wanted the critical and provocative input of reformist zeal, whose social and political attacks provided not only the substance of "news" for the papers but a ready market of readers as well.

Thus the relationship of Progressives to the press differed in a number of ways from the Populist-press relationship. First, no "Progressive press," in the sense that there was a "Populist press," existed. At no time did a group of editors, journalists, or writers coalesce into a formal association like the National Reform Press Association to further a partisan cause in such a manner. While one can speak of individual journalists, newspapers, or magazines as being "Progressive," a "Progressive press" as a collective entity did not exist. Even when a "Progressive party" emerged in 1912, counting among its leaders a host of Progressive editors, it failed to organize any propaganda organ equivalent to those of the Populists.[36] Second, strong antiorganizational attitudes held by many (but not all Progressives), and strains of individualism and elitism shared by various Progressives, made it difficult if not impossible for them to achieve the structural unity and philosophical cohesiveness needed to make a party press operate effectively. Third, their very freedom from identification with partisan labels enabled many Progressive ideas and interests to penetrate the pages of vast numbers of newspapers—Republican and Democratic—with frequency and ease. One sees in the first two decades of the 20th century

---

[36] Perhaps the closest approximation to the Populists' National Press Reform Association was Herbert Croly's magazine, the *New Republic,* founded in 1914; see Charles Forcey, *The Crossroads of Liberalism: Croly, Weyl, Lippmann and the Progressive Era* (New York: Oxford University Press, 1961).

no organized Progressive propaganda network but, rather, a significant though informal array of Progressive reformers whose criticisms of social, economic, and political ills had generally easy access to the broadest channels of political communications in part *because* of the informal and inchoate nature of their movement. The style, substance, and nature of the Progressive movement, together with the particular needs of mass journalism at that moment in time, opened wide the channels of political communications.

The advent and rapid proliferation of popular magazines at the turn of the century markedly facilitated the Progressive's access to a national audience. Prior to 1893 only four magazines might claim national prominence, and their circulations were small because very high prices sharply narrowed their potential appeal. But that year *McClure's* reduced its price to fifteen cents per issue and the rapid rise of the popular magazine commenced. Within the same year *Cosmopolitan* and *Munsey's* had reduced their prices to ten cents, and readership soon skyrocketed, rising from a half million in 1893 to three million readers in 1898.[37]

The rise of the popular magazine exerted important political influence during the Progressive era. As newspapers continued to emphasize reportorial rather than editorial content, and news became less organized—less "shaped" as to be self-explanatory—by partisan points of view, increasing numbers of readers turned to magazines in search of guidance to gain meaning and order out of the morass of apparently disconnected bits of news. Magazine editors soon discovered this market of searching readers and sought to exploit it. In consequence, major articles about political corruption and the need for reform appeared with increased frequency along with stories of social and economic criticism. Probably even more than newspapers, magazines organized and structured political

---

[37] C. C. Regier, *The Era of the Muckrakers* (New York: Peter Smith, 1957), chapter 2; Louis Filler, *Muckraking* (College Park: Pennsylvania State University Press, 1976), p. 30; Mott, *American Journalism,* pp. 605–7; Martin Mayes, *The Development of the Press in the United States* (Richmond, Missouri: Missourian Press, 1935), p. 77.

perceptions in an age when besieged political parties, without benefit of their own partisan news organs, found it difficult to synthesize and spread their own political messages.

The "literature of exposure" (that is, articles on political and economic corruption at all levels) provoked the curiosity of millions of readers and became the staple of national magazines. High levels of circulation were sustained by serialized feature articles whose titles tell much in themselves: Lincoln Steffens's "The Shame of the Cities" and Ida M. Tarbell's "History of the Standard Oil Company" in *McClure's;* Thomas W. Lawson's "Frenzied Finance" in *Everybody's;* and Samuel H. Adams's "The Great American Fraud" in *Collier's.* [38] Such "muckraking," as this type of reporting was pejoratively called, rapidly became a kind of socially conscious sensationalism of the middle class, offering an exciting and acceptable variant of earlier newspaper exposés in the years of "yellow journalism." As it had for the daily press, sensationalism paid off, at least for a time, in the marketplace, and the readership of primarily muckraking journals reached an estimated twenty million readers at its peak. [39]

The social exposés that appeared in magazines, and in newspapers, as well, strongly influenced mass opinion and helped to shape demands for political reform. Perhaps the most politically efficacious series of articles was David Graham Phillips's "The Treason of the Senate," published by *Cosmopolitan* in 1906. These articles consisted of censorious personal biographies of senators detailing their irresponsibility, corrupt practices, and loose morals. Although the general press criticized Phillips's articles as extremist, there is little doubt that his series focused public attention on what had become known as the "Millionaires' Club," with—eventually—important results. Like many journalists, Phillips had offered many criticisms but few proposals for systemic reform. However, a few magazines and the

---

[38] For discussions on the origins of each "Muckraker" see Louis Filler's *Muckraking.*

[39] Regier, *The Era of the Muckrakers*, p. 196.

then reformist Hearst papers used his articles to force action on long-stalemated reform efforts to move the election of senators away from state legislatures to direct, popular, statewide votes. Resolutions proposing the direct election of senators had come before the House without legislative success since 1826, but six years after Phillips's series the combination of exposure and political pressure was able to secure this major institutional reform with the passage of the Seventeenth Amendment in 1913.[40]

Because self-styled Progressives, heavily represented in the business and professional classes, were not perceived as at all radical, the movement and the journalists connected with it were not viewed as a threat to existing economic and social structures. Unlike the Populists, they offered few if any solutions that involved a major redistribution of economic resources, focusing on reform and modification of existing political and economic formulas.[41] Their approach as Progressives to the political and economic systems was more narrowly procedural in nature, seeing "bad trusts," poor working conditions, and political corruption, as signs of inefficient operation of systems needing rectification, rather than as deep-rooted problems endemic to the systems themselves.[42]

The Progressives' interest in improving the efficiency of the existing political system was heightened by their concern with managerial expertise. Such expertise could, they thought, be used to regulate political as well as business matters. Experts chosen because of education and professional skill would act as "nonpolitical" preservers of the public interest, in marked contrast to the supposedly cor-

[40] For a historical account of this political reform see David Graham Phillips, *The Treason of the Senate* (New York: Quadrangle Books, 1964). Also see Louis Filler, *Muckraking*, chapter 19.

[41] David Mark Chalmers, *The Social and Political Ideas of the Muckrakers* (New York: Citadel Press, 1964), p. 111.

[42] For an interesting analysis of the economic approaches of Progressive presidents Theodore Roosevelt and Woodrow Wilson, see William Letwin, *Law and Economic Policy in America: The Evolution of the Sherman Anti-Trust Act* (New York: Random House, 1965), pp. 195–207, 244–47, 271–73.

rupt behavior of officials appointed by party leaders. Progressive belief in the value of "experts" reflected an elitism linked to the socioeconomic and educational background of the Progressives themselves. A supposedly "depoliticized" view, it resembled the attitude adopted by John Quincy Adams's supporters when Jackson appointed party loyalists to governmental positions.

A tension thus existed within progressivism, created by its belief in greater democratic participation within a framework of political activity carefully advised and administered, however, by bureaucrats or managers with sophisticated skills and training.[43] The tension between these reform values was manifested, most importantly, in their tentative and cautious attitudes toward organizations capable of mass mobilization from below, such as parties and labor organizations, and it was not resolved until a new approach to political mobilization was taken in the New Deal.

Though the Progressives borrowed a number of earlier Populist reforms, such as direct election of senators and referendum and recall, they rejected those that challenged in any direct way the middle-class hegemony which largely underpinned liberal reformism during this period. In essence, progressivism during the early decades of the 20th century was good, sound politics, capturing the social sympathies and restless demands for change among the fast-growing middle classes.[44] The success of Progressive reform appears to be inextricably linked to the brief but impressive period of access it had to the channels and sources of political information during and after the turn of the century. But it is clear that this access to the channels of the commercial mass press—a courtship of press and progressivism—was also dependent on the ability of Pro-

---

[43] See John Morton Blum, *The Progressive Presidents: Roosevelt, Wilson, Roosevelt, Johnson* (New York: W. W. Norton, 1980), pp. 49–50. For a clear reflection of Progressive ideas see Walter Lippmann, *Public Opinion* (New York: Harcourt, Brace, 1922), pp. 234–52.

[44] Hofstadter, *The Age of Reform*, p. 241; Marc Karson, *American Labor Unions and Politics* (Carbondale, Ill.: Southern Illinois University Press, 1958), pp. 71–73.

gressive reform to continue to meet the needs of an "independent" and profit-making press. Because Progressive reform did not threaten the commercial interests or the underlying socioeconomic values of the press, and retained a posture that, though critical and political, was yet nonpartisan, it was able to achieve unparalleled access to both new and old channels of political communications.

Progressivism's very success in gaining such access, however, not only tells us something of the nature of Progressive reform but also helps us to better understand the development of the popular press as an institution of influence in American politics. Already freed from party control by the first decade of the 20th century, the press proclaimed itself politically "independent" and a guardian of the "public interest." But large-scale newspapers were in reality constrained by their corporate and commercial relationships to support only a relatively narrow range of conflict in American politics. "The press," V. O. Key, Jr., wryly observed, "could serve, in the large, the commercial interests, or it could remain neutral."[45] But in either case, its placement within the commercial community and its dependency on advertising revenues seemed to have limited the scope of political reform it would support from its position astride the major channels of political communications.

Not by coincidence, this period of growth in the press's political power accompanied a penetrating and sustained attack on political party organizations, during which most Progressives and most of the press challenged the partisan method of mass mobilization by "machine" politics. While it is important to note that in motive all Progressives were not "antiparty"—some were clearly not against parties as institutions but against those that were leading the political organizations[46]—the consequences, of widespread attacks

---

[45] V. O. Key, *Public Opinion and American Democracy* (New York: Knopf, 1963), pp. 395–404.

[46] David P. Thelen, *Robert M. LaFollette and the Insurgent Spirit* (Boston: Little, Brown, 1976) pp. 179–94; John D. Buenker, *Urban Liberalism and Progressive Reform* (New York: Scribner's Sons, 1973), pp. 198–239.

on party leaders made this distinction difficult to define in practice. The new "independent" press and the "good government" challenges of the Progressives seemingly shared a convenient common enemy—the party organization— whose "private" or "closed" organizational methods were attacked and contrasted with "public" and "open" politics of the press-Progressive alliance.

Both press and Progressive reformers sought to reduce the influence of the party organization, which they perceived as an inefficient and corrupt mediator between governmental leaders and the people at large. Could not the combination of a public-spirited press, "independent" political leaders, and an informed voter accomplish, without party mediation and without partisan structuring of information, the vital function of democratic control over government? The vast increase in available political information and public awareness fostered by reformist criticism and press revelation would serve to strengthen the direct links of individuals to their government and reduce, if not eliminate, the role of the parties. Should not democratic reforms contribute to closer electoral ties, to an increase in public participation, and a strengthening of the electoral connection?

Party Demobilization: Redefining the Electoral Connection

Progressive efforts to reform existing electoral institutions—to change the rules of the game—had both intended and unintended effects on the American political system. In varying ways, all significant changes in political procedures influence the flow of issues and power interests into and out of the political arena. The very nature and method of political organization produces political bias, as E. E. Schattschneider has remarked, because organization "is itself a mobilization of bias in preparation for action." The actual organization of the electoral processes, then, precludes certain points of view from reaching the political arena, ensures that others reach it in weakened and ineffective condition, and permits still others to reach it in a position of dominance. As Schattschneider put it, "some issues are organized into politics while others are organized out."[47]

Since the political parties had long played an important role in organizing the arena of American politics, many scholars linked the changes in the structure, organization, and competitiveness of the parties just before and after the turn of the 20th century to a subsequent decline in popular electoral participation. The significant drop-off in voting has been viewed by many as seriously weakening the electoral system as a legitimate means of political expression. Although there is continuing argument among scholars as to the origins and timing of this electoral decline, the evidence is clear that the political parties themselves failed to sustain the high levels of mass mobilization—particularly among new voters and large numbers of recent immigrants—achieved during the 19th century.[48]

From the 1896 presidential election to the New Deal, a series of party-related factors produced substantial changes in both the qualitative nature and quantitative levels of public participation in American elections: the disenfranchisement of blacks in the South; the elimination of two-party competition in most areas of the country; technical changes in the voting process itself; and concerted attacks

---

[47] E. E. Schattschneider, *The Semi-Sovereign People* (New York: Holt, Rinehart and Winston, 1960), pp. 30–71.

[48] Walter Dean Burnham, *Critical Elections and the Mainsprings of American Politics* (New York: W. W. Norton, 1970), pp. 71–90; see also his article "Theory and Voting Research: Some Reflections on Converse's 'Change in the American Electorate,'" *American Political Science Review* 68 (1974): 1002–23, also in that issue see Phillip Converse, "Comment," pp. 1024–27, the "Comment" by Jerrold Rusk, pp. 1028–49; and Burnham, "Rejoinder," pp. 1050–58. See, generally, Richard Jensen, *The Winning of the Midwest: Social and Political Conflict 1888–1896* (Chicago: University of Chicago Press, 1971), pp. 2–11; and Samuel T. McSeveney, *The Politics of Depression: Political Behavior in the Northeast 1893–1896* (New York: Oxford University Press, 1972), pp. 7–8.

on the resources, power, and legitimacy of parties as mobilizing organizations.[49] An important source of partisan
demobilization was clearly the very cleavage established in
the election in 1896 itself. The aftermath of the sharply
polarized sectional split between the urban North, on one
hand, and the rural South, on the other, brought about a
new electoral configuration of one-party domination—a
dominant Republican party in the Northeast and Midwest,
and a dominant Democratic party in the South. With the
minority party in each region badly defeated and relegated
to apparently unalterable second position, effective competition between the two major parties, which had already
ceased throughout the South now, with the exception of a
few eastern industrial states, halted in the North as well.
This cessation of two-party competition at the local level
severely weakened the organizing potential of the chronic
minority party, eliminated much of the dominant party's
need for responsiveness and organizational efficiency, and
effectively "organized out" of politics those groups and
interests not linked to the dominant party.

At a time when almost all nominations were made in
party conventions by party leaders (with the exception of
incipient primaries in a few southern states), control of the
nomination process gave the leaders of one party—which-
ever was dominant in a specific area—effective control over
politics and left no organized outlet through which the
mass public could express opposition. Without an effective
mechanism for opposition, there was no clear popular sanction against corrupt or inefficient public officials or dis-
agreeable policies, since the absence of two-party
competition brought the locus of power to the organizational leadership of a single party "machine."[50] Opposition

---

[49] For a detailed analysis of the mobilization of immigrants see Kristi
Andersen, *The Creation of a Democratic Majority: 1928–1936* (Chicago:
University of Chicago Press, 1979). On other aspects of party demobilization see Austin Ranney, *Curing the Mischiefs of Faction: Party Reform
in America*, passim.

[50] V. O. Key, *American State Politics* (New York: Knopf, 1956), pp.
85–196, and "The Direct Primary and Party Structure," *American Political Science Review* 48 (1954): 1–26.

to these locally dominant party leaders and their political allies eventually became a position shared by all those groups, interests, and individuals not in power who, while not necessarily agreeing with one another on specific policies, could nevertheless agree on the need for "reform" of political power. The Progressives' pursuit of procedural changes reflected their need to reopen the contest for power.[51]

Certain of the reforms initiated to prevent such local party dominance or electoral corruption were effective in rooting out blatant illegalities, and simultaneously weakened the party organizationally. The introduction of the Australian ballot, for example, providing for secret voting and a publicly printed ballot listing all candidates by the office they sought, markedly reduced (though it did not eliminate) electoral fraud. By eliminating the practice of using each party's privately printed ballot of all its candidates on one single slate, the new system, as Jerrold Rusk notes, also encouraged nonparty, short-term forces, such as candidate and issue appeal, to play an enlarged role in determining the vote.[52] A voter could now support his favorite candidate without voting for a party's other candidates. However, the Australian ballot vastly complicated the act of voting itself, which now came to involve various alternative candidates for numerous offices, all listed separately. Party cohesiveness was weakened by the increased ability of a candidate to win without his fellow party candidates winning as well. By loosening the concept of "the slate," the new ballot effectively increased the costs and difficulties of party mobilization, increased the "personalization" of elections, and, in consequence, enlarged the role of the press in the electoral process.

The imposition of new eligibility rules, such as registration or other voter qualifications, also made the act of vot-

---

[51] On this point see: Martin Shefter, "Party, Bureaucracy, and Political Change in the United States" in *Political Parties: Development and Decay*, ed. Louis Maisel and Joseph Cooper. (Beverly Hills, California: Sage Publications, 1978), 4: 229–37.

[52] Jerrold G. Rusk, "Comment," *American Political Science Review* 68 (1974): 1028–49.

ing more complicated and more difficult than it had been
before. These regulations required greater voter effort
throughout a two-stage rather than a one-stage voting process and discouraged the marginal voter from participating
by raising the costs in time, energy, and knowledge. Lit-
eracy tests, poll taxes, and grandfather clauses, rapidly
eliminated the principal part of a substantial black electorate in the South between 1890 and 1910. In the North,
registration requirements tended to depress immigrant
and working-class participation, although by no means to
the same extent, by strengthening barriers to corrupt voting practices and simultaneously weakening the traditional
mobilizers of these groups—the political parties.[53]

Although it is clear that the corruption of local party
organizations—in large measure due to the absence of two-
party competition—led to the reforms that weakened them
organizationally, corruption was not the sole motive of the
assault on party power. The attack on party organizations
as mobilizing agents and durable intermediary institutions
was also a question of power—to determine *who* should
have power as well as *how* power should be properly exercised, for the parties' loss of political power meant that
other organizations and interests could gain power. Attacking the concentrated power of machines through such
reforms as the primary, the recall, the initiative, and the
referendum strengthened the relative ability of other centers of power—civic organizations, professional and business groups, and, of course, the press itself—to organize
and mobilize electoral activity. Legitimate attacks on the
parties for their corruption or unresponsiveness were inevitably mixed with attempts to gain power for new sets of
leaders and for different groups in the mass electorate.

The most important, most direct, and most durable
attack on party organizational strength during this period
of reform was the development of direct-primary legislation. The primary was a crucial mechanism for breaking the
party organization's monopoly over the nomination pro-

---

[53]*Ibid.*

cess. Before primaries, when the party organization controlled elective and appointive offices, all those in opposition in the many one-party localities had no electoral check on arbitrary political power. But primaries could break party elite control over the candidate selection process and make "popular" rather than organizational decisions the determining factor in a nomination. In addition, they permitted those in opposition an opportunity to gain access to power from *within* the party.[54]

The groundswell of reform that brought the primaries into most state and local party processes reached into presidential nominations as well. The parties and the state legislatures together had to deal with growing popular demands that delegates to the national conventions be popularly rather than organizationally selected. In 1904, competition between LaFollette and anti-LaFollette groups of Wisconsin Republicans to represent the local party nationally resulted in legislation (enacted in the following year) providing for popular election of all Wisconsin delegates to the national convention. Pennsylvania followed suit in 1906, and in 1910 Oregon legislated the first presidential *preference* primary, which linked the presidential candidate and aspiring state party delegates by name on the ballot itself. By 1912, the number of states with some kind of presidential primary had reached fifteen, and by 1916 nine more states had added primary legislation, bringing the total to twenty-four out of forty-eight states.[55]

The growth of presidential primaries paralleled, not coincidentally, the growth and interest in the presidency, the increased scope of that office, and the presence of popular presidential candidates who could convert procedural reforms into dramatic political confrontations. The candidacies of both LaFollette and Theodore Roosevelt against Taft in 1912 helped escalate interest in the primaries as a

---

[54] Louise Overacker, *The Presidential Primary* (New York: Macmillan, 1926); James W. Davis, *Presidential Primaries: The Road to the White House* (New York: Thomas Y. Crowell, 1967).

[55] Ranney, *Curing the Mischiefs of Factions*, p. 121. See also Louise Overacker, *The Presidential Primary*, pp. 137–46, 244–51.

new mechanism for injecting popular participation into the nomination process. But the eventual failure of Theodore Roosevelt to convert primary victories into the nomination at the Republican convention, the absence in subsequent contests of popular and charismatic challengers, and the decline of reformist zeal in general, all encouraged participation in presidential primaries to drop precipitously. By 1920, one-quarter of the states that had enacted presidential primary laws at the height of participation in 1916 had let them lapse, and many states that retained enabling legislation entered a sustained period in which, because of lack of interest, party primaries simply were not held.[56]

The decline of popular participation in internal party affairs was part of a general decline in electoral participation. Average turnout in presidential general elections was about 78 percent of the potential voting population from 1876 to 1896, but declined to 65 percent from 1900 to 1916, and to 52 percent between 1920 and 1928; in both 1920 and 1924 only slightly over 43 percent of the eligible population voted in the presidential elections.[57] Although the precise effect on voter turnout of the Australian ballot, voter registration and qualification processes, and the eligibility of women to vote is still debatable, the overall evidence indicates that a significant part of the American people's decreased participation in the electoral process was due to the parties' decreasing efforts to register and mobilize new members of the potential electorate.

Certainly one of the factors involved in the decline of voter interest—in the primaries as well as in the general election—was the electorate's inability to sustain its interest in the ad hoc types of coalitions that much of the press

---

[56] Richard L. Rubin, "Presidential Primaries: Continuities, Dimensions of Change, and Political Implications," a paper delivered at the American Political Science Association annual meeting, 1977; also reprinted in *The Party Symbol: Readings on Political Parties*, ed. William Crotty (San Francisco: W. H. Freeman, 1980).

[57] Walter Dean Burnham, "The Changing Shape of the American Political Universe," *American Political Science Review* 59 (1965): 7–28, esp. 10.

and many reformers hoped would replace party-mobilized coalitions.[58] During the Progressive era ad hoc political organizations were transient at best and they proved to be incapable of generating and sustaining mass mobilization. Even party organizations themselves which, with the decline of reform interest and activities, had rapidly reasserted their power in local politics, did not mobilize voters as they had in the prereform period. Their experience with the party primary as a mechanism for political challenge, and its continued existence (even if only "on the books"), kept party leadership wary of mobilizing too many rank-and-file voters, fearful that large numbers of regularly mobilized voters might create too ready a market for later insurgent primary challengers. Therefore, care was exercised by the party organizations (particularly in one-party dominant areas) to mobilize voters only to the extent that they were needed to maintain the party in office in the general election; and they frequently made efforts to keep registration and primary turnout low so that the party organization could control the nomination process with a relatively small expenditure of resources and a small number of faithful voters.[59]

Those areas where, before the Progressives, party machines had enjoyed substantial popular support returned to firm organization control of local politics after the cooling of reformist zeal in the 1920s.[60] But even though party organizations regained control of electoral resources, Progressive reforms left an important imprint on the operation of elections, party deliberations, and, most importantly, on the party leadership's approach to popular mobilization. Many of the reforms designed to monitor or

[58] Mosei Ostrogorski, *Democracy and the Organization of Political Parties* 2 vols. (1902; rpt. New York: Quadrangle Books, 1964), esp. 2:350–400.

[59] Harold Foote Gosnell, *Machine Politics* (Chicago: University of Chicago Press, 1968), pp. 83–84.

[60] Martin Shefter, "Party Organization, Electoral Mobilization, and Regional Variations in Reform Success," a paper delivered at the American Political Science Association annual meeting, 1978.

by-pass the parties, such as the referendum, recall, and initiative, fell into general disuse, and primary elections were either discontinued or lightly contested. But the nature of the electoral connection had, in fact, been redefined. The return of party organizational power was now linked to low levels of public interest in elections and a more careful approach to mass mobilization than had typified earlier party systems. The experience of attack on the parties from *within* had apparently redefined the party organization's relationship to the functions of mass mobilization. The reaffirmation of the parties' organizational structure during the postreform period depended on a more inhibited, less dramatic style of political mobilization than that characteristic of the pre-1896 Jacksonian model.

As the pressures of political reform waned, as the presidency moved into unassertive hands, and as the activists of reoriented party organizations collectively promoted the broad depoliticization of the 1920s, the political relationship of various groups in the electorate changed as well. Lowered levels of mass participation in the electoral system did not affect all groups and interests equally, for the broad depoliticization of the period served to increase the existing electoral advantages of certain classes of society. In the South, Jim Crow laws rapidly demobilized blacks as an electoral force. In the North, the decline of strong two-party efforts to mobilize new voters did not exclude but weakened the relative position of immigrants, workers, and minority groups in the major cities.[61] Whereas the middle and upper classes, with the organizational advantages of developing professional and business associations behind them, could more easily mobilize themselves electorally on an ad hoc basis, the lower classes had to rely primarily on the weakened political parties to promote their interests. Progressive leaders proved unwilling to exploit certain social cleavages upon which new broad electoral coalitions could be based, and in the absence of strong presidential

[61] Walter Dean Burnham, *Critical Elections*, pp. 71–90; and E. E. Schattschneider, *The Semi-Sovereign People*, pp. 76–83. Also Otis L. Graham, *Encore for Reform: The Old Progressive and the New Deal* (New York: Oxford University Press, 1967), p. 174.

leadership and strong party organizations capable of drawing potential voters into the electoral arena, popular participation declined substantially.

The agenda of politics in the years before the Great Depression was consequently far less influenced by voters than it had been in the past, working against those classes victimized by a rapidly industrializing society. An already large pool of nonvoters, particularly among factory workers, immigrants, blacks, and newly eligible voters continued to grow.[62] The distribution of actual voters was skewed in favor of the conservative, laissez-faire political interests of the middle class, resulting in public policies that served to perpetuate and deepen the grave social and economic disparities developing in the system. With the presidency and party in a state of relative unassertiveness, significant change in public policies produced by the electoral system would emerge only when both the presidency and the party were mobilized once again.

What role the press played in the coming shift in the political agenda—from an inactive and conservative national government under Republican leadership to an interventionist and liberal government under Democratic New Dealers—reveals much about the interplay between electoral institutions and mass communications. Did the press help advance or retard the new social and economic demands that were seeking public expression? What were the relationships between the print press and the new mass medium—radio—to the presidency of Franklin Roosevelt? How, in fact, were centralizing changes in mass communications linked to the vast mobilization of presidential power in the New Deal realignment and the setting of a new and different political agenda?

[62] Kristi Andersen, "Generational Change, Partisan Shift, and Realignment," in Norman Nie, Sidney Verba, and John R. Petrocik, *The Changing American Voter* (Cambridge, Mass.: Harvard University Press, 1976) pp. 74–95. See also Kristi Andersen, *The Creation of a Democratic Majority*, esp. chapter 10: "Growth of the Non-immunized Population"—i.e., those citizens without party identification or prior voting experience.

6

Presidential Mobilization
and the Political Agenda

Substantial changes in the political agenda of American politics have occurred relatively infrequently throughout U.S. history, and scholars link many of these significant shifts in the course of American politics to major realignments of the coalitions of voters. During periods of heightened political tension, the parties polarize and present more distinct political alternatives. The voter's choice is then more closely linked than usual to the policy actions of governmental leaders. Political leaders become more responsive to socioeconomic problems—or risk being removed by an aroused electorate—and governmental elites are pressed to respond with solutions that are beyond the normally narrow range of policy discourse. It is not that "the people" directly define new policy solutions during the realignment of coalitions, but rather that political leaders, increasingly aware of shifts among voters and potential voters on whom they depend for survival, must become increasingly sensitive to the policy needs of the electorate.

Although scholars frequently argue over some of the specific characteristics of major realignments—e.g., whether they are cyclical in pattern, or whether they cover more than one presidential election—they generally agree that when there is a major realignment of the electorate, it marks a relatively clear and enduring transformation of the political agenda.[1] The New Deal realignment under Franklin Roosevelt, for example, massively increased direct intervention by the national government in the operations of the economy and redefined the topics of political argument, created new combinations of political interests, and produced new public policies reflecting the interests of the new alignment.[2]

The explanation of past major realignments is a subject of great complexity and beyond the scope of this book. In broad measure, however, the durable realignment of voters apparently grows out of powerful tensions over issues of public policy—issues that have *not* been adequately resolved within the existing framework of normal two-party politics. Because the parties do not address these issues effectively enough to produce meaningful governmental response, a great disparity develops between economic and social demands, on the one hand, and governmental policy actions, on the other. The tension of this disparity forces previously unexpressed issues into the national electoral arena, provoking dissatisfaction with existing leadership and prompting different elite responses to newly recognized problems and subsequent shifts by voters behind the new stands of party leadership.

In the formative stage of realignment, partisanship—an individual's party loyalty built up over years of relatively stable politics—tends first to loosen, and then to sharpen along the new lines of cleavage. Traditional party loyalty—what V. O. Key calls an individual's "standing decision"—weakens and permits new and different party loyalties to be made. Also, as Kristi Andersen points out, the dynamic

---

[1] See, for example, Walter Dean Burnham, *Critical Elections and the Mainsprings of American Politics* (New York: W. W. Norton, 1970), pp. 6–10; James Sundquist, *Dynamics of the Party System* (Washington, D.C.: Brookings Institution, 1973), chapters 1–3, 13–14, pp. 1–38, 275–307; Everett Carll Ladd, Jr., *American Political Parties: Social Change and Political Response* (New York: W. W. Norton, 1970), *passim.*

[2] Ladd, *American Political Parties*, pp. 1–2, for an interesting development of the concept of a political agenda.

of the forces unleashed in such unstable times brings unaf-
filiated voters into the political process and arms them with
a newfound partisan allegiance that shapes their future
votes as well as their present ones.

The enveloping tension, the emerging issues, and the
leadership reactions all combine to create new political
symbols, such as the "New Deal." Even long after the
years of peak politicization during the realignment, moreover, as Burnham notes, these simple patterns remain the
"dominant elements of political persuasion and rhetoric"
and a powerful remnant of the language of past policy conflict.[3] A policy crisis by itself is not a sufficient cause of
realignment; the rise of crucial new issues may weaken the
existing basis of party competition. But no durable realignment will occur until and unless both the public and political elites develop a common understanding of the *basis* of
the new realignment. A new vocabulary for discussing politics—a new set of popular symbols—is needed to facilitate
the development of such an understanding.

The New Deal political transformation—considered by
most scholars a clear example of the nexus of socioeconomic
tension, party realignment, and new policy dimensions—
offers an opportunity to examine the role of the press in the
process of realignment and the setting of a new political
agenda. The process of realignment is, in a sense, a process
of political communication, and a scenario of that process
would be as follows: Prior to a major realignment, normal
channels of communications from voters to political leaders
and from leaders to voters break down. Two-party competition fails to reflect salient divisions in public opinion,
party identification weakens, and unrelieved tension propels new political forces into the electoral system in pursuit
of policy changes. As a partisan realignment develops, lines
of communication between the electorate and leaders

---

[3] Walter Dean Burnham, Jerome Clubb, and William H. Flanigan,
"Partisan Realignment: A Systemic Perspective," in *The History of
American Electoral Behavior* ed. Joel H. Silbey, Allan G. Bogue, and
William H. Flanigan (Princeton, N.J.: Princeton University Press,
1978), p. 71.

expand to accommodate more and varied political information. Parties then offer clearer choices to voters, and voters are better able to express their preferences.

The press is, of course, a major means of spreading political information, establishing broad public awareness of new issues, and developing the symbols and language of new political divisions.[4] But what are the dimensions of its role? How powerful is it in shaping political action, and under what circumstances does it have (or not have) independent influence on politics?[5] Does the press, in fact, directly influence the precipitation, timing, or results of realignments and the new agenda they bring—or does it primarily reflect or ratify the activities of other institutions? Do significant changes in the political content of mass communications actually occur in a buildup period prior to realignment that can induce or propel the coming of a major new policy agenda?

The New Deal realignment is used here as an important test case in probing some of the limits of the press in shaping the political agenda under pretelevision circumstances. The Great Depression revealed severe, unresolved problems in the ecopolitical system and produced, first, demands for governmental action, second, political polarization by both political elites and mass population over proposed solutions, and, third, a new, clearly defined policy

[4] Murray Edelman, *The Symbolic Uses of Politics* (Urbana: University of Illinois Press, 1967).

[5] For discussions and case studies on the agenda-setting function of the press, see Maxwell McCombs and Donald Shaw, "The Agenda Setting Functions of the Mass Media," *Public Opinion Quarterly* 36 (1972): 176–87, and their book, *The Emergence of American Political Issues: Agenda-Setting Functions of the Press* (St. Paul, Minn.: West, 1977); see also Marc Benton and P. J. Frazier, "Agenda-Setting Function of the Mass Media at Three Levels of Information Molding." *Communications Research* 3 (1976): 261–74; McLeod, Becker, and Byrnes, "Another Look at the Agenda-Setting Function of the Press," *Communications Research* 1 (1974): 131–58; R. W. Cobb and C. D. Elder, *Participation in American Politics: The Dynamics of Agenda-Building* (Boston: Allyn and Bacon, 1972); Shanto Iyengar, "Television News and Issue Salience: A Reexamination of the Agenda-Setting Hypothesis, *American Politics Quarterly* 7 (1979): 395–416.

agenda in the Democratic New Deal. These stages offer, then, a sequence in which we can examine the press's role as a political force in the relatively recent past and as a benchmark for examining later journalistic impact on the political process.

In brief, what was the nature of mass communications in the important decades before, during, and after the New Deal? What, if anything, can we learn from this period about the role of the press in shaping broad shifts in the political agenda?

News and the Political Communications Process

Assessments of the role and influence of the press in shaping the public agenda during the New Deal requires knowledge of the content of news coverage. By raising certain political questions in the public forum, the press can bring issues to heightened public consciousness, emphasize one political conflict at the expense of another, and influence the range and substance of national debate. The press alone may not determine what the public will think on any particular issue, but it goes a long way toward determining what the public will think about.[6]

To grasp the relationship of the press to the political process during the New Deal we need to know whether any significant changes in the relative prominence and emphasis of different kinds of news stories occurred, and how these may have changed over time: for example, were certain kinds of news, such as economic stories about massive unemployment, bank failures, or labor unrest given increased coverage by the press in the New Deal period? And when did increased coverage of stories of this kind actually occur—if it did? We need to find out whether news coverage of the depression by the mass press accelerated political action, retarded it, or merely reflected the actions of political leaders.

---

[6] Bernard Cohen, *The Press and Foreign Policy* (Princeton, N.J.: Princeton University Press, 1963), p. 13.

While such an effort at understanding the press's role in political change is difficult, a serious attempt can be made through a systematic content analysis of major newspapers over time. Examination of front-page news stories of major circulation newspapers between 1920 and 1940 sheds much light on the relationship between the press's own news agenda and the specific political agenda as it unfolded during the New Deal. What topics did the press treat during this period, what did the newspapers deem important, and how can we link the press's sense of a news agenda—the content of mass communications—to the political activities of the period?

Figure 1, concerned with the content of news coverage in major American dailies from 1920 to 1940, firmly reflects the shift of a partisan political press to one concentrating on varied human interest and nonpolitical stories.[7] News of a "political" nature—e.g., stories of elections, party activities, and congressional and administration maneuverings—hovers at a relatively low level of approximately 20 percent of the total stories, rising in frequency during election years, but with no other trend detectable. Some papers—the *New York Times*, for example—were more politically oriented than most others during the period examined (and after). But the overriding thrust of the evidence is that, unlike the years of a fiercely partisan press, political news lags well behind nonpolitical news in the competition for prominence and space in the decades before, during, and after the New Deal realignment.

Had the press's news agenda played an independent role

---

[7] See Richard L. Rubin and Douglas Rivers, "The Mass Media and Critical Elections: A First Report," a paper delivered at the 1978 Northeastern Political Science Association convention. In the original study the top three stories on the front pages of six major newspapers were analyzed for content over a ninety-year period starting in 1885. While the sample used was by no means representative of all newspapers—different geographic regions were included but no small town newspapers were included—it was broad enough to catch any major trends in mass communications. If anything, the data would *overstate* national news content because of the absence of small local papers. The figures that follow utilize only the data from 1920 to 1940.

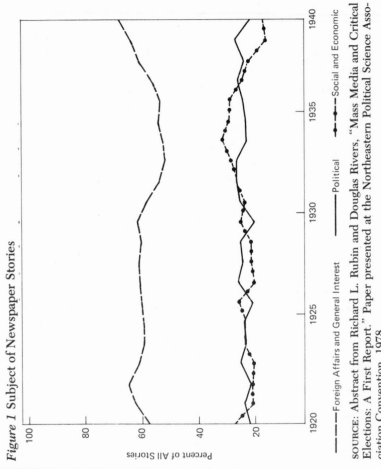

Figure 1 Subject of Newspaper Stories

Percent of All Stories

————— Foreign Affairs and General Interest   ————— Political

——●—— Social and Economic

SOURCE: Abstract from Richard L. Rubin and Douglas Rivers, "Mass Media and Critical Elections: A First Report." Paper presented at the Northeastern Political Science Association Convention, 1978.

in forming the major political agenda of this era, we should expect the nature of press coverage to have changed *prior* to the actual establishment of the New Deal. News about economic or social problems prior to the realignment of the Great Depression should have markedly increased, as tensions building in the system became "news." If the press directly and significantly influenced politics during this period, then we should detect a significant increase in social and economic stories before 1929, or, at the latest, shortly after the depression had begun. This is clearly *not* the case, since the acceleration in social and economic stories found in figure 1 follows well after the beginning of the Great Depression rather than signaling or responding quickly to the onset of the crisis.

The Roosevelt administration's response to the depression crisis clearly defined a relationship between the national government and the operation of the economic system different from what had previously existed. Economic issues once left to private firms for resolution became subject to direct governmental intervention. Areas such as farm production, labor relations, and the pricing of manufactured products, hitherto local problems, now attracted national regulation. The economic system, heretofore largely independent of large-scale federal influence, became, in the New Deal realignment, both the central focus of American politics and the main subject of political cleavages, both between opposing political leaders and between large segments of the population at large. Economic and social issues concerning the capitalist system itself became included in the political debate.[8]

We would expect, had the press at this time actually possessed any substantial direct agenda influence, that its own "news agenda" would have indicated new economic priorities by increases in the number of stories bearing on the

---

[8] Everett Carll Ladd, Jr., with Charles D. Hadley, *Transformation of the American Party System: Political Coalitions from the New Deal to the 1970s*, 2nd ed. (New York: W. W. Norton, 1975), pp. 31–104, 166–67; William E. Leuchtenburg, *Franklin D. Roosevelt and the New Deal* (New York: Harper and Row, 1963).

economy: stories about declining production and the ravages of high unemployment, for example. We might also
expect some increase in the *political content* of previously
neutral or purely descriptive economic stories. For
instance, descriptions of farm failures or plant closings
might link these events to proposals by a national leader or
congressional committee for a political remedy to such economic problems. But the evidence again denies the expectation on both counts. Figure 2 traces the change in press
coverage of economic issues, showing a definite expansion
of economic stories from a predepression frequency of
about 10 to 15 percent of all stories to a high of 26 percent,
which occurs, however, *in 1935.* Clearly, no marked
increase in press stories on economic matters begins until
1931, after at least a year and a half of a deep depression.
This leisurely response indicates that, rather than anticipating the new agenda, or at the least moving the economic
crisis quickly onto the political agenda, the press at this
stage was merely reflective of the actions and interests of
political leaders and not a provocative force.

While this study of news content does not incorporate
any in-depth analysis of the actual news stories themselves,
it nevertheless suggests certain important qualitative elements. The dotted line in figure 2 indicates the frequency
of major economic news stories during this period, local or
otherwise, tied to a political proposal or to the action of
either a national political figure or a national institution
such as Congress, the president, or the political parties.
Thus the data portray not only the frequency of news stories on economic issues, but also the extent to which the
press *politicized* economic stories by taking them out of the
category of mere description of economic events and placing them within the arena of political action.

The low level of economic stories with clear political
linkages (only between 3 to 5 percent of all prominent stories prior to the depression) is not at all surprising when
one recalls that laissez-faire was still the dominant economic ideology. In terms of the press's role in placing economic issues more prominently on the political agenda—

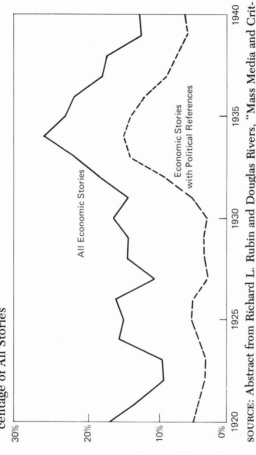

Figure 2 Economic Stories with Political and Nonpolitical Reference as a Percentage of All Stories

All Economic Stories

Economic Stories with Political References

SOURCE: Abstract from Richard L. Rubin and Douglas Rivers, "Mass Media and Critical Elections: A First Report." Paper presented at the Northeastern Political Science Association Convention, 1978.

telling the public what to think about—the data underscore
the slowness with which the press politicized the very
issues that were to become the basis of the New Deal
realignment. The growth in politicized economic stories
clearly escalates in the 1930s, rising sharply in the election
year of 1932 and reaching a peak in the 1935–36 period.
Rather than anticipating the politicization of heretofore
"neutral" issues, the press during this particular period
merely reflected, *belatedly,* a new agenda set instead by
opposing political leaders in electoral competition.

Thus the actions of politicians, most notably at the presidential level, defined the new political priorities—with
voters responding to the new lines of cleavage. At this stage
of its development, the press clearly lacked any major
political agenda-setting power. Moreover, with the exception of certain individual newspapers, the press as a whole
was not yet ready to advance or accept many of the New
Deal's apparently threatening economic and social reforms.
Much of the newspaper publishing industry, grown large
in scale and economically powerful, was itself part of the
old order and deeply linked to established economic power
and the status quo it reflected. One of the most significant
findings, both objective and subjective, of this survey of
newspaper stories is how little economic coverage the early
years of America's greatest depression received and how
reluctant the press was to politicize economic issues and
bring new, unorthodox solutions into the political arena.

Shaping the Channels of Communications

Although Theodore Roosevelt and Woodrow Wilson
both possessed deep insight into the role and potential of
the press in a modern political system, neither rivaled
Franklin Roosevelt's grasp of the complexities of press
operations and his concentrated efforts to deal with the
press as a part of an overall system of political communications. Zealously opposed by a substantial majority of newspaper publishers throughout most of his career, Roosevelt's

four consecutive victories suggest not only sharp limits to press power in ordering political choices but also emphasize a president's potential to reshape the channels of mass communications to serve his own ends. While the influence of the print press seems to have detracted from the margins of Roosevelt's victories in certain localities,[9] Roosevelt's active utilization of a variety of communications strategies neutralized much, if not all, of the press's negative efforts. Roosevelt recognized the importance of the presidency not only as the center of government but also as the center of political information.

Roosevelt's diverse strategies for communicating favorable political information to the people encompassed both a powerful grasp of the internal dynamics of newspaper publishing and a subtle understanding of the political relationship of newspaper readers to their regular newspapers. His strategies, directed at minimizing the impact of hostile news stories and interpretations, forced coverage of positive actions of his own, and reached, whenever possible, over the head of the newspapers to the people directly. Roosevelt faced a press which, though not nearly as consistently hostile as he claimed it to be, was, nevertheless, significantly more antagonistic to him than was the population at large.[10] To pierce what he considered was the screen of a "Tory" press required both a strong will and skills to manipulate mass popularity to achieve his own programmatic objectives.

The newspapers, particularly the largest and most important chains, had become increasingly conservative since the Progressive era. No longer predominantly reformist, muckraking enterprises, they had become strong, reinforcing forces in maintaining the economic and social status quo. Despite three years of depression and financial crisis, only 38 percent of the nation's dailies supported

[9] Harold F. Gosnell, *Machine Politics: Chicago Model* (Chicago: University of Chicago Press, 1937), pp. 156–76.

[10] For a discussion of the hostility of the press to Roosevelt see Graham V. White, *FDR and the Press* (Chicago: University of Chicago Press, 1979), pp. 68–84.

Roosevelt in 1932, and this support even declined slightly in 1936.[11] If total newspaper *circulation* is compared rather than just numbers of papers, his support in 1936 was, in reality, considerably less. Hearst and several other high-circulation urban chains, furious with Roosevelt and the New Deal, shifted to Republican Alf Landon. Considering that Hearst alone had 13.6 percent of all the total daily circulation in the country and 24.2 percent of all Sunday circulation, Roosevelt's perception that he had to mobilize his own resources against such influence is easily understood.[12]

Several important trends in the nature and structure of newspaper ownership posed major problems for Roosevelt. First, the ownership of newspapers was becoming concentrated in fewer and fewer hands. Second, local papers in the large newspaper chains had less autonomy from their ownership (in regard, for example, to questions involving support for national candidates) than some do at present.[13] Not only did the majority of the most powerful chains come to oppose Roosevelt editorially but also some, like Hearst, tightly controlled the slant of news and the very use of political phrasing in their subsidiary newspapers. Thus a Hearst executive of the parent organization advised both individual editors and Hearst's national news services:

The Chief instructs that the phrase Soak the Successful be used in all references to the Administration's tax program instead of the phrase Soak the Thrifty hitherto used, also he wants the words Raw Deal used instead of New Deal.[14]

While Charles Michelson, Democratic public relations director, had stimulated hostile press treatment of Hoover with a series of vicious attacks, no Republican encourage-

---

[11] Frank Luther Mott, *American Journalism*, 3rd. ed. (New York: Macmillan, 1962), p. 719.

[12] Edwin Emery, *The Press and America*, 3rd ed. (Englewood Cliffs, N.J.: Prentice-Hall, 1972), p. 701.

[13] See "The Great Press Chain," *New York Times Magazine* (April 8, 1979), pp. 41–50, for a discussion of how the Gannett chain handles local political editorials.

[14] James MacGregor Burns, *Roosevelt: The Lion and the Fox* (New York: Harcourt, Brace, 1956), p. 241.

ment of the press was apparently needed in 1935. The reaction of many of the large papers to Roosevelt, and particularly to the New Deal economic reforms, was negative—far more so than their response to his foreign and trade policies. But because many of these hostile papers were located in the major cities of the North, Roosevelt considered it vital to counter their influence over the flow of political information. The large cities had become a battleground of the New Deal realignment, a critical base for a new coalition. Since only approximately 20 percent of the papers in large northern cities other than New York supported Roosevelt in 1936, he needed various strategies and mechanisms to penetrate the political screen of a broadly hostile press.[15] His efforts to parry the thrust of the print media and manipulate other means of mass political communications resulted in a dazzling display of new and old public relations techniques and innovations.

Roosevelt was keenly aware that the size, complexity, and internal structure of newspapers afforded him a number of means to counter press opposition. He understood that news reporters, and even many editors, did not share the same political convictions as owners and publishers. In consequence, he went to great pains to service the needs of reporters and develop a close and intimate rapport with them as a whole—while simultaneously keeping up a drum beat of charges against the owners for distortions and omissions in the stories that ultimately appeared. Speaking before the American Society of Newspaper Editors he noted:

In the newspaper game those boys down here in Washington have as high a standard of ethics and morals and fair play as any profession in the United States. I take off my hat to them. But a lot of them labor under a very big handicap. It does not trace back, of necessity, to their editors. It traces back to the owner of the paper essentially.[16]

---

[15] Arthur M. Schlesinger, Jr., *The Politics of Upheaval: The Age of Roosevelt*, vol. 3 (Boston: Houghton Mifflin, 1960), p. 63; and White, *FDR and the Press*, p. 73.

[16] James Pollard, *Presidents and the Press* (New York: Macmillan, 1947), p. 806.

Roosevelt's generally close relationship with news reporters continued throughout his presidency. Despite some strains in their relationship, primarily in the last four years of office, the relationship was one of mutual respect and warmth. One well-known Washington reporter, Raymond Clapper, concluded that, even if the working press was only 60 percent for the New Deal, they were 90 percent for Roosevelt personally.[17a]

Roosevelt's strong links to news reporters—those who created political stories at the entry level—were consistently reinforced by professional factors as well. Professionally, Roosevelt provided reporters with a constant stream of interesting news from the White House, even though most reporters were soon aware that he was trying to frame stories favorable to him.[17b] With only a few exceptions, for example, he stuck faithfully to his promise to hold two press conferences every week, meeting publicly with the press 337 times during his first administration, 374 times in the second, 279 in the third, and 8 times in the three months of his fourth term.

Prior to Franklin D. Roosevelt's administration, the presidential press conference had been an uncertain tool as a creator of news. Presidents Harding, Coolidge, and Hoover, for example, all required written questions in advance of the conference, which severely limited the range, spontaneity, and newsworthiness of the event. Despite the initially friendly and mutually supportive relationship of these presidents and the press, either personal or political circumstances eventually led to the erosion of the relationship and a decline in the quality and quantity of press conferences.[18]

Roosevelt, in contrast, developed his own political formula, eliminating the restrictive practice of requiring written questions in advance, furnishing reporters with much

---

[17a] Raymond Clapper, quoted in Pollard, *Presidents and the Press*, p. 780.

[17b] Leo C. Rosten, *The Washington Correspondents* (New York: Harcourt, Brace and Co., 1937), pp. 47–60.

[18] See Pollard, *Presidents and the Press*, pp. 710–12, 728–33, 766–70.

background information both off and on the record, and answering their questions frankly whenever he could. With a professional's nose for news headlines, Roosevelt often suggested in the news conference itself what the lead for the story about the conference might be. He provided the Washington press with a major organized source of interesting, printable national news.

Part of Roosevelt's political communications strategy was based on creating a tight link with the news process at the reporter level so that he could minimize the impact of subsequent omissions and distortions made by top management. While he could not stop warped front-page editorializing—a *Chicago Tribune* headline in 1936 read, for instance, "Roosevelt Area in Wisconsin Is Hotbed of Vice"—he could and did try to create news stories that would be of such interest to the mass public that even papers hostile to him would have to carry them.[19] By multiplying the number of important stories emanating from the presidential office and from the public information offices in the growing executive agencies, he dramatically increased the total flow of political information involving himself and his programs, and, aided by the crisis atmosphere, force-fed some, if not all, of his activities and intentions onto the front page of the newspapers.[20]

Though he obviously could not "get out" to the public all the news he wanted, and many of his domestic programs were treated in distorted fashion at higher editorial levels by his opposition in the press, Roosevelt and his programmatic presidency did markedly escalate the total flow of political information. The evidence presented in figure 2

[19] Burns, *Roosevelt: The Lion and the Fox*, p. 633.

[20] Elmer E. Cornwell, Jr., "The Presidential Press Conference: A Study in Institutionalization," *Midwest Journal of Political Science* 9 (1960). And for a more general discussion see his *Presidential Leadership of Public Opinion* (Bloomington, Ind.: University of Indiana Press, 1965). For historical analyses of presidential use of the media see Glenn Mark Barkan, "The President and Broadcasting: Governing Through the Media," unpublished Ph.D. dissertation, Claremont Graduate School, 1972; and John Knox Boaz, "The Presidential Press Conference," unpublished Ph.D. dissertation, Wayne State University, 1969.

confirms, for example, the dramatic increase in the volume of politicized economic news generated by Roosevelt and his actions after 1932, indicating that the press as a whole was prompted to respond to the establishment of his new domestic political agenda even if, on balance, it rejected the direction it took.

Among Roosevelt's press strategies was his cultivation of the idea that the newspaper reader should not believe unfavorable stories about his administration. Singling out the issue of credibility repeatedly, Roosevelt noted:

There is a growing tendency on the part of the public not to believe what they read in a certain type of newspaper. I think it is not the editorial end, because, as you know, very few people read the editorials. . . . Lack of confidence in the press today is not because of the editorials but because of the colored news stories and the failure on the part of some papers to print the news.[21]

Seeking to undermine the credibility of unfavorable news, Roosevelt attacked the AP and UP news services. Claiming to detect subtle bias in their treatment of his administration, he often singled them out for direct criticism of their prejudicial view of national political news. In general, however, the evidence points to the fact that Roosevelt was not as heavily opposed in the press as he perceived (or claimed), though opposition to him on the basis of his domestic initiatives was far more marked than on other issues of leadership. Roosevelt repeatedly used the figure of 85 percent to denote the percentage of the press against him, though the actual percentage was probably about 20 percent less than that; and some who opposed his reelection did not oppose him on all issues of leadership.[22] Roosevelt felt, however, that the press did not at all reflect the opinion of the country as a whole, and therefore saw the press's influence as a distorting influence. Even so, his exaggerated stance against press leaders probably did serve

[21] Franklin Roosevelt, quoted in Pollard, *Presidents and the Press*, pp. 783–84.

[22] White, *FDR and the Press*, pp. 69–74, 82–84.

to blunt adverse criticism and put the press in a somewhat defensive posture.

Roosevelt viewed the press's proper function as a channel through which information about government should flow to the people to keep them well informed. He saw the government itself as a major but not exclusive source of those "facts," and any "opinion" added to those government "facts" he perceived as a political distortion. Though perhaps naive (or self-serving), his hostility to the press's interpretation of straight "fact" was characteristic of his presidency and made him particularly antagonistic to the growing band of political columnists. His disdain for columnists as a whole even spilled over to those who favored his administration.[23]

In getting the administration's broad point of view out to the public at large, Roosevelt's wife, Eleanor, also proved a valuable asset. A woman whose activities underscored the president's concern for the suffering and hardship of ordinary people, she too created and focused news and opinion. Whether answering questions in magazines, making visits and speeches, or writing her column, "My Day," for 135 newspapers, she spread the underlying themes of the Roosevelt administration to a wide audience. As a result, Eleanor Roosevelt served as a handy target for anti–New Deal caricature by certain papers. But even hostile treatment of her worked to FDR's advantage, hardening the political cleavages that the president felt would benefit his new coalitions and his programs.[24]

Roosevelt's most powerful single weapon blunting the impact of hostile criticism in the print media was his extraordinary use of radio. Radio linked him personally and directly to the people. No interpretive screen mediated between Roosevelt and people receiving his voice, as it did with the print press. Radio gave Roosevelt the opportunity to present his program, his voice, and his personality directly to his constituency. For Roosevelt, radio served as

[23]*Ibid.*, pp. 31–32; 129–31.
[24]Joseph P. Lash, *Eleanor and Franklin* (New York: W. W. Norton, 1971), pp. 418–33.

an effective communications alternative, a mechanism of
direct, person-to-person contact by which he could bypass
a hostile commercial press. It was, in essence, an electronic
adaptation of Bryan's national lecture program, and it
enabled Roosevelt to reach his audience directly and
instantaneously.

Presidential candidates had first used radio in any significant way in 1924. In the 1928 campaign both sides spent
approximately a half million dollars apiece to beam their
candidates to the approximately nine million radio sets
then in use. By 1932, however, the number of radio sets in
use had leaped to over eighteen million, and it jumped to
twenty-six million by 1935. Not only could radio reach a
total audience of approximately fifty to sixty million listeners, but also two radio networks, NBC and CBS, had
enough affiliates to blanket the country and give simulta-
neous nationwide coverage to a single speaker.[25] Thus
radio gave Roosevelt a communications channel similar in
part to the presidential keynote newspaper of the earlier
partisan press era: in both, the presidential side of a story
could be assured transmission with its content undiluted.

Roosevelt, long sensing the opportunities radio could
afford his personal career, was an early practitioner of radio
politics. He had used the radio as early as 1924, and
employed it extensively in his campaign for Al Smith's
nomination as the Democratic presidential candidate in
1928, during his terms as governor of New York State from
1928 to 1932, and in his presidential campaign in 1932. In
campaign speeches and formal radio addresses Roosevelt
was an impressive performer; but it was in his direct personal conversations with his listeners—the "Fireside
Chats"—that Roosevelt opened an entirely new channel of
political communications with his audience. Designed to
be uncomplicated, explanatory, and addressed to a specific
policy objective, these talks—referred to by Roosevelt as
"heart-to-heart" talks—were meant to inform and per-

[25] Erik Barnouw, *Mass Communication: Television, Radio, Film,
Press*, 2nd ed. (New York: Holt, Rinehart and Winston, 1960), p. 34;
Historical Statistics (Washington, D.C.: Bureau of the Census, Depart-
ment of Commerce, 1976) 2: 796.

suade. Only six days after his inauguration, Roosevelt made his first Fireside Chat to explain why he had temporarily closed the banks, what he expected to do, and what behavior he expected from nervous depositors. The next day the banks reopened, large amounts of hoarded currency were returned, the banking crisis was averted, and Roosevelt had established himself as a close and interested "friend" and leader to each of millions of frightened listeners.[26]

Roosevelt was careful not to impose himself too frequently in his homey, intimate manner, delivering fewer than thirty Fireside Chats over his twelve years in office. Most, though not all, were considered very effective in serving Roosevelt's political objectives, which were, first, to establish for himself a close, unscreened, and favorable relationship with each listener; second, to enable the president to move or lead public opinion in a direction he wanted to go; and, third, to stimulate mass opinion to express itself strongly to other governmental institutions and leaders in favor of his initiatives.

Basically Roosevelt sought to take advantage of the new context of mass communications by using radio broadcasts—whether Fireside Chats, presidential addresses, or political speeches—to reach his audience directly with his own messages and to solicit political opinions from his listeners in return. As a result, in his first term in office Roosevelt's mail ran on average between thirty-five thousand to fifty-five thousand pieces per week, which was approximately ten times the mail received by Hoover at the end of his administration. With the exception of what presidential secretary, Louis Howe, considered organized "pressure" mail—mail inspired by organizations and stereotyped in wording—all personal letters to Roosevelt received a prompt and individual reply.[27] A few personal letters to

[26] Ernest Brandenberg and Waldo Braden, "Roosevelt's Fireside Chats," *Speech Monographs* 22 (1955): 294. See also Edward W. Chester, *Radio, Television, and American Politics* (New York: Sheed and Ward, 1969), p. 33.

[27] Leila A. Sussman, "FDR and the White House Mail," *Public Opinion Quarterly* 20 (1955): 5–8; also her *Dear FDR: A Study of Political Letter Writing* (New Jersey: Bedminster Press, 1963).

him (some of questioned authenticity) later would be quoted in a subsequent address or press release, providing new assurances of the personal interest and closeness of the president to the ordinary people of the country. In the absence of sophisticated polling techniques presently available to presidents, this incoming White House mail served as a valued "feedback" linkage for a president deeply interested in the dimensions of public opinion on both specific issues and his personal image.

In order to gain as much political insight as possible into the characteristics of public opinion, the White House actually kept a daily count of incoming mail by subject categories—such as National Recovery Administration (NRA), Social Security, Supreme Court plan, and so forth—with subjects constantly revised to reflect the shifting relevance of political topics. Also monitored was the rise or fall of interest in particular issues, which offered the president a running analysis of trends in public concern. With "mail briefs" measuring support for and opposition to presidential activities, the president reinforced his direct link to the ordinary citizen.

Aware as he was that much of the upper socioeconomic stratum of American society felt increasingly threatened by New Deal reforms, Roosevelt used his strong public support to resist efforts by political representatives and lobbyists for these interests to obstruct his programs in Congress. He realized, of course, that the flow of mail he was generating to support his recovery program could be directed to others beside himself and encouraged letter writers not only to inform him of their needs but also to remind their House and Senate representatives as well. The mail generated to members of Congress, particularly in Roosevelt's first term, was an effective weapon in building local constituent awareness and subsequent pressure in the battle to enact his programs.[28]

---

[28] For a detailed discussion of election politics, see James T. Patterson, *Congressional Conservatism and the New Deal* (Lexington, Kentucky: University of Kentucky Press, 1967), pp. 211–87. See also Leuchtenburg, *Franklin D. Roosevelt and the New Deal*.

Before Roosevelt's presidency, much of a president's knowledge of public opinion came to him indirectly, from congressional assessments of local district opinion, from estimates by various politically knowledgeable activists, and, of course, from the press as a "stand-in" for public opinion. Before the confident use of opinion surveys or polls, presidential assessments of the public mind were, therefore, at least a step removed from their source and subject to dilution or distortion by intervening carriers. Roosevelt not only wanted to go over the heads of newspaper owners to communicate directly with the mass public, but he also wanted a direct link in the other direction, i.e., from the public to himself. A major change in the transmission of political information *to* the president as well as *from* him was thus initiated by Roosevelt's utilization of new communications technology. By claiming and holding a newly central position in mass communications, by orchestrating mass support for his public policies, and by symbolizing in his office the aspirations of political reform, Roosevelt effected a significant change in the relationship of the presidency, mass communications, and the public at large.

The Press, Reform, and Realignment

Assessing the relationship of the press to New Deal reforms, we must recall that, while Roosevelt and the New Deal had some important press support throughout his presidency, the commercial press as a whole did not serve to stimulate political change. Unlike the period less than two decades earlier, when the press had been closely involved with Progressive reform movements, mass-circulation newspapers—despite the ravages of the deepest and most durable depression in the country's history—largely resisted Roosevelt and New Deal reforms, allying themselves instead with the forces defending the political and economic status quo.

Reasons for the press's resistance include important

changes in the nature of press ownership and, also, a shift of political attitudes by important press leaders. First, the press had rapidly been affected by the growing consolidation and concentration that had already spread throughout industry as a whole. Newspaper chains were now commercial giants, spanning huge markets and encompassing newspapers, magazines, and wire and movie news services. As the trend toward newspaper consolidation deepened, a new trend toward *concentration*—i.e., the elimination in many cities of competition between differently owned newspapers—rapidly changed the communications environment. Not only did the total number of newspapers decline between 1915 and 1935, but also many continuing papers acquired by large chains no longer retained their independent political voice, thus limiting the range and variety of press opinion in many localities.

The strongest wave of newspaper consolidation and concentration took place during and after World War I and continued into the 1920s. By 1930, only 20 percent of 1,400 cities with daily newspapers had any newspaper competition, and in many of these the competition was badly skewed in favor of a single dominant paper. During the depression period, from 1931 to 1936, several hundred additional papers suspended publication, affected by business's slashed advertising budgets, so that in 1935 only 63 companies controlled 328 newspapers with 41 percent of all daily circulation and 52 percent of all Sunday sales.[29] Newspapers, as Munsey had predicted, were businesses: they conformed to the broad corporate trends in the economy as a whole.

The concentration of press power in fewer but larger corporate organizations seems to have had a significant role in making the press increasingly businesslike and conservative. But it was not the sole factor producing a strong commitment to the socioeconomic status quo against the growing outline of New Deal reforms. The owners and dominant personalities behind some of the largest chains,

---

[29] Emery, *The Press and America*, p. 629.

people such as Scripps and Hearst, had shifted markedly the political positions they had espoused in earlier years. The Scripps chain, one of the three largest, was founded originally as a group of liberal "people's papers." It shifted steadily toward the right under Roy W. Howard, who took control of the chain in the 1930s. The Scripps chain had supported Robert M. LaFollette, the Progressive party candidate in 1924, and championed organized labor throughout its formative years. Under Howard's more conservative direction, it moved steadily away from its early New Deal support of Roosevelt and became the New Deal's enemy. Although the chain permitted somewhat more "local autonomy" than Hearst, Howard's attitudes on national affairs were made clear to all subsidiary newspapers.[30]

Hearst kept an iron grip on his newspapers' political positions. As his own views shifted from Populist left to strongly reactionary, the chain reflected his transition. Whether from political conviction, ambition for public office, or both, Hearst had encouraged strong Populist and reform-oriented positions around the turn of the century. His papers fought strongly against monopolies and concentrated economic power of all kinds, and he was the only major publisher in the entire Northeast who supported Bryan's Populist-Democratic 1896 campaign. In addition, he championed the cause of the working classes and was aggressive in his support of labor unionization.[31] By the 1930s, however, Hearst had moved sharply rightward. Although he supported Roosevelt's bid for a first term, when Hearst saw the broad outlines of the New Deal's domestic programs he turned his chain to an all-out attack on the administration. With almost one out of four of Sunday, and one out of eight of all daily, newspaper readers in the country, Hearst sought to punish New Deal leaders for programs that challenged Hearst's now ultraconservative politics.

---

[30] Mott, *American Journalism,* pp. 641–42.

[31] W. A. Swanberg, *Citizen Hearst: A Biography of William Randolph Hearst* (New York: Charles Scribner's, 1961), p. 198.

The same publisher who had once regularly fought the concentration of business and economic power in American society now fought Roosevelt's proposals to limit business concentration through government controls over holding companies. Attempting to undermine public confidence in the Social Security program, Hearst carried front-page, eleventh-hour claims just before the 1936 election that contributing wage earners would never get their money back. His headline read: "DO YOU WANT A TAG AND A NUMBER IN THE NAME OF FALSE SECURITY?"[32] His early support for the working man evaporated, transformed into savage attacks on such New Deal legislation such as the Wagner Act, a statute that encouraged the organization of labor unions. Hearst claimed that the Wagner Act was "vicious class legislation," a violation of the Constitution and American principles, and, in effect, "betray[ed] the country."[33] A front-page story attacking the activities of the Works Progress Administration (WPA) claimed "Taxpayers Feed 20,000 Reds on New York Relief Rolls."[34]

While the two largest newspaper organizations in the country had moved from support of liberal reform to staunch defense of the social and economic status quo, the third, McCormick's *Chicago Tribune*, did not reverse its political perspective at all. Starting from a politically conservative position toward social reform and business regulation, it simply kept becoming more conservative as New Deal reforms were implemented. The *Chicago Tribune* was not merely reactionary. Like Hearst, it was also strident, strongly opinionated, and biased. As a result, a poll of Washington correspondents rated it the runner-up to the Hearst papers as "least fair and reliable" in reporting the news.[35]

Thus the top news organizations in the country eventually opposed the economic initiatives of the New Deal.

---

[32] Schlesinger, *The Politics of Upheaval*, p. 636.

[33] *San Francisco Examiner*, May 29, 1935.

[34] *San Francisco Examiner*, October 30, 1936.

[35] Emery, *The Press and America*, p. 710.

Although a majority of smaller southern papers remained in support of Roosevelt and the Democrats, a significant majority of larger northern papers, as well as the three chains, opposed the New Deal reforms. As a result, Roosevelt found the largest segment of the press opposing his reform efforts and making it more difficult for him to communicate "his side" of the discussion of new initiatives through regular newspaper channels. Speaking over radio in a 1937 Fireside Chat, Roosevelt's pointed omission of the print press as a means of political education clearly indicated the negative role he felt that newspapers and news services played in New Deal reform. "Five years of fierce discussion and debate—five years of information through the *radio and moving pictures*," he observed, "have taken the whole nation to school in the nation's business."[36]

Clearly the press's response to reform differed markedly in the Progressive and New Deal eras. Equally clearly, the change in the press by itself does not give a full explanation of press/reform relationships during the New Deal realignment. Not only had the press changed its attitudes toward political reform, but also certain fundamental aspects of reform itself had changed. Comparison of reform characteristics in the Progressive and New Deal eras is beyond the scope of this study. However, certain differences between the two periods—in political strategies and, most importantly, in leadership use of social cleavages as a basis for political mobilization—tell us much about the changing character of reform.

During the Progressive era, neither of the two major political parties was willing or able to articulate the demands or to mobilize the support of expanding working-class and immigrant populations. Republicans grew increasingly conservative and antilabor between 1900 and 1930. The Democrats, still dominated by their strong "provincial" roots, were not capable of capitalizing on the widespread dissatisfaction among laboring groups. Even the

---

[36] Pollard, *Presidents and the Press*, p. 800 (italics mine).

American Federation of Labor, the largest labor organization at the time, was more anti-Republican than genuinely
pro-Democratic in 1920. Southern, rural support for pro-
hibition and the Ku Klux Klan, for example, widened the
differences between the southern and northern wings and
kept the Democratic party from capitalizing on its growing
urban constituency. The strength of urban ethnic groups
and workers within the Democratic party eventually
helped bring about the nomination of Al Smith as the presidential nominee in 1928, but urban working-class influence was still largely diluted in the electorate as a whole by
the relative weakness of labor unions and the lack of significant differences between the two major parties on working-class issues.[37]

Most of organized labor's leadership backed Robert
LaFollette's Progressive presidential challenge in 1924,
and some evidence suggests that the rank and file also supported his candidacy at the polls.[38] But the principal social
and economic gains made by Progressive reforms between
1900 to 1916 were made with labor little more than the
very minor partner of primarily middle-class reformers.
Although some settlement house reformers were, at times,
successful in mobilizing poor laboring *people* for local political action,[39] labor *unions* and Progressives formed only
tentative and irregular alliances.

The fear felt by many Progressives of large-scale organized power, whether in the form of corporate trusts, interlocking directorates, or political parties, carried over to a
substantial degree in their attitude toward labor unions.

---

[37] David Burner, *The Politics of Provincialism: The Democratic Party
in Transition 1918–1932* (New York: W. W. Norton, 1968), p. 71. See
also J. David Greenstone, *Labor in American Politics* (New York: Vin-
tage, 1969), pp. 36–37. On the New Dealer's attitude toward the political use of social cleavages, see Otis L. Graham, *Encore for Reform* (New
York: Oxford University Press, 1967), p. 174.

[38] Roger Wyman investigates working-class electoral support for Progressives in Wisconsin, in "Middle Class Voters and Progressive
Reform," *American Political Science Review* 68 (1974): 488–504.

[39] Allen F. Davis, *Spearheads for Reform: The Social Settlements and
the Progressive Movement 1890–1914* (New York: Oxford University
Press, 1967).

Labor's own economic imperative—to develop a large and tightly linked organizational structure through which it could "collectively" bargain with employers—ran against the "individualist" grain of Progressive thought, despite broad sympathy in the movement for the problems of laboring people in general.[40] Many Progressives felt genuine concern about the implications of strong unions for society, should unions become another "combination" of great economic power. That Progressive political reformers considered labor unions a mixed blessing was in part due also to their fear that concentrated labor might join with concentrated capital to squeeze the consumer, the small businessman, or both. The rise in the price of coal after the great anthracite strike of 1902, for example, fed Progressive concerns about the unions themselves. In some cities where organized labor was genuinely powerful, Progressivism often took on an antilabor tinge.[41]

Despite their sympathy for the lower classes and legislative efforts to alleviate some of the suffering of unprotected and exploited workers, Progressives made little, if any, effort to mobilize the masses of working people into any on-going political activity *led by organizations of their own*. They felt an undercurrent of concern about the political direction an organized, aroused, and self-conscious working class might take. Positioned as a buffer between the demands of unregulated capitalism on the right and the threat of socialism on the left, the Progressive movement, basically middle class in its economic base and outlook, sought to protect the free enterprise system by trying to limit the system's ravages—but without encouraging the mobilization and organization of potentially dangerous portions of the ethnic and working-class population.[42]

---

[40] Mancur Olsen, *The Logic of Collective Action*, 5th ed. (Cambridge, Mass.: Harvard University Press, 1975), pp. 66–76; and Richard Hofstadter, *The Age of Reform* (New York: Knopf, 1955).

[41] Hofstadter, *The Age of Reform*, p. 241; and Marc Karson, *American Labor Unions and Politics* (Carbondale, Ill.: Southern Illinois University Press, 1958), pp. 71–73.

[42] See Ronald Steel, *Walter Lippmann and the American Century* (Boston: Little Brown, 1980), pp. 40–41, 47–48. To a significant extent,

The two eras of reform thus differed substantially in their approaches both to labor organizations and to political parties. Many Progressives had attempted to weaken the organizational power of established party leaders. The New Dealers, however, mounted no concerted attack on the political party as a vehicle of organization. Instead, Roosevelt utilized party leaders on the basis of how they could further his personal and political objectives. Political "bosses" such as Ed Crump of Memphis, Ed Flynn of the Bronx, and Frank Hague of Jersey City cooperated with Roosevelt and received substantial distributions of federal patronage and favors. A few who opposed him, or who were considered a political liability, he sought to eliminate.[43] In any case, the link between the Roosevelt administration's actions and the Democratic party's leadership and organization was always based on Roosevelt's pragmatic assessment of their ability to help or hinder him and his objectives. He made no effort to reform the parties such as the Progressives had undertaken. Roosevelt saw party organizations as tools for mass mobilization to be rewarded or punished depending on what they could do for him or his programs—as a means of extending his political reach.

In gaining the nomination in 1932, for example, Roosevelt and his campaign manager, James A. Farley, pursued and then bargained with the party organizational leaders, making it a strict rule not to challenge or interfere with favorite-son endorsements.[44] His campaign for the nomination depended on dealing with established organizational leaders and convincing them to support him, and was not in any significant way a "party reform" candidacy. His original backing for removal of the obstructive two-thirds rule—which required support of a *large* majority of delegates for the nomination—was, in fact, dropped when it

---

Progressive attacks on political party organizations—the prime vehicles for mobilizing ethnic and working-class groups—also served to insulate lower-class groups from potential organization.

[43] Lyle W. Dorsett, *Franklin D. Roosevelt and the City Bosses* (Port Washington, N.Y.: Kennikat Press, 1977), pp. 112–17.

[44] *Ibid.*, p. 14.

seemed clear that he could be nominated under the old rule, and that his continued support for a rule change would jeopardize support he had already gained among southern delegations.[45]

Roosevelt eventually tried to extend his system of support for his organizational friends and punishment for his enemies to fellow party members in congressional office, but here he met with far less success. After refraining from opposing the party's local choices for Congress in his first term, Roosevelt's frustration with obstruction of his program objectives by congressional Democrats in 1938 aroused him to actively intercede in an effort to deprive certain congressmen of the Democratic nomination. This attempt to eliminate Democratic incumbents from national office failed. With the exception of a single congressman from Manhattan, the candidates he opposed—Smith in South Carolina, Tydings in Maryland, George in Georgia, McCarren in Nevada, and Lonergan in Connecticut—all won.[46]

Although his attempt to "nationalize" the congressional nomination process met no success, Roosevelt and the New Deal served to reinvigorate the party system as a whole. Whereas Progressive reforms attacked party organizational resources and encouraged—intentionally or not—the weakening of both party organizations and voter ties to the major parties, the New Deal accepted and used strong (and supportive) organizations and encouraged new party loyalties. With the exception of the elimination of the two-thirds rule, a rule change aimed at strengthening, not weakening, the national Democratic party, the New Deal made no significant effort at reform of the parties as political institutions.[47]

---

[45] See Richard L. Rubin, *Party Dynamics: The Democratic Coalition and the Politics of Change* (New York: Oxford University Press, 1976), pp. 114–15.

[46] See James M. Burns, *Roosevelt: The Lion and the Fox*, pp. 363–64.

[47] Richard L. Rubin, "Presidential Primaries: Continuities, Dimensions of Change, and Political Implications," a paper delivered at the American Political Science Association annual meeting, 1977, p. 8.

If the New Deal did not revive the party reform spirit of the Progressives, it is because, in a certain sense, party organizational reform was crowded off the political agenda by the sharp social and political cleavages that developed *between* the two parties. Sharp lines of conflict between the two parties on issues critical to the well-being of large numbers of Americans left the issue of party reform subordinate to politically polarized economic and social cleavages.[48]

It is important to emphasize several critical distinctions in the nature of political coalitions during these two different reform periods. In the New Deal era, major policy differences on substantive issues clearly divided the two major parties, and reform elements clustered almost entirely within the Democratic party. In the Progressive era, though progressivism emerged largely from the Republican party, both parties—Wilson's Democratic administration included—embraced substantial parts of the philosophy of Progressive reform. As a result, the parties did not polarize around reform issues. Less directed than New Deal reforms at major substantive programs, unaggressive in risking changes of the capitalist system itself, Progressive reforms were not only heavily procedural but also, most importantly, based upon and protective of the broad active middle class in both parties.

Unique in New Deal reforms was Roosevelt's and his supporters' efforts to use different tools to enfranchise, and gain the support and loyalty of, large numbers of hitherto nonparticipant and unorganized groups.[49] However it resembled the earlier movement, Roosevelt's New Deal differed from the Progressives in daring to exploit social

---

[48] E. E. Schattschneider, *The Semi-Sovereign People* (New York: Holt, Rinehart and Winston, 1960), pp. 62–73; Graham, *Encore for Reform, passim.*

[49] Kristi Andersen, "Generational Change, Partisan Shift and Realignment," in Norman Nie, Sidney Verba, and John R. Petrocik, *The Changing American Voter* (Cambridge, Mass.: Harvard University Press, 1976), chapters 5, pp. 79–95. See also Kristi Andersen, *The Creation of a Democratic Majority, 1928–1936* (University of Chicago Press, 1979), *passim.*

and economic class cleavages in its quest for voters, encouraging the political mobilization of the working class by its own leaders.[50] In this sense Roosevelt was certainly a "traitor to his class," for in reaching out to organize a then impoverished working class to self-conscious political self-assertion, he was endangering a political structure whose institutions tended to dilute—*not* encourage—a class basis to politics.

The New Deal differed from the Progressive era, then, primarily because of Roosevelt's efforts to expand the area of political conflict, to entice large numbers of citizens into the national political arena, and to utilize both the political parties and organized labor as on-going mobilizing tools. Unlike the outcome of Progressive reform, New Deal reform worked to increase an individual's sense of party loyalty rather than weaken it. Despite fears among some of his allies, Roosevelt's mobilization of large numbers of working-class voters behind his leadership both revitalized and nationalized the electoral system, bringing into the electoral arena many who were outside, and restabilizing the system at a new and different level of governmental involvement. Underlying Roosevelt's actions was, of course, his own political self-interest. In addition, his interest in knowing what the "people," not just the "experts," thought about an issue, encouraged New Deal reform to "organize into politics" unmobilized important groups.

The New Deal realignment tells us much about the relative effectiveness of press influence when such influence is opposed by that of other strong institutions. The print press undoubtedly had political influence—Roosevelt's majorities probably would have been even larger than they were had he had greater newspaper support. But its ability to direct and convince public opinion on major issues was severely constrained by the countering activities of other political institutions. In this case, the major expansion of

---

[50] For an example of Woodrow Wilson's fears of exploiting class cleavages see James W. Caeser, *Presidential Selection*, p. 192.

the presidential role in the structuring of political communications established a significant counterforce to newspaper influence over popular opinion. In his manipulation of the print press, and particularly in his use of radio, Roosevelt opened new channels of political information. He established a faster, more centralized and more direct circuitry between the mass public and the presidency than possible before him and used the unique personal qualities of radio to deeply penetrate into a vast new listening audience.

The evidence lends support to several ideas that have important bearing for the future. When the issues arouse large numbers of voters, when leadership responds aggressively and parties polarize, then the independent influence of the press appears limited to sharpening (but not initiating) the lines of battle. Where the print press's information is opposed either by alternative sources of information (such as radio) or by strong personal or group experiences, the power of the press is also limited. In effect, the stronger the force of political parties and the presidency as mobilizing institutions and the greater the strength of electoral realignment, the less powerful the press is either in influencing the shape of political opinion or in structuring the political agenda.

From a small, economically and politically dependent appendage to the political parties, the press had grown by the 1930s into an institution of great, concentrated economic power. Fearful of Populist demands, enthusiastic in its support of Progressive modifications, and then resistant to the apparently threatening policy changes proposed by the New Deal, the mass press's overall influence on the political system served—unsuccessfully—as a resistance to the pressures for change in the economic and political status quo and to narrow the range of political alternatives. Clearly, the press's relationship to the parties and the presidency had changed significantly from its dependent beginnings and, with the development of television, it would change substantially again.

7

Television Journalism
and the National Arena

The press's failure to significantly alter the political outcomes of the 1930s and 1940s cannot be regarded as the
continuing level of press influence in the political process.
In fact, the rapid development of television after World
War II has served to change once again the relationship
between mass communications and political institutions.
By broadening the range and intensity of the press's overall
impact on politics it has destabilized existing political institutions and changed the structure and style of American
political conflict.

Television followed, in essence, an exceptionally brief
"age of radio." It took less than one generation for radio to
suffer a virtual eclipse by television as a prime political
instrument, one which offered not only immediacy and
voice but also visual presence. Impressions about a politician—images of personality, leadership, values, and suc-
cessfulness—are now brought together visually. We do not
just read about or hear about politicians but we also see
them and they speak (or appear to speak) to us directly.
The new medium has facilitated a new direct and *seemingly
intimate* relationship between the politician and the audi-

ence and produced, as we shall see, significant changes in the operations of our election system.[1]

The growth of television as a new communications medium was extremely rapid. Whereas only 940,000 American households had television sets in 1949, by 1956, 34,900,000 homes had at least one television. This extraordinary expansion of television's presence was translated into dominance as the medium was soon looked upon as America's prime source of election information. Although one-third of all Americans had claimed that radio was their most important source of campaign information in 1952, by 1960 only 6 percent chose radio, while 65 percent named television as their most important source.[2] In addition to its rapid replacement of radio as the dominant electronic medium, it quickly became the most trusted source of political news for the American people. A 1959 Roper poll found 32 percent claiming newspapers as their most believable news source while 29 percent claimed television, but by 1968 only 21 percent still claimed newspapers and 44 percent felt television the most trustworthy.[3] Importantly, another series of surveys has also shown that Americans believe that television gives the clearest understanding of national news and electoral candidates, with newspapers and other mass media following far behind—a belief that is by no means documented in fact as yet.[4]

While the growth of television as a communications medium was very rapid, the development of television journalism was significantly slower than that of the entertainment side of television. Clearly one of the retardant features on the early credibility and influence of television

[1] For further discussion of the relationship see James David Barber, *The Pulse of Politics: Electing Presidents in the Media Age* (New York: W. W. Norton, 1980), particularly pp. 319–22.

[2] For data on households with television sets see *Historical Statistics* (Washington, D.C.: Bureau of the Census, Department of Commerce, 1976) 2:796; also see Herbert B. Asher, *Presidential Elections and American Politics* (Homewood, Illinois: Dorsey Press, 1976), pp. 222–27.

[3] Described in Asher, *Presidential Elections and American Politics,* p. 226.

[4] *Ibid.*

news reporting was that, unlike print journalism, it developed out of the entertainment industry. Except for unusual (and dramatic) events, such as the Kefauver Senate crime investigations and the Army-McCarthy Senate hearings, regular network news coverage in the 1950s was brief (fifteen minutes per evening), lacking in visual highlights, and most often presented a reporter reading written news reports that were initiated by journalists of other media. The network news divisions were, in fact, severely limited in the amount of resources that the network would allocate to them and were viewed by management initially as a "prestige" but money-losing part of the business.

Over the last two decades, however, the news side of television has become a much larger part of press coverage as a whole, a money-making division of the networks, and a substantial new influence in changing how the political game itself is played. Though only a small part of the total press coverage of presidential nominations, conventions, and elections in the 1940s and the 1950s, television journalism's reach and influence grew particularly rapidly in the early 1960s. Michael Robinson has identified 1963 as a pivotal year in the development of television journalism when the major networks increased their evening programming from fifteen minutes to a half hour.[5] The networks not only doubled the amoubt of national news broadcasting but signaled, in effect, a commitment to extensive news coverage and their coming of age as a serious news medium.

The increased role of television and the press as a whole in electoral politics was largely recognized by politicians and audience alike after the Kennedy administration. Perhaps in recognition of the growing press influence that stemmed from television, a dramatic and symbolic incident at the 1964 Republican convention occurred. There, the perceived intrusion of the press in the political process exploded in a major convention demonstration by the del-

---

[5] Michael J. Robinson, "Television and American Politics, 1952–1976," *Public Interest*, Spring 1977, 14–15.

egates *against the press*. Triggered by a scornful reference to the press in an address by ex-president Eisenhower, the rage of the Goldwater delegates culminated in a noisy, long, and furious demonstration. James David Barber described that scene as follows:

When at last the furor died down, the reading of the platform went forward . . . Brinkley switched to his colleague John Chancellor on the floor of the convention. Chancellor loomed up on the screen, saying, "Well, I'd try if I could, David, but I wonder if I may be under arrest." The television audience saw Chancellor, in respectable suit and tie, being forceably carried out of the hall, reporting as he went, "This is John Chancellor, somewhere in custody."[6]

Events themselves (and television's coverage of them) have played a continuing role in enlarging the public's interest in television journalism, and the increased public interest has, in consequence, promoted television's growing influence in American politics. The presidential debates in the 1960 presidential election, the assassination of President John F. Kennedy, civil rights marches, urban rioting, and the Vietnam War have all provided the kind of dramatic raw materials which stimulated viewer interest in televised journalism. Of equal if not of greater importance, the Watergate investigations and the subsequent impeachment proceedings—together with the thousands of evening news stories generated by the special news coverage of these events—have brought increased credibility to the press as well as a new assertiveness to its self-prescribed role in the political process.

With the development of television, the combination of the print and electronic "press" has brought about, then, a new and distinct phase in the relationship of the press, the party, and the president. To better understand the contemporary relationship of these institutions, we must ask: First, what is the distinctive character of television journalism? Second, how is television news shaped and organized for its mass audience? And, third, what is the impact of the

---

[6] Barber, *The Pulse of Politics*, p. 179.

addition of television to overall press influence on political behavior?

The Changing Nature of News

The significance of television journalism in the political process lies not just in its special visual qualities but also in a distinctiveness derived largely, but not exclusively, from its national *network* linkages. Television news not only reaches a huge audience simultaneously, but the content and presentation of its news is different in specific ways from that of newspapers.[7] Besides obvious differences in immediacy and personal visibility between news received from television and newspapers, for present purposes the most important distinction between these two most pervasive sources of mass communications is that network television, in particular, is not primarily directed at a specific local community audience. While local television news is firmly grounded in local community happenings and closely parallels local newspaper reporting in its content and focus,[8] network television, like national news weeklies such as *Time* and *Newsweek*, builds upon a national audience. Whereas the over six hundred local stations that have become affiliates of the three major networks cater separately to the local news interests of their constituents, when they link into network news programming they reach a much enlarged national audience that can only be addressed as a single unit.

We have already seen that localism and parochialism have been the essential characteristics of the American print press over time. Unlike the more nationally oriented newspapers of, for example, Great Britain, the American newspapers—with the exception of a few nationally ori-

[7] Paul A. Weaver, "Newspaper News and Television News," *Television as a Social Force*, ed. Douglass Cater and Richard Adler (New York: Praeger, 1975), pp. 84–88.

[8] See David L. Altheide, *Creating Reality: How TV News Distorts Events* (Beverly Hills, California: Sage Publications, 1974), pp. 13–14.

ented newspapers—are economically and politically linked to a specific community, the local marketplace which provides its circulation and advertising, local personalities and events.[9] The economics of reaching a national audience, we will see, impel the network news to deal with this audience in a way unlike that of newspapers or local television stations. In short, television has created an enormous national audience of approximately fifty million nightly viewers, and in meeting the needs of those viewers who receive their local news elsewhere it has given a new and different thrust to the content and presentation of news and, in consequence, to the nature and flow of political information as a whole.

A comparison between the three leading stories on the CBS *Evening News* between 1963 and 1975 and the three leading front-page newspaper stories over the same period illustrates some of these distinctions between the different media.[10] Figure 3 shows most strikingly that network television news is not simply more national in outlook, as one might expect, but is *much more* national than newspaper news. More importantly, it is also far more political in the amount of attention it gives than newspapers. The data show that by a two- or three-to-one ratio over the newspapers, network television focuses its audiences' interest not only on national stories but on stories that are linked to either national political figures or institutions—e.g., the activities of congressional committees, actions taken by the president, or other partisan activities going on in Washington.

Newspapers, on the other hand, focus their most prominent attention on nonpolitical events, such as crime or other types of human interest stories, much more than net-

---

[9] David Butler and Donald Stokes, *Political Change in Britain* 2nd ed. (New York: St. Martin's Press, 1974), pp. 115–19.

[10] Random samples of the first three television stories from *CBS Evening News* were drawn covering a thirteen-year period (CBS was the only network with sufficient transcript data to cover such a span). The data were then compared with the three most prominent newspaper stories covering the same period. See Rubin and Rivers, "Mass Media," for methodological details, pp. 17–18.

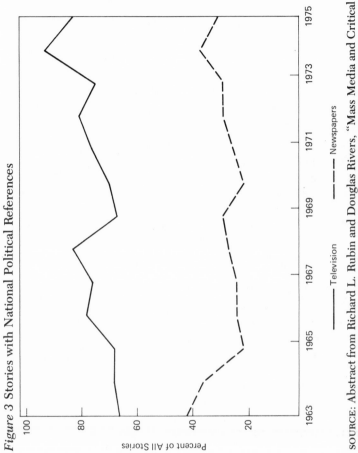

Figure 3 Stories with National Political References

SOURCE: Abstract from Richard L. Rubin and Douglas Rivers, "Mass Media and Critical Elections: A First Report." Paper presented at the Northeastern Political Science Association Convention, 1978.

work television. Over time, the differences between the
two have widened significantly. Whereas only 60 percent
of all lead stories on network television had political topics
in 1963, by 1975 about 80 percent of all top news stories
reaching the air were "political." In contrast, the newspapers' lead headline stories were political (either local or
national) in only a little over 25 percent of the cases, and
the trend between 1963 and 1975 indicates, if anything, no
increase in political news stories.

The far greater emphasis on politics in the news stories
presented by network television is important in that it
spreads an additional body of information that has political
emphasis more similar in structure to weekly news magazines like *Time* and *Newsweek* than to newspapers and local
television.[11] This body of information assures a substantial
increase in the familiarity of the mass audience with politically oriented issues and personalities, and also markedly
increases the likelihood of a common frame of reference for
political topics. As a result, television broadens the scope
of political conflict by spreading interest in a particular
topic, political incident, or political personality over a vast
audience in just a few moments of viewing each night. An
example of the rapidity of change in the salience of an issue
is the swift shift in the perceived importance of "civil
rights" after heavy television emphasis of dramatic civil
rights confrontations in the South. The percentage of the
public placing civil rights on the top of the country's political agenda as "the most important problem facing America" rose from 4 percent in late 1962 to over 50 percent just
after the massive August 1963 rally of an estimated 300,000
civil rights sympathizers in Washington, D.C. Such an
extraordinary and rapid shift in public awareness and public priorities could not have occurred without an already
highly developed national audience and the means to reach
it quickly and dramatically.[12]

No claim is made that a change of such magnitude was
brought about solely because of television news. Civil

---

[11] Paul A. Weaver, "Newspaper News and Television News," pp. 89–
91.

[12] Robinson, "Television and American Politics."

rights activists had spent years seeking to raise national awareness of regional injustices; and, in addition, newspapers and weekly news magazines played crucial roles in fleshing out events and fostering popular consciousness as well. What is claimed, however, is that without national television news coverage of sit-ins, marches, beatings, and other race-related actions, efforts to capture the attention of Americans outside the South and to crystallize opinion as to political priorities would have taken far longer.[13] Television coverage magnified the velocity of political information, the range and personal intensity of the messages of the civil rights movement, and permitted groups of activists who normally lacked easy access to the public at large to penetrate deeply and rapidly into mass political consciousness.

The tendency of network television to cover more prominently a higher percentage of political stories than newspapers may well be linked to the fact that other kinds of stories are better covered by print media or local television. To capture viewer interest networks cannot merely repeat news available elsewhere and, of course, there is little time on the network for long descriptions of events. Political analysts have speculated that in order to distinguish itself network television news, more often than newspaper stories, focuses on a political theme that runs throughout the story, organizing information, narrative, sound, and picture to build impact and meaning.[14] A recent study of presidential election stories on network television, in weekly news magazines, and in daily newspapers confirms that television—and news magazines as well—contains four times the number of purely interpretive "theme" stories than do newspapers and far fewer simply descriptive stories.[15]

The claim made is not simply that network television

---

[13] See David J. Garrow, *Protest At Selma: Martin Luther King, Jr. and the Voting Rights Act of 1965* (New Haven: Yale University Press, 1979), pp. 161–78.

[14] Weaver, "Newspaper News and Television News."

[15] Thomas E. Patterson, *The Mass Media Election: How Americans Choose Their President* (New York: Praeger Publishers, 1980), p. 26.

news covers a higher percentage of political stories than newspapers do, but that its coverage of the *same* kind of issue is usually more politicized than theirs. The kind of information dispensed to fifty million network news viewers each night is not simply a large dose of the same kind of information received elsewhere, but tends to add through its special qualities a more personalizing, politicizing, and "nationalizing" element of news coverage than other media provide.

Figure 4 shows the proportion of economic stories with references to political leaders or political institutions both in newspapers and on television over a thirteen-year period.

Content analysis makes clear that the above hypotheses are grounded in fact, specifically that network television news tends to both nationalize and politicize specific types of news stories far more than newspapers even in nonelection periods. Despite the fact that the newspapers examined were large, metropolitan dailies—and more cosmopolitan in outlook than smaller rural and suburban dailies—the difference in perspective is exceptionally large. For example, a story on the front page of a newspaper about an increase in the rate of inflation is more likely to be treated on a local and nonpolitical basis—i.e., how much inflation went up in the local area and what items caused the increases in the consumer price index. Network television treatment of the same inflation story, in contrast, is much more likely to link the specific facts in the story to a response (or a demand for a response) from a national politician, one either demanding political action by the president, Congress, or national government, or decrying past actions by government that allegedly brought about the increases. Very high proportions of television's economic stories (over 80 percent on average) contain a specific national political reference to a political leader or governmental institution, whereas newspapers tend to retain a more factually descriptive perspective, politicizing their stories only about 30 percent of the time in their reporting.

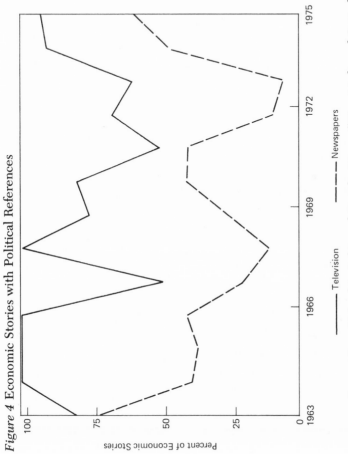

Figure 4 Economic Stories with Political References

——— Television   - - - - - Newspapers

Percent of Economic Stories

SOURCE: Abstract from Richard L. Rubin and Douglas Rivers, "Mass Media and Critical Elections: A First Report." Paper presented at the Northeastern Political Science Association Convention, 1978.

By adding political, national, and personal "color" to stories, by frequently seeking reactions to economic events from national politicians, and by directing attention to and implying an *expectation of action* from the national government in Washington, television news tends to shift political discussion disproportionately to national political institutions. National political personalities are, as a result, quickly and firmly linked to events and, not unexpectedly, viewer expectations for corrective actions by the national government are likely to be heightened. Network television news thus organizes information in a somewhat different manner, closer (though still different) to the style and emphasis of national news magazines than newspapers, stressing broad themes and linkages rather than detailed information, and personalizing and politicizing the news stories themselves.

The close analysis of economic stories covered by both network television and major newspapers discussed above also revealed that there are, at times, significant differences in the prominence of topics covered. Figure 5 depicts the proportion of economic stories to all stories covered in both newspapers and television from 1963 to 1975, and certain features immediately strike one's attention. During the prosperous period of the 1960s, newspapers gave front-page attention to economic stories (between 10 percent to 17 percent of all major stories), while television lead stories averaged about half that much. But during the 1970s, television's own news agenda markedly changed and by 1975 economic stories accounted for nearly one-third of the top TV news stories, exceeding the 20 percent level that was reached and maintained by newspapers during this same period.

The relative surge in economic stories was, of course, directly related to the energy crisis and its ramifications, and the lack of direct U.S. involvement in Vietnam. But while the print media maintained a relatively stable proportion of economic stories, increasing their emphasis moderately with the coming of the crisis, television vastly expanded the prominence and frequency of its coverage of

Figure 5 Economic Stories

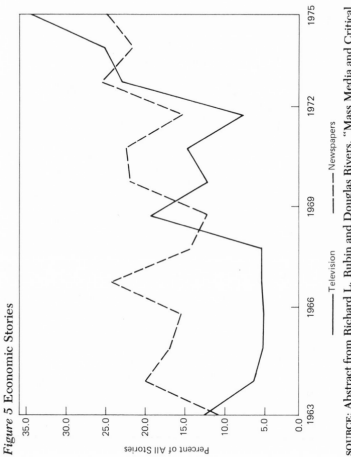

SOURCE: Abstract from Richard L. Rubin and Douglas Rivers, "Mass Media and Critical Elections: A First Report." Paper presented at the Northeastern Political Science Association Convention, 1978.

economic stories in 1973 and 1974, increasing fourfold its coverage of such stories over the levels of the 1960s. Considering that only the top three stories in each medium are counted (and thus the greater size of a newspaper's "news hole" is discounted), newspapers and television networks indicate that television news coverage is far more volatile than print, and may in the course of years shift more rapidly from subject to subject. In particular, the evidence indicates that television was responsible for magnifying the amount of total economic information available to the mass public in the 1970s. Not only did television emphasize economic affairs, but the nature of its coverage ensured that the public would view economic issues in increasingly active political terms.

Through a comparison with newspapers certain distinctive features of television news have been examined but some specific questions remain unaddressed. For example, how are network stories developed, selected, and presented? As a result of the method of news selection and story line requirements are there significant biases that permeate the television news process? What is the influence of the commercial and organizational structure of network television on the medium's news output? How do the professional values of journalists themselves shape the nature and style of news? In brief, what is organized into the network news channels and what is organized out?

Shaping the Network News

V. O. Key, Jr. has remarked that "attention to the economic aspects of the communications industries serves to emphasize the fact that they consist of commercial enterprises, not public service institutions."[16] The network's structure, its relationship with affiliate stations and advertisers, the budget and size of the news department, as well as the percentage of "air time" devoted to news, all reflect

---

[16] V. O. Key, Jr., *Public Opinion and American Democracy* (New York: Knopf, 1961), pp. 378–80.

the fact that the news is developed within an enterprise connected to profit making and, thus, the economic and organizational considerations that influence the process of news production. These considerations by a business organization determine substantially when the news is aired (and to what extent regularly scheduled broadcasting can be interrupted for special news events), the amount of money allocated to develop the news, and the range and depth of news coverage. In fact, were it not for federal statutes and Federal Communications Commission guidelines that mandate a percentage of air time for news and public affairs programming, it is probable that business logic has retarded the growth of network news divisions—at least until they became profitable.[17]

Federal statutes also influence the structure of network television within which news production takes place. Federal Communications Commission regulations permit each of the three major broadcasting companies to own only five local television stations, while additional independently owned local stations are induced to become affiliates of one of the three national networks by voluntarily relinquishing varying amounts of their local commercial time in exchange for network programming. The network structure of the three national broadcasting companies is, therefore, extended to a chain of over six hundred local television stations and blanket the nation.

Although the transmission of television is fundamentally decentralized by government regulation of station ownership, the organization of the network news production process is exceedingly centralized. The power to assign correspondents to stories within the United States and overseas is centrally located within the management division of a network news department. In addition, since network news is primarily national and international in its perspective, there is little input from local stations' news departments to the network news production center.

---

[17] Edward Jay Epstein, *News From Nowhere* (New York: Random House, 1973), p. 61.

Except for important breaking stories, the relatively small, centralized network news department (compared to newspapers), having network constraints on resources (time, staff, expertise, and money), must make a series of decisions about what news gets on the air and how the story is done.

Why network news is nationally oriented is not hard to grasp. The answer results directly from the relationship between networks, affiliates, advertisers, and the audience. If network news were only little more than local news from a few different cities, affiliates would be less likely to yield valuable time for news with a similarly local perspective much like their own. To encourage viewers to make the transition from the preceding local news to network news is, of course, in the interest of all: the audience wants something different and interesting to view, network advertisers want a broad *national* audience for their product, and local affiliates want to serve their "public interest" requirements under FCC regulations and still maintain the level of local viewer interest.

Economic and intraorganizational considerations are also a factor in determining what film stories appear on the news each night. Aside from major breaking stories that compel immediate coverage, a substantial number of stories on network news are prepared in advance. To utilize film units economically, network producers commission stories they intend to use in advance and send the cameras to what Daniel J. Boorstein has called "pseudo-events," i.e., news events scheduled well in advance and specifically organized for the media.[18] Other news that cannot be so induced, such as governmental hearings, can still be planned for well in advance. This greater hierarchical control over news stories on network television (and in weekly news magazines) compared to newspapers has been concretely documented by Stephen Hess's study of Washington news reporting by the different media.[19]

---

[18] Daniel J. Boorstin, *The Image: A Guide to Pseudo-Events in America* (New York: Harper Colophon, 1961), p. 11.

[19] Stephen Hess, *Washington Reporters and Their World* (Washington: Brookings Institution, 1981), pp. 7–8.

Much of the cost control involved in producing usable news film thus lies in "anticipating" events and keeping limited personnel constantly busy with stories of broad viewer interest. While recent technological developments, such as the minicamera, have given much greater range to local news reporting than before, network news is not similarly affected since the vast geographical area covered still makes planning a necessity. Outside of a few top stories that make news on their own, e.g., revelations of high-level corruption or international incidents like the taking of American hostages in Iran, a substantial part of regular news production involves important organizational decisions that are made every day about which stories are to be covered and which potential stories, by lack of coverage, shall never make the television screen at all.[20]

Certain principles operative during the search for suitable stories strengthen the tendency of television news to be more "planned," more nationally oriented, more thematic, and more political than newspaper coverage. First, at least part of the cosmopolitan emphasis attributable to network news programming stems from the fact that the network-owned local affiliates of CBS, NBC, and ABC are in large cities, such as Washington, New York, Los Angeles, and Chicago. Since these network-owned affiliates contribute a certain amount of film for use on the parent network economically, news film from these major cities is more likely to reach the screen than from smaller stations not owned by the networks. Both because of economies of transmission between the major cities and because camera personnel are geographically based in these cities as well, a substantial and more than proportionate amount of news originates from a few large and nationally oriented cities such as Washington and New York.

There are few regular "beats" for television correspondents besides the White House, for example, and reporters are usually moved from place to place and story to story. While television's reliance on "generalist" correspondents rather than "specialists" (whom newspapers rely on),

---

[20] Epstein, *News from Nowhere*, pp. 103–4.

makes for efficient use of news personnel, it also limits correspondents' ability to develop the depth of knowledge
possible when specializing in certain topics. As Edward J.
Epstein noted:

The alternative of permanent assignments, or beats, would not
satisfy the networks' basic problem of creating "national news";
since network news, unlike local news media, is expected to
cover the nation, if not the entire world, hundreds of camera
crews would be needed to cover even the most prominent
sources of potential news. Yet networks need only a limited number of stories—usually no more than a dozen or so—to fill programming requirements.[21]

In a curious way the use of generalists rather than specialists also tends to politicize more of the news. Rather
than digging deeply into a subject—the vertical approach
of a specialist toward knowledge—the generalist moves
horizontally, attempting to integrate different bits of
knowledge into some kind of cohesive (and usually
national) theme. For example, an incident of unrest in a
major city becomes part of a national theme of urban decay,
an indictment on corruption becomes an example of the
decline of national morality. Quite possibly the need to
reach and hold a disparate yet national audience accounts
for the strong tendencies of network news to link together
pieces of information and "causes" and "effects," and the
thematic demands of network reporting seems to translate
into greater politicization of news as a whole. To report
straight news factually and without integration with other
events is, in fact, no longer seen professionally as the function of the television correspondent, whose obligation now
is, as Walter Cronkite clearly put it, "to report events
*markedly significant beyond the moment, and to relate sto-
ries to each other.*"[22]

Both organizational necessities and the national orienta-

---

[21]*Ibid.*, p. 136.

[22]*Ibid.*, p. 243 (emphasis added). For an analysis of informal journalistic codes and practices on news outputs see Gaye Tuchman, "Objectivity as Strategic Ritual: An Examination of Newsmen's Notions of
Objectivity," *American Journal of Sociology*, January 1972, pp. 660–79.

tion of network news apparently enlarges the interpretive, thematic, and political contents of network news. In addition, the narrative style of television, in contrast to newspaper reporting, is intensely personal; a voice that describes the news and its meaning consequently offers television journalists far more room than newspaper reporters to impart some of their own personal sensibilities (however delicately and difficult to measure) to the news story itself.[23]

In addition to the important organizational or professional constraints that influence the shape of network news, several other factors may bias either the selection of news content or its treatment. While there is some reported evidence of attempts by commercial sponsors to influence the content of network news in the early years of television, this kind of direct interference is rarely attempted.[24] Effective commercial pressure has most often been applied to documentaries or to "specials" and not to the network news itself. Although the separation of the business from the editorial side of news production may not fully protect network news from sponsor pressure, the combination of professional independence and the growing corporate strength of the networks has kept the news (though not programming in general) relatively free of sponsor intimidation.[25] Unlike local television, for example, which is highly dependent on a few local advertisers, network news can draw on a large number of potential sponsors, and editorial inhibition is more likely to come from the anticipation of sponsor antagonism than from direct intervention.[26]

The influence of governmental regulation is, however, clearly more recognizable than sponsor influence in its effect on the ultimate style and shape of news content. Although elected or appointed government officials occa-

---

[23] Weaver, "Newspaper News and Television News," p. 86, 89–91.

[24] Herbert Gans, *Deciding What's News* (New York: Pantheon, 1979), pp. 251–68.

[25] *Ibid.*

[26] David L. Altheide, *Creating Reality*, pp. 125–38.

sionally attempt direct political intimidation—Vice-presidential Spiro Agnew's attacks on network "analyses" of President Nixon's administration, for example[27]—the most pervasive and persistent of political influences on the content and style of television reporting comes from the FCC's statutory power to regulate and license the use of airwave channels. Besides stipulating the amounts of weekly television time to be devoted to news and other public affairs broadcasting, the FCC standards and guidelinee, such as fairness in news coverage, equal time for political candidates, and the right of any person to respond to aired personal attack, have served to contain strident partisanship and strong opinionated reporting on television. Unlike the newspapers and national news weeklies, which have no equivalent requirements or standards of regulation, the editorial posture of television news reporting—the networks traditionally do not endorse political candidates or take controversial issues—reflects its deep concern for FCC doctrines in its news style and approach.[28]

Added to these legal pressures for nonpartisanship are other pressures from the marketplace. The very size of the networks' national audience tends to diminish any flagrant partisanship or consistent favoritism on simple economic grounds, since strong political preferences by newscasters might well lead some of the "offended" viewers to turn to another channel—similar if not identical in news programming—and reduce subsequent advertising revenues. As a result, the network news approach tends to be both *political and critical, but not partisan or ideological.*[29]

---

[27] David Halberstam, *The Powers That Be* (New York: Knopf, 1979), pp. 655–63. See also William E. Porter, *Assault on the Press* (Ann Arbor, Michigan: University of Michigan Press, 1976).

[28] For a discussion of the FCC see Barry Cole and Mal Oettinger, *Reluctant Regulators: The FCC and the Broadcast Audience* (Reading: Mass.: Addison, Wesley, 1978) and Erwin G. Krasnow and Lawrence D. Langley, *The Politics of Broadcast Regulation* (New York: St. Martin's Press, 1973).

[29] This does not mean, as Colin Seymour-Ure has noted, that random bias in the press as to what topics and themes journalists feature in a particular campaign cannot favor coincidentally one candidate over

Despite claims made in some early studies of network news that "liberal" networks displayed flagrant partisan bias against Richard Nixon in 1968, extensive research by C. Richard Hofstetter shows little, if any, consistent pattern of political bias in election reporting. While structural or organizational bias was found to be a shaping influence, i.e., on who, what, and how news was covered, little persistent political favoritism was uncovered and a good news story could always penetrate the media bureaucracy. Nothing close to the kind of favoritism frequently found among newspapers and magazines was uncovered by various analyses of the networks, and though the networks did vary somewhat in their treatment of the candidates, there was little, if any, discernible pattern of bias in network news. While favoritism or the expression of an individual journalist's political values do surface on occasion, no consistent trend was uncovered.[30]

If anything, the bias in news reporting remains the broad professional tendency to favor action and controversy because they attract attention and sustain interest. Since "news" is clearly what is new and not "old," there is, of course, a professional imperative to favor change in the activities of society rather than sameness. If there is any one journalistic value that clearly dominates others it is this professional need to generate stories of change, movement, and something happening—a need strongly reinforced by the demands of a visual medium such as television. As a result, the various demands made upon network television force a unique critical perspective. Unable, regularly, to project a strong position on candidates, parties, and policies, as do newspapers, but needing a strong provocative posture from which to dramatize events, network television has tended to emphasize the political in the news and couple it with a strong critical tone toward those who practice politics. Politicized and critical reporting is not, of

another. *The Political Impact of Mass Media* (Beverly Hills, Calif.: Sage, 1974), pp. 202–239.

[30] Richard Hofstetter, *Bias in the News* (Columbus, Ohio: Ohio State University Press, 1976).

course, a new journalistic tradition in America, but the intensity, range, and national focus of television have raised serious questions about the cumulative but as yet unmeasured effect of such reporting on our political institutions and leaders.[31]

While much of the foregoing has stressed what is unique about network television news, it is crucial to understand that print and electronic journalists do not operate independently of each other, but are, rather, both part of a *newly enlarged political information process.* Not only do journalists of the print and electronic media share professional values and interests, but also they often rely on common sources to provide the framework for many news stories. While the treatment of a story may vary somewhat according to the imperatives of each medium, we can also find them sharing much common ground in their judgments of newsworthiness, as well.[32] In addition, the different sectors of the collective "press" are strongly interactive, cuing each other with ideas and "running with" stories that other media have broken. Certain columnists in opinion-leadership papers, for example, often set the story line for other reporters in both print and electronic media with their "interpretation" of what is really going on.[33] With their much larger staffs and greater depth and breadth in reporting, the newspapers and wire services continue to generate the largest amount of source material. What television contributes to the overall information process, however, is an intensified national and political thrust to news, and, as Hess recently substantiated, greater interest in the presidency as a source of news stories than is found among newspapers.[34]

---

[31] Michael J. Robinson, "Public Affairs Television and the Growth of Political Malise: The Case of the Selling of the Pentagon," *American Political Science Review* 70 (1976): 409–32. For some contrary data about the relationship of television and negative attitudes compared to newspapers see Doris A. Graber, *Mass Media & American Politics* (Washington, D.C.: Congressional Quarterly Press, 1980), pp. 174–75.

[32] See Robert G. Meadow, "Cross-Media Comparison of Coverage of the 1972 Campaign," *Journalism Quarterly* 50 (1973): 482–88.

[33] Timothy Crouse, *The Boys on the Bus* (New York: Ballantine, 1973).

[34] Stephen Hess, *op. cit.*, p. 98.

A brief examination of what was considered Jimmy Carter's most dangerous mistake in his 1976 campaign offers some insight into the interaction between elements of the press in terms of news organization and magnification. In answering a reporter's question about the location of subsidized low-income housing, Carter questioned the wisdom of injecting a different racial group into an existing suburban community and stated, "I see nothing wrong with ethnic purity being maintained." Carter's "ethnic purity" remark was originally made in an interview with a *New York Daily News* reporter, Sam Roberts, and appeared in the sixteenth paragraph of his nineteen paragraph story on a back page of the Sunday edition. The quotation was seen by a CBS news editor who suggested to the network's correspondent traveling with Carter that he question Carter further on the meaning of his statement. Eventually, a clarification and apology forced from Carter after six days of probing and questioning made many millions of voters aware of a remark that had been hardly noted (if at all) by readers of local newspapers.[35]

Though there are clear and important distinctions to be made between the different communications media, the impact of network television has clearly been to dramatically expand the political information process and to enlarge the role of the press, as a result, in the political system as a whole. The tremendous coverage of the "collective" press offers, on the one hand, a greater degree of surveillance over political elites than was possible in the past. Such surveillance may well inhibit certain questionable actions because of the greater costs of discovery.[36] On the other hand, the presence of such a powerful communications medium as television, in addition to other channels of political communications, has markedly increased the potential "reach" of political leaders in gaining public attention, thus yielding new opportunities for diverse elec-

[35] Details of this incident can be found in Jules Witcover, *Marathon: Pursuit of the Presidency 1972–1976* (New York: Viking, 1977), pp. 302–09.

[36] See Leon V. Sigal, *Reporters and Officials: The Organization and Politics of Newsmaking* (Lexington, Mass.: D. C. Heath, 1973), p. 184.

toral elites to present both particular issues and their own
personalities more directly than in the past. How the new
interplay between political leaders and the press has
actually affected individual attitudes and beliefs becomes a
central question, then, in understanding how the actual
production of news translates into "media effects." In brief,
what do we know about the impact of the press, what does
it mean, and how does it affect American politics?

The Effects of Mass Media

In assessing the impact of media on individual political
behavior, a striking and disturbing disparity becomes
almost immediately apparent. On the one hand, practicing
politicians and rank-and-file voters alike believe that both
print and television journalism are important and very
influential in affecting politics. On the other, the broad
weight of social science research has, until recently, found
little *measurable* evidence to substantiate such major
claims. For example, tests of mass media effects on individual political attitudes and subsequent voting behavior have
generally shown only small, marginal impact, results that
do not apparently square with either elite or mass perceptions of the press's role in "making" and "breaking" practicing politicians.

Until the mid-1960s, most social scientists—particularly
political scientists—generally accepted preliminary claims
that television and its predecessor, radio, were primarily
transmitters rather than shapers of political influence and
had not, as V. O. Key noted then, "become institutions of
political influence in their own right."[37] The direct impact
of mass media information on the individual, i.e., its
"micro-effects," were considered to be very limited, and,
where found, were thought to be almost entirely "reinforcing" of existing attitudes rather than capable of actually
changing them. In addition, most students of politics ini-

[37] V. O. Key, Jr., *Public Opinion and American Democracy* (New
York: Knopf, 1961), p. 374.

tially accepted the "two-step flow model" of information, which claimed that people did not get much political information directly from the mass media, but, rather, received it indirectly after processing or filtering by the leadership strata in society. Not only was an individual's exposure to, retention and perception of political information regarded as screened by secondary groups to which he belonged, such as unions, trade associations, and social organizations, but also certain more than ordinarily active individuals or "opinion leaders" were thought to be necessary "translators" of information to the ordinary voter.[38] With a few exceptions, the direct impact of the mass media was considered by researchers to be minimal, and direct media influence as an important political factor received little sustained interest until the close of the 1960s.[39]

The events of the turbulent 1960s—the civil rights revolution, the war in Vietnam, the urban violence—and the substantial destabilization of existing social and political institutions, values, and modes of activism of that period brought renewed interest to the mass media, particularly to television journalism. What was seen on network news

---

[38] Paul F. Lazarsfeld, Bernard Berelson, and Hazel Gaudet, *The People's Choice: How the Voter Makes up His Mind in a Presidential Campaign*, 3rd ed. (New York: Columbia University Press, 1968), pp. 120–36; Bernard Berelson, Paul F. Lazarsfeld, and William N. McPhee, *Voting: A Study of Opinion Formation in a Presidential Campaign* (Chicago: University of Chicago Press, 1953), pp. 49–51, 151–52.

[39] A vast literature examines the effects of mass communications on political behavior. For particularly good surveys of research findings see Sidney Kraus and Dennis Davis, *The Effects of Mass Communications on Political Behavior* (University Park, Pa.: Pennsylvania State University Press, 1976); *Political Communication: Issues and Strategy for Research*, ed. Steven H. Chaffee (Beverly Hills, California: Sage Publications, 1975); and William Adams and Faye Schiebman, *Television Network News: Issues in Content Research* (Washington, D.C.: George Washington University Press, 1978). Four more general surveys of mass communications studies are Joseph T. Klapper, *The Effects of Mass Communication* (Glencoe, Ill.: Free Press, 1960); George Comstock, et. al., *Television and Human Behavior* (New York: Columbia University Press, 1978); Doris A. Graber, *Mass Media and American Politics;* and W. Phillips Davison, James Boylan, and Frederick T. C. Yu, *Mass Media: Systems and Effects* (New York: Praeger, 1976).

and how the subject was treated became a subject of intense research, for the rapidity of shifts in public opinion on traditionally slow-changing issues such as race relations, foreign policy, and confidence in government made continued acceptance of such a static role for the mass media as a mere "reinforcer" of established values an idea difficult to hold. New explanations of change were sought by political observers to make some sense out of the growing volatility of social and political life. As a result, the mass media, particularly the role of television journalism, came under renewed and more detailed scrutiny by political scientists as a possible "cause" for some of the apparent social instability and individual political alienation in evidence.[40]

Some scholars, like Kurt and Gladys Lang, had long argued that television could markedly change the political climate and, in consequence, an individual's subsequent political beliefs.[41] But it was only as a new volatility struck American society that television and the press as a whole were again sought out by political scientists as "independent" explanatory influences. Part of the difficulty in determining the significance of media effects is that any real change in underlying political *attitudes* created by the mass media would be likely to be relatively small. One would hardly expect individual political attitudes built by family ties, social and economic associations, and through an individual's own life experience to be changed easily by journalism of any kind. Substantial evidence already exists to show that broad political attitudes, unlike individual preferences for consumer products, are not, in fact, easily changed.[42] Further, the measurement of the political

[40] See Robinson, "Television and American Politics," and Edward C. Dreyer, "Media Use and Electoral Choices: Some Political Consequences of Information Exposure," *Public Opinion Quarterly* 35 (1971): 544–53.

[41] Kurt Lang and Gladys Engels Lang, *Television and Politics* (Chicago: Quadrangle Books, 1968).

[42] The literature making this point is substantial. See, for example, Lazarsfeld, et. al., *The People's Choice;* Berelson, et. al., *Voting;* Angus Campbell, "Has Television Reshaped Politics?" *Columbia Journalism Review*, Fall 1962; Jay Blumler and David McQuail, *Television in Politics* (Chicago: University of Chicago Press, 1969).

effects of the mass media is hindered by the fact that our tools and methods are, as yet, imprecise; and, in addition, even where strong correlations between media variations and behavioral variations are found they do not clearly define which causes which.[43]

The difficulty in defining the media's direct effects on political attitudes and subsequent voting is accentuated by the limited time frame of most research, which does not measure the cumulative effects of media exposure over a long period but considers only relatively short-term effects. Even where sample panels are used, i.e., following the same sample group of people and repeatedly examining them as their opinions form and shift over time, cost and other limitations of data collection have severely curtailed the time frame over which the research has been conducted. As a result, even though an increasing body of evidence tends to support claims of increased mass media effects on individual political behavior, unambiguous evidence of such direct effects has not been developed.

Recent research has found that strongly critical news presentations and editorials in different newspapers can affect the political perceptions of readers depending on whether they have read critical or noncritical papers.[44] In another instance, network reporters' critical "instant analyses" following some of President Nixon's speeches were found to dull some viewers' favorable impressions by comparison with the impressions of viewers who saw and heard Nixon's speeches but did not see the "instant analyses" that followed.[45] Even in these cases demonstrating significant direct effects, however, one does not know whether the effects are lasting or just fade away in the following weeks or months—or just how the information itself is digested

---

[43] See Arthur H. Miller, Edie N. Goldenberg, and Lutz Erbring, "Type-Set Politics: Impact of Newspapers on Public Confidence," *American Political Science Review*, March 1979, p. 68.

[44] *Ibid.* Also see John P. Robinson, "The Press as King Maker," *Journalism Quarterly*, 1974, 51, pp. 587–94.

[45] See David L. Paletz and Richard J. Vinegar, "Presidents on Television: Effects of Instant Analysis," *Public Opinion Quarterly*, Winter 1977–78, pp. 488–97.

and ultimately converted into some overt political response.

On the other hand, a significant study of the political effects of television journalism by Patterson and McClure has, in fact, contradicted many of the positive findings by other media scholars. Their examination of the last eight weeks of the 1972 general election campaign concluded that steady viewers of nightly network television newscasts learn almost nothing of importance about the election, either about the candidates' positions on issues or their personal characteristics, change very few if any votes, and that "the only noticeable effect of network campaign news is an increased tendency among voters to view politics in the same trivial terms that the newscasts depicted."[46]

These findings of the "noneffects" of television journalism, however, also suffer in generalization from being timebound, and are subject to criticism on the basis that the single election studied and the limited time frame of the panel during the general election campaign limit the scope of any claims. As a matter of fact, in a later study that incorporated the 1976 presidential *primary* period, Patterson found that television coverage was a very important factor—particularly in the early primary period—in developing and in spreading a positive image of a little-known candidate, Jimmy Carter, to the disadvantage of other candidates.[47] These findings taken together tend to identify the limitations of any evidence covering only short specific periods; for at what point in the election process (i.e., in the formative early stages or in the later stages) one examines media and voter relationships is of critical importance and can produce markedly different results.

The specific situational factors in a given election, i.e., unique events and special characteristics of one campaign versus another, also play a role in whether or not journal-

---

[46]Thomas E. Patterson and Robert D. McClure, *The Unseeing Eye* (New York: Putnam, 1976), p. 22.

[47]Thomas E. Patterson, *The Mass Media Election: How Americans Choose Their President* (New York: Praeger, 1980), pp. 119–30, 133–52.

istic treatment is found to be influential. Whether the candidates nominated are the preferred choices of the rank
and file of the parties that nominated them, how long and
strong the feelings of support may be for a particular candidate by the public, and how intense and important the
key issues of a particular campaign may or may not be are
only some of the factors that can enlarge or diminish the
influence of the press in a campaign.

Patterson and McClure also examined political advertising in the 1972 campaign and found it to have only a small
effect on behavior, although, counter to conventional wisdom, the authors indicated that advertising did increase
voters' issue awareness, and, in special cases, seems to
have had a small but definite effect on their votes.
Although the manipulative effects of presidential advertising were estimated to be effective on only between 1 and
2 percent of the 1972 electorate, even such a small margin
could have been sufficient to change the winner of the
presidential election in three of the last six elections.[48]

The small amount of demonstrated manipulation may
obscure larger potential but unmeasured effects. First, as
noted, both the late stage of the campaign in 1972 when
these measurements were made and the polarized circumstances of the 1972 campaign itself probably minimized
potential advertising effects. Second, both sides in this
campaign were able to commit substantial funds for advertising, and we do not know how much unmeasured advertising impact was canceled out by the counterinfluence of
opposing political commercials. Nor do we know what the
effect might be when one side is able to spend considerably
more than the other, or when one side's political advertising is qualitatively better than the other's.

Some recent research has focused not on the attitudinal
or voting effects of mass media but upon changes of perceptions and awareness by exposed individuals at the beginning stage in the development of political ideas. Such
research has foregone tests of the directive or "convincing"

---

[48] Patterson and McClure, *The Unseeing Eye*, pp. 111–20.

ability of journalism on a specific issue or vote. It has examined, instead, the press's role in raising the *salience* of an issue in the public consciousness, an increase which it is assumed would eventually prompt a new evaluation of political information by individual members of the public. The press, Theodore White cogently noted, "sets the agenda of public discussion. . . . It determines what people will talk and think about . . ." and thus identifies as important certain ideas, issues, and personalities. In effect, it puts claims on our attention to confront certain kinds of news while ignoring other information.[49]

A large and promising body of research has begun to form around this "agenda-setting" concept, which argues that, to a certain extent, the press's agenda of political importance influences the structure of an individual's political agenda.[50] By affecting the public prominence of political topics, the mass media sharply influence what candidates talk about, what issues are more or less ventilated in public discussion, and which political leaders gain or lose by the public's new awareness. This kind of effect, while it may not necessarily cause immediate changes in our political *attitudes*, produces individual change in *perceptions* of what is politically at stake, and what events and which candidates seem to be important.[51] For example, if a voter perceives that inflation rather than unemployment is the more crucial problem—a perception in part related to increases in press coverage of specific economic devel-

---

[49] Theodore White, *The Making of the President, 1972* (New York: Bantam, 1973), p. 327.

[50] Two useful overviews of the agenda-setting research are *The Emergence of American Political Issues: The Agenda-Setting Function of the Press*, eds. Donald L. Shaw and Maxwell E. McCombs (St. Paul, Minn.: West, 1977) and R. W. Cobb and C. D. Elder, *Participation in American Politics: The Dynamics of Agenda-Building* (Boston: Allyn and Bacon, 1972). For a recent analysis see Shanto Iyengar, "Television News & Issue Salience: A Reexamination of the Agenda-Setting Hypothesis," *American Politics Quarterly*, October 1979, pp. 395–416.

[51] See Maxwell E. McCombs and Donald L. Shaw, "The Agenda-Setting Function of the Press," in *The Emergence of American Political Issues: The Agenda Setting Function of the Press*, ed. Donald L. Shaw and Maxwell E. McCombs, pp. 6–16.

opments—then he may, without changing his political attitudes toward both topics be more likely to vote for the
candidate better able to handle inflation.

Although the press's agenda and the public's agenda may
not coincide at any moment of time, there is, to the extent
that politicians respond to journalism's important stories, a
pressure toward the eventual coordination of the press's
and the public's agenda. The dynamics of agenda-setting
are not completely clear as yet, but the extraordinary range
of the print and electronic media combined clearly tends to
tie the press, political leaders, and the public into a more
intimately linked environment than at any time in the past.

Closer ties among a press agenda, an individual political
agenda, and a leadership agenda seem in large part a feature of both increases in the speed and the centralization of
mass communications initiated first by network radio and
then heightened enormously by network television. While
studies of the actual information people gain from reading
newspapers versus watching television show newspapers to
be a deeper and more detailed influence on knowledge of
specific issues, television not only reaches over fifty million
viewers each night, but also reaches millions of people who
do not read newspapers at all and for whom network television news is the only source of mass communications.[52]
Thus newspaper readers and nonreaders receive a heavy
additional dose of news, disproportionately national and
political, from television *over and above* all other mass
communications.

Although it is of value to define the similarities and differences between mass media, these should not obscure
the most important question, namely, the total impact of
the press—print and electronic media—on American politics. Even though the different media contribute uniquely,
in a qualitative sense, they do not act in isolation. Rather,
they interact with one another, sharing much common
ground in their news topics, and, as in the building of the
"ethnic purity" story, they feed and reinforce one another.

[52] See Gary Wamsley and Richard Pride, "Television Network News:
Rethinking the Iceberg Problem," *Western Political Quarterly* 25 (1972):
434, 450.

Newspapers clearly provide more "specifics" and more depth on political issues than television, but television spreads a common core of news (often but not exclusively originated by print journalists) more rapidly than newspapers are able through the system, collectively providing a vast and swift mechanism for politicians directly and personally to reach their potential market.

Clearly, the public's perceived political environment is now subject to much more rapid change than in the past. Of equal importance, the potential strategic environment for political candidates has been substantially changed as well. Political attitudes may still not be particularly susceptible to effective media manipulation by candidates, though only future research can unravel the extent of its susceptibility. Yet the tremendous direct exposure that the electronic media provide aspiring candidates offers an important mechanism by which popular *beliefs about the candidates' stance* vis-à-vis established issues and attitudes can be subtly but effectively altered. Television has the capacity to make an impact during an election campaign not by being used to induce change in underlying political attitudes but, rather, by convincing a small but significant percentage of the audience that it has "misperceived" certain aspects of the candidate's stance about a particular issue.

An individual's underlying issue preference, e.g., his or her attitude on relations with the Russians, seem only slightly manipulable by the mass media during an election campaign. A campaign seems to offer, however, far more room to change the voter's perception of how a particular candidate might act as president in relation to those issues. While a candidate's stance, as presented on the news or in political advertising, is not at all likely to prove effective if it grossly misrepresents his earlier positions—a tiger can hardly be turned into a lamb—the "shading" of the public's perception of his stance can be accomplished, i.e., toughening up the candidate's soft spots or softening up his perceived rigidities. Much of the campaigning in the 1980 election focused on just this type of shading—Carter toughening his posture on Russia and defense issues and Reagan softening his perceived posture on economic issues of unemployment and social welfare.

Moreover, the great range and direct impact of electronic media enhance a candidate's ability to influence the public's actual "weighting" of issues. That is, the electronic media may make a candidate better able to displace the prominence of one issue (on which he feels he loses votes) by providing him with a forum to convince the electorate of the greater importance of another political issue (on which he feels he gains votes). What the electronic media now uniquely offer candidates is a much enhanced ability to directly affect the public's perception of the "right" agenda (i.e., which issues *should* dominate the public's attention) by giving them an opportunity to direct the electorate toward what it should "think about."

Generally, picking leaders rather than deciding a large number of complex issues seems to be what the electorate is most comfortable with. It is constrained by only a very few "must" issues in a campaign, and places a premium on the leadership abilities of presidential candidates as a basis of choice. As a result, the range of specific information required by voters need not be high to be "sufficient" across a spectrum of "nonessential" or discretionary issues.[53] With much discretion offered or delegated to a president over many complex and less than crucial issues, it should not be surprising that the voter and the press are both more interested in the personal qualities of aspiring leaders than in their detailed discussion of a variety of less gripping issues during a campaign. If all but a few key issues are, in fact, subsumed within the voter's choice of a particular candidate—what Doris Graber has termed a "rational politico-choice model"—then it is logical for presidential politicians to devote enormous efforts to developing an image—real or manufactured—of their personal leadership qualities.[54]

Even though some promising avenues of research exist

---

[53] See Doris A. Graber, "Press Coverage and Voter Reaction in the 1968 Presidential Election," *Political Science Quarterly* 89 (1974): 85–91.

[54] *Ibid.*, pp. 94–98.

in sorting out the relationship of perceived candidate qualities, issues, and events, the complexity of the process of individual political decision-making, composed of diverse sources of political information and varying individual predispositions, makes it difficult to separate causes from effects. However, the present lack of conclusive evidence about direct media effects does not mean that discussion of television's impact on American politics as a whole must be confined to what may only be the present limitations of social science research. Individual responses to media messages, i.e., their micro-effects, may be presently small and hard to sort out with the tools we have. But the *indirect* influence of television on our key electoral institutions, i.e., its macro-effects, are already large, measurable, and crucial in reshaping, rechanneling, and reorganizing American political power.

Despite the limited scope of behavioral findings about the political impact of the mass media, practicing politicians of all kinds *believe* that the impact of the press is substantial, not small, and they *act* on that basis. By acting on the grounds of what they perceive to be the new realities created by television, they are changing the framework of political competition and forcing significant changes in the key operating institutions of American politics—specifically the political party and the presidency. Mass media effects are clearest and strongest when we consider how media changes—particularly the addition of television to print journalism—affect political leaders and the electoral institutions within which they work, and how the changes in these institutions, in turn, reshape the nature and range of individual political choices.

As E. E. Schattschneider has observed, "the definition of alternatives is the supreme instrument of power."[55] And it is here, by rechanneling the flow of political information, and changing both candidate strategies and voter alternatives, that the mass media will be seen to have had their clearest influence on American politics.

---

[55] E. E. Schattschneider, *The Semi-Sovereign People* (New York: Holt, Rinehart, and Winston, 1960), p. 66.

8

Party, Media,
and Presidential Primaries

No public institutions have been more affected by the immensely heightened impact of the mass media than the presidency and the political parties—the presidency because of its ability as an institution to respond to major changes in the processes of mass communications, and the parties because they have not been correspondingly able to adapt. Examining the party first, it is clear that many, though not all, of the functions of the political party have been lost to the new mass media, specifically the party's primacy in electoral mobilization and, to an increasing extent, in identifying, "recruiting," and "testing" potential candidates.[1] Particularly because American parties have functioned throughout their history primarily as electoral rather than policy organizations, the influence of the press as organizer of information, mobilizer of voters, and recruiter of potential candidates directly challenges much of the traditional strength and functional underpinnings of the parties.

---

[1] David Broder, *The Party's Over* (New York: Harper & Row, 1972) discusses the various party functions. In his subsequent newspaper columns he has clearly identified the increasing role of the press in many of those same functions, particularly in the nomination recruitment process.

Of course, evidence is available to indicate that the decline of the party commenced long before the development of television increased the impact of the press as a whole. Many additional factors—the decline of available patronage, the fragmentation of the party slate in local and national politics, the weakening of party loyalty, the increase in levels of education, among others—help to account for what Walter Dean Burnham has termed partisan decomposition over the last eighty years.[2] But even if the decline of the party has several long-term causes, a major change in mass communications such as television must be viewed as a critical factor in the vastly *accelerated* rate of the party's decline.

Can we, then, define the impact of current mass media changes on, first, the parties and, subsequently, on the presidency, the very institutions that have structured our political choices by defining for large numbers of individuals the range and nature of their political alternatives? If the parties and their leadership lose political power, do others gain it? Does the loss of influence by party elites mean that the rank and file have captured it, or do media elites or other political activists gain a new and decisive role in determining political choices? How does the new power relationship between the press and the party affect presidential candidates, and how does the new strategic environment in which aspiring presidents must compete influence their effectiveness once in office? What, then, are some of the critical changes in the institutional relationships of press and party, and how have the changing dynamics of political communications altered the structure, organization, and opportunities for political conflict.

The Press and Nomination Politics

The weakening of the American political party is a theme that runs consistently through the work of academics and

[2] Walter Dean Burnham, *Critical Elections and the Mainsprings of American Politics* (New York: W. W. Norton, 1970), chapters 4 and 5, pp. 71–90.

journalists alike. The deterioration of the party as an important American institution may not be irreversible, but the evidence is overwhelming that the party has declined substantially in strength as a mediating institution standing between the people and the government. The party has not only been weakened organizationally by its loss of important patronage resources since the advent of the welfare state, but many of its traditional activities, long regarded as its principal functions, are now performed by competing political organizations of independent candidacies.[3] The term machine, which once adequately described local, state, and, at times, even national political organizations, seems clearly inappropriate to the parties at present.

The party as a symbol and organizing cue for individual voting has also weakened measurably. Research clearly documents a significant decline in the number of potential voters identifying with either the Democratic or Republican party—from 76 percent in the mid-1950s to 62 percent by the mid-1970s—and a concomitant increase in self-proclaimed independents from 24 percent to 38 percent over the same time period. Even more importantly, the last two decades in particular have been marked by large-scale and frequent voting defections from one's self-declared party preference.[4] As a result, the strength of party as a shorthand source of information and as a symbol giving political direction for the individual has significantly diminished.

Certainly one of the most important media-related changes that has affected the political party as an organization has been the development of the presidential primary system. Primaries have, over time, both democratized the internal processes of choosing a party's presidential candidate and simultaneously weakened the traditional structure

[3] Anthony King, "The American Polity in the Late 1970s: Building Coalitions in the Sand," in *The New American Political System,* ed. Anthony King (Washington, D.C.: American Enterprise Institute, 1979), pp. 371–95. See also Burnham *Critical Elections;* David Broder *The Party's Over;* Gerald Pomper, *Voters' Choice: Varieties of American Behavior* (New York: Dodd, Mead, 1975).

[4] Norman M. Nie, Sidney Verba, and John R. Petrocik, *The Changing American Voter* (Cambridge, Mass.: Harvard University Press, 1976), pp. 43–73.

of the party. By breaking the party leadership's control over the presidential nomination, and by opening the internal deliberations of the party to broad public participation, primaries have also opened a way for the press to gain a major role in the nomination process that it previously lacked. Primaries expand the nomination arena from one dominated by established party leaders to a more fluid and volatile combination of contesting political activists and ordinary party voters. Thus they enable the press to serve as a crucial link between candidates seeking nomination and a party's rank and file. When all candidates run under the same party banner, the value of the party as a cue of voter information is virtually worthless. The press has moved into this vacuum to organize information, appraise candidates' qualities, and evaluate trends and outcomes, and the importance of its role in filling these functions— once the functions of the party—has grown with the increase in the importance of the primaries in the nomination process.

The initial explosion in the number of presidential primaries during the Progressive era had a number of triggering causes. Not least was the direct role that the press played in demanding that closed proceedings be opened to public scrutiny, and that open and direct lines of political communication—the primaries—be established between the people and their governmental leader.[5] However, though the press then began to enjoy a role that permitted it some influence in the preliminary stage of the selection of American presidents, the power of party organizational leaders was still strong enough to leave the actual selection of delegates to the national conventions predominantly in the hands of established local, state, and national party leaders. Despite the increase in the numbers of presidential primaries in the period from 1912 to 1920, party elite structure still retained much strength, as Taft's defeat of primary victor Theodore Roosevelt made clear. As public

---

[5] See Louise Overacker, *The Presidential Primary* (New York: Macmillan, 1926).

and press enthusiasm for the primaries waned, they became a party mechanism of presidential influence that was more important in form than in consequence.

However, the political environment has changed substantially since the first wave of primaries. The advent of television, the reemergence of primaries, and new intraparty dynamics have brought new shape and content to nomination politics. The combination of print and electronic journalism has contributed significantly toward the institutionalization of the presidential primaries by which the control of the presidential nomination has become less of a party function and more of a public process.

The expansion of the decision-making arena of nominations in American parties is a clear indication of an inherent American ambivalence toward political parties. On the one hand is an acknowledged need to have partisan organizations serve functionally in organizing both elections and government. On the other is the widespread popular belief, as Austin Ranney notes, that "political parties are, at best, unavoidable evils whose propensities for divisiveness, oligarchy, and corruption must be closely watched and sternly controlled."[6] And in no other democracy has the combination of the need for party mechanisms and antiorganizational spirit been more fully and uniquely utilized than in the development of presidential primary elections in the United States.[7]

The antiorganizational sensibility that periodically surfaces in American politics—most noticeably in the Progressive era and again in the "New Politics" reforms of the late 1960s and early 1970s—can be linked to two phenomena of importance. First, in both these periods the amount and

[6] Austin Ranney, *Curing the Mischiefs of Faction: Party Reform in America* (Berkeley, California: University of California Press, 1975), p. 22.

[7] While some other nations show some small-scale parallels to the direct primaries in the selection of legislators (West Germany and Belgium), at the executive level the presidential primary system is unique. For an analysis of cross-national similarities and differences in the primary process, see Leon D. Epstein, *Political Parties in Western Democracies* (New York: Praeger, 1967), pp. 201–32.

quality of political communications as a whole substantially changed, and the press as an important filter and shaper of political information consequently played a more central role in the political process. Whether it was the "journalistic mind" of progressivism together with the rapid growth of nationally oriented magazines, or the broadening and politicizing scope of network television in the recent reform period, the amount of political communications not only increased markedly, but these communications also received a heightened *national* political emphasis. Thus major increases in public access to information about political ideas and competing candidates in these periods coincided with both party reform and the disruption of traditional party loyalties.[8]

Second, in both these periods of high primary election activity, the policy differences between the two parties were not clear or durable and the strength of the existing majority coalition—the Republicans in 1912 and the Democrats in 1968 and again in 1972—was already in decline.[9] The articulation of political programs by the two parties was not distinct, as it was during the New Deal realignment, and, in the absence of such political definition by parties, the press found an opportunity to define the structure and content of political information. In a certain sense, the press, the parties, and the president are competitors in channeling public opinion; the weakness of one institution in this three-way competition has clearly had an impact on the relative strength of the others and on the political system as a whole.

In examining the relationship of the press to the presidential primaries, it is important to understand that, though states using primaries reached an initial high level

---

[8] See Phillip E. Converse, "Information Flow and the Stability of Partisan Attitudes," *Elections and the Political Order,* eds. Angus Campbell, Phillip E. Converse, Warren E. Miller, and Donald E. Stokes (New York: John Wiley, 1966), p. 141.

[9] For a theoretical analysis of majority party dynamics see Samuel Lubell, *The Future of American Politics,* 2nd ed. (Garden City, New York: Doubleday, 1955), p. 217.

as early as 1916, the number of primaries alone does not adequately distinguish the first phase of primary reform in the Progressive era from the second explosive phase that began in the late 1960s and still continues. Other critical differences—such as the proportion of convention delegates chosen by primary methods, how delegate slates are formed, at what level the unit rule (or "winner take all" rule) may be used, and how close and binding are the ties between delegate slates and the candidates themselves—have all played a major role in making the changes resulting from the contemporary phase of primary elections of greater significance to the party and the party system than the changes of the Progressive period.[10] Over time, the nature, meaning, and impact of the presidential primaries have changed, and the press itself has played a unique role in the depth and rapidity of the transformation.

Recent changes are, of course, the result of a complex series of events, among them changing power relationships of key groups such as the strengthening of blacks and the weakening of labor unions within a diminishing Democratic coalition, major policy challenges over the Vietnam War, rising racial conflict, and the extraordinary increase in the ability of candidates to mobilize followers *without* the help of established party leadership. The principal political tensions of the 1960s and 1970s were also not a major subject of division *between* the two major parties, and conflict on key issues was played out most visibly within the majority Democratic party. First, the rising tide of conflict on racial issues brought commitments in 1964 to change party rules that had permitted all-white, segregated southern delegates to be seated at the Democratic conven-

---

[10] See Dennis G. Sullivan, Jeffrey L. Pressman, Benjamin I. Page, and John J. Lyons, *The Politics of Representation* (New York: St. Martin's, 1974); James I. Lengle and Byron Shafer, "Primary Rules, Political Power, and Social Change," *American Political Science Review*, March 1976, pp. 25–40; Gerald M. Pomper, "New Rules and New Games in Presidential Nominations," *Journal of Politics*, August 1979, pp. 784–805; James W. Davis, *Presidential Primaries: The Road to the White House* (New York: Thomas Y. Crowell, 1967).

tion. Then the anti–Vietnam War challenge of an incumbent Democratic president, Lyndon Johnson, by Senator Eugene McCarthy in 1968 set the stage for a major reform of convention rules.[11]

According to one of its members, Austin Ranney, the McGovern-Fraser commission (formed in the aftermath of the turbulent 1968 Democratic convention to reexamine party rules) did not originally intend to foster primaries at the expense of state convention methods. But in the political environment of the time it seemed both practical and acceptable for increased numbers of states to adopt a primary election.[12] To achieve compliance with the Democratic party's new and complex rules, state party officials not only found it simple to hold a presidential primary, but also found that they as leaders would be less vulnerable to charges of "bossism," private dealings, and restrictive practices if they did so. In the face of criticism that "closed" practices at the 1968 convention had somehow exacerbated existing cleavages in the party, "primary fever" came to dominate the party deliberations prior to the 1972 convention. The change in the political environment was clear: whereas Hubert Humphrey could be nominated by established party leaders in 1968 without having run in a single primary election, both the new rules and the prevailing psychology of 1972 clearly encouraged increased public participation through presidential primaries.

The major difference between the contemporary phase of primary reform and that of the earlier period clearly lies in the ability of present-day primaries to ultimately produce a nomination victory for an insurgent candidate. The failure of an enormously popular Theodore Roosevelt to gain the nomination in 1912, despite his dominance over Taft in the presidential primaries, stands in marked con-

---

[11] Theodore H. White, *The Making of the President, 1968* (New York: Bantam, 1969); Richard L. Rubin, *Party Dynamics: The Democratic Coalition and the Politics of Change* (New York: Oxford University Press, 1976), pp. 107–43.

[12] Austin Ranney, "Turnout and Representation in Presidential Primaries," *American Political Science Review* 66 (1972): 21–37.

trast to the role of the primaries as a route to recent nomination success. Both "outsiders," McGovern in 1972 and Carter in 1976 were successful primary challengers among Democrats, while Ronald Reagan's primary challenge in the Republican party in 1976 almost took the nomination from a sitting president.[13]

What has occurred has been a series of rules changes seeking to provide a greater opportunity for political expression by different groups within the parties. These changes have resulted, in addition, in a major transformation of the role of presidential primaries in the nomination process. The presidential primary system no longer simply consists of a few symbolic tests of a candidate's popularity among rank and file in a few isolated states, which then encourage or discourage support from party elites. Rather, primaries have become a full-blown *electoral system*, one that has largely (though not totally) replaced the decision-making power of state organizational leaders with popular elections. This change has made the nomination process basically a series of rank and file state elections, each with critical national overtones, rather than a consensus process "negotiated" by the party's established organizational leadership.

Of course significant individual primary battles were crucial to candidates like Willkie, Dewey, and Stassen in the 1940s, Eisenhower in the 1950s, and Kennedy in the 1960s. But these contests were essentially used by candidates to "convince" undeclared or uncommitted delegates. Most importantly, the significant audience for these primary fights consisted of party activists rather than rank-and-file voters. Elite evaluations rather than public electoral decisions were the essence of decision-making, and conflict between activists, though often intense, did not attract much public involvement until the conventions themselves began.

The recent transformation of the presidential primary system has been dramatic. Fifteen states held presidential

---

[13] Jules Witcover, *Marathon* (New York: Viking Press, 1977).

primaries in 1968. The number increased to twenty-one by 1972; and, of crucial importance, the percentage of delegates that could be won in primaries reached the point of a critical mass needed for nomination. Whereas only 41 percent of the delegates to the 1968 Democratic convention were selected by primaries, the opening and "democratizing" of party procedures in 1972 resulted in selection of a majority of delegates (66%) from primary states.[14] The number of states with primaries increased to thirty in 1976, and thirty-five states utilized primary elections in 1980. Importantly, 75 percent of all delegates to the Democratic convention were chosen in primary states in 1976, increasing to approximately 80 percent in 1980. While the percentages for the Republicans are slightly lower, and their ground rules for delegate selection are slightly different, the changes in rules in both parties place the prime requisite for candidate success on public, press-related electoral activities rather than on nonpublic party elite negotiations.

The arena of decision-making has thus been opened to allow not only more public participation in the selection of the parties' presidential nominees but also more *decisive* participation. The new "rules of the game" have encouraged various kinds of less established political aspirants to enter the race by putting a premium on campaigning abilities rather than preexisting support among state, local, and national party leaders. Clearly, under the rules that existed as late as 1968, neither McGovern's nor Carter's nomination victories as outsiders would have been possible nor Reagan's challenge in 1976 and Kennedy, in 1980 attempted. Thus, within a decade, the number of primaries had doubled, the proportion of delegates that could be won in primaries had more than doubled, and the primaries themselves linked delegates more uniformly to a presidential candidate. Most importantly, the variety of changes in primary and convention rules have changed the entire stra-

---

[14] F. Christopher Arterton, "The Strategic Environment of Primaries for Presidential Campaign Organization, 1976," a paper delivered at the New England Political Science Association Convention, April 1976, Table 1.

tegic environment for an ambitious candidate. Public preferences rather than party-leadership assessments has
become the ultimate determinant in nomination politics.

The swift transformation of the nomination system to a
more volatile public arena has promoted the value of electoral entrepreneurs and their organizers, and permitted
the press (as well as the public) a much more central position in the political process. What *was*, in fact, the press's
role in making the critical reforms that have changed the
process of choosing candidates, and what *is* its role at present in shaping the present scope of intraparty conflict and
the political outcomes? How does the press structure the
political environment in which candidates act and rank-
and-file voters respond? What, then, are the critical linkages between the press, the primaries, and the political
parties?

Television: Legitimating the Primary Process

The transformation of the presidential nomination process into an essentially mass electoral system is surely
linked in important part to television and the new political
environment it has helped create. The precise relationship
between the new electronic medium and the institutionalization of presidential primaries is, of course, not easy to
define. Nevertheless, several important aspects of television's impact on the spread of presidential primaries can
be identified. First, a thorough examination of network
television news transcripts from 1967 to 1976 clearly shows
that renewed interest and demand for primaries came first
from candidates challenging entrenched politicians, not
from any pressures by television journalists.[15] Second, the
evidence also shows that, once television journalists
grasped the professional opportunities offered by expanded
primary politics, they were quick to capitalize and expand

---

[15] Charles Skop, "*CBS Evening News* Transcripts: The Presidential
Primaries, 1968–1976," unpublished student paper, Columbia University, 1979.

on a process economically and politically advantageous to the medium.

Rather than initiating renewed interest in primaries, the prime political role of television during the period studied was in legitimating the primary process as *the* genuinely democratic way to choose convention delegates. The basic political posture of television journalism toward alternative nomination processes was to favor primaries versus state caucus/convention methods, both in amount of coverage and in the positive nature of story treatment. The positive treatment of the primaries *as a process* was in part due to the fact that television, compared to print journalism, had (and still has) far more difficulty in covering stories of complex elite negotiations (such as occur in caucuses and state conventions) than election campaigns and action-oriented events. Its need to show filmed events in each news presentation make primaries "reportable" and newsworthy events for network television.

Indicative of network television's preference for primaries is the fact that, though CBS news coverage of the primaries in 1968 was the most extensive at that time, only once did the network evening news run a feature story on nonprimary delegate selection procedures—despite the fact that almost six out of ten delegates and the nominee himself were chosen by these methods rather than in primaries.[16] In 1972, the same network aired a four-minute segment on the Iowa caucus in January—and, after that, nonprimary methods of selection were not given more than casual coverage again until the Texas convention was examined in June of that year.[17]

Indications that television journalists might perceive primaries as "the right way" to choose presidential candidates became apparent only toward the end of the 1968 campaign. Initially, networks news teams had shown little interest in exploring insurgent charges that "organization" politics unfairly restricted their ability to transform claimed

---

[16] Arterton, "Strategic Environment of Primaries."
[17] Skop, "*CBS Evening News* Transcripts."

political support into actual delegate strength. Through most of the campaign, television news treated the primaries as games in themselves, as an exciting series of events largely distinct from other, less exciting (but more determinant) caucus/convention processes. Senator Eugene McCarthy's efforts to draw attention to the "closed" methods of choosing delegates—some were chosen a year before the convention—got little treatment and even less analysis from the network news until almost the end of the campaign. Only in June, when the primaries were over and before the convention began, did the network news teams begin to genuinely question the existing nomination process and probe ideas such as a "fair share of delegations" and "the will of rank-and-file Democrats."

Though television journalists did not initially favor primaries as *the* appropriate democratic process, their efforts to legitimate the primary process were very strong by 1972. Not only was their affirmation of primaries clear from the vastly disproportionate air time given primaries compared to other selection methods, but also numerous phrases attributing inherent democratic values to primaries appeared, sprinkled liberally throughout network news. These alternately described primary results as "the people speaking," "a democratic voice," and "open decision-making," despite the fact that the mechanics of multicandidate primaries often made for ambiguous results.[18] Overall, the networks treated McGovern's nomination victory as a clear and overwhelming "popular" choice; as it happens, later analyses of the 1972 Democratic results showed only approximately one-third of the primary voters supporting McGovern, one-third George Wallace, and one-third a combination of Humphrey, Muskie, and other centrists.

Network support for "pure" democratic processes, though usually subtle in form, occasionally became direct. One network television correspondent, critical of certain "organizational" constraints in the "at-large" selection of only twenty Massachusetts delegates, offered the thought

[18] Rubin, *Party Dynamics*, pp. 147–71.

that such arrangements "may have been promoted by someone who had a grudge against the democratic system."[19]

Television's preference for primaries and action rather than caucuses and negotiations is, of course, rooted in its advantages (and disadvantages) as a medium. It is a preference reflected by the medium's broad use of sports analogies (such as the "horse race") to describe primary campaigns. Television needs a shorthand method to compress and dramatize events, and has settled comfortably on sporting phrases to describe and simplify a complex process. Candidates are "leading the pack," "closing fast," "sagging in the stretch," and "gaining ground," as the medium strives to treat their competition in language suggestive of movement and vitality.

The "game" analogy is prominent in the treatment of all media, but its prominence, as Thomas Patterson has demonstrated, is greater on television (and in weekly news magazines) than in newspapers. The looser story line in newspaper versus television reporting and a larger "news hole" enables it to move beyond these analogies to cover intricate, complex, and talky political activities in more detail than television easily accommodates.[20] One media analyist found that the script of an entire half hour network news segment would fill only several columns of the front page of the *New York Times*.[21] The pressure to eliminate words and shorten stories, and its fear of a "talking head"— a television journalist just speaking without action film clips—force television to develop themes and personalize stories so that it can capitalize on its uniqueness as a powerful and visual communications medium.

Television's impact on the primary process itself can thus be seen in perspective. Television journalists did not initiate renewed public interest in presidential primaries by

[19] Morton Dean, reporting on the *CBS Evening News*, April 24, 1972.

[20] Thomas E. Patterson and Robert D. McClure, *The Unseeing Eye* (New York: Putnam, 1976), pp. 49–58.

[21] Gary Paul Gater, *Air Time: Inside Story of CBS News* (New York: Harper, Row, 1978), p. 144.

conscious actions. But finding primaries professionally beneficial, they subsequently promoted them as the proper,
democratic, and "American way" to deal with intraparty
representation. Interest in primary elections was reawak-
ened by competition between aspiring politicians, but their
treatment by network television fostered, exaggerated, and
finally helped to legitimate the new trend. By offering
almost exclusive coverage of primaries in reporting the
nomination process, network news implicitly devalued
other processes that could be open and democratic as well,
and consequently down-played methods that were consensus—rather than conflict—oriented. The initial object of
the McGovern-Fraser commission reforms was to make all
procedures—state caucus/convention rules as well as primary rules—open and democratic. The persistent thrust of
network television, however, was to favor primaries as if
they were the *only* legitimate way to do party business,
and, consequently, encouraged existing plebiscitarian
tendencies within the parties.

Though it may not necessarily have been conscious of
doing so, or arbitrarily self-aggrandizing in the process, the
fact remains that television's contribution to the organization of the contemporary political environment has
increased the impact of the press as a whole on political
decision-making. Because of the importance of the press to
the candidate in influencing public opinion in primaries,
because cues for voting from the party organization are
weak or nonexistent, and because traditional sources of
information are either unclear or unsure during much of
this phase of a campaign, media assessments of what's
going on and who is "winning" or "losing" take on a greater
importance than under the more stable circumstances of a
general election.[22] Particularly when outcomes are uncertain, when candidates are just beginning to make a connection with relatively inattentive segments of the rank-and-
file electorate, the press's influence in structuring popular

---

[22]Thomas E. Patterson, *The Mass Media Election: How Americans
Choose Their President* (New York: Praeger, 1980), pp. 107–147.

perceptions is greatest. Paradoxically, the media appear to have their most significant impact on outcomes when their audience knows the least about politics and pays little attention.[23]

Campaign Organizations and the Press

During the primary campaign, competing candidate organizations not only make use of new and old communications processes to reach their electoral "markets," but are also, in fact, part of the communications process itself. Where in the news process candidate organizations leave off and the press begins is not always clear, for the press uses candidates to generate news for its own journalistic purposes while the candidates of necessity must use the press to reach and persuade their potential publics. Some political scientists have seen this interaction between political actors and the press as an "exchange process" by which each seeks to advance its own professional interest, producing as a result of the interaction, a news outcome.[24] Whatever the appropriate model, however, both primary candidates and the press clearly seek to develop news that will suit their own professional and organizational purposes.

Traditionally, political parties have supplied candidates with financing and organization as well as the party label— the rubric under which candidates could be identified with certain party causes and aspirations. The party organizations acted as mediators and evaluators between electorates, with relatively low levels of exposure to political communications, and candidates, who, without a party's

---

[23] Donald R. Matthews, "Winnowing: The News Media and the 1976 Presidential Nominations," in *Race for the Presidency*, ed. James David Barber (Englewood Cliffs, N.J.: Prentice-Hall, 1978), p. 57; and V. O. Key, Jr., *Public Opinion and American Democracy* (New York: Knopf, 1961).

[24] Michael Grossman and Francis Rourke, "The Media and The Presidency: An Exchange Analysis," a paper delivered at the American Political Science Association annual meeting, September 1975.

label and organization, could seldom hope for a bid for the presidency. But since primaries have become essential to the nomination process, and state and local party organizations greatly weakened in their cuing and mobilizing capacities, campaigning through the media has become an organizational necessity. Now candidates for presidential nominations must mobilize millions of voters without an on-going organization behind them, and their electoral ambitions are thus dependent on their own ad hoc campaign organizations.

These ad hoc organizations formed by all primary contenders, financed independently of traditional party sources, are built initially upon a candidate's personal contacts, volunteer assistance, and whatever hired services the organization can afford, including advertising agencies and polling services, direct mail, and door-to-door canvassing teams.[25] Furthermore, these ad hoc organizations are entirely dependent upon the particular candidate's personality and actions. Defeat ends both candidacy and organization; victory leads to the organization's absorption into the new presidential administration. In the very short time in which these organizations exist, they must reach millions of potential supporters with the candidate's message and policies and mobilize them to vote in the primaries. The only effective way to mobilize a potential electorate quickly, in the absence of a permanent campaign apparatus, is, of course, through the media. Consequently, large amounts of free media coverage (i.e., "uncontrolled" press coverage) and lesser but significant amounts of political advertising (i.e., "controlled" media) have become the staple of presidential primaries.[26]

Particularly before the primaries have begun, and at the early stage during them when numerous candidates are competing, the press's evaluative influence on ad hoc organizations can be critical, since the press's assessment of whether one's candidacy is serious has much to do with

---

[25] Robert Agranoff, *The Management of Election Campaigns* (New York: Holbrook Press, 1976), pp. 181–216.

[26] *Ibid.*, chapter 13; pp. 323, 361–78.

whether a candidate gets the necessary coverage to actually *become* serious. While press assessments of contenders are not generally made capriciously, coverage decisions may deeply affect the eventual outcome. By contributing to the early demise of candidates who do not appear to be in the mainstream, press assessments restrict certain kinds of candidacies by quickly drying up potential campaign resources. Thus, though putatively describing the winnowing of candidates for the public, the press becomes part of that winnowing process.

In the early campaign stages, when most traditional political indices have weak predictive value, the widest latitude seems to be given the professional judgments of print and television journalists. The initial events in the long nomination process are, as F. Christopher Arterton notes, the first "hard news" stories; they tend, consequently, to receive inflated emphasis.[27] For example, in the three months before the 1976 primaries began fully 54 percent of all print stories and 60 percent of all network television time devoted to the presidential race dealt *only* with the opening primary in New Hampshire. This tendency to exaggerate coverage of early primaries is also indicated by coverage of individual candidates: for example, while Jimmy Carter narrowly won the New Hampshire primary over Morris Udall (28 to 22 percent), in the week following the election Carter received four times the amount of column space in newspapers and five times more exposure on the three television networks than his major rivals. Because of such exaggerated coverage, the number of Americans knowing more about Carter than just his name went from less than one-fifth in February to over four-fifths only two months later.[28]

[27] F. Christopher Arterton, "Campaign Organization Confronts the Media Political Environment," in *Race for the Presidency*, ed. Barber, p. 4.

[28] Thomas E. Patterson, "Press Coverage and Candidate Success in Presidential Primaries: The 1976 Democratic Race," a paper delivered at the American Political Science Association annual meeting, September 1977, p. 8. See also Michael J. Robinson and Karen A. McPherson, "For Better or Worse, News Content Can Make a Difference," unpublished paper, 1976.

How a candidate is *perceived* to fare in the primaries' early stages has much to do with how he can *actually* campaign in the future, since his ability to raise funds and maintain organizational stability for subsequent primaries is heavily dependent on the appearance of campaign progress.[29] Particularly in 1972, the press unabashedly participated in the interpretation of victory and defeat, deciding, for example, how big the Muskie edge over McGovern in New Hampshire had to be to make what was, in fact, both a popular and delegate victory into a "real win." As the *New York Times* simply put it:

Nearly all Democratic pros believe Senator Edmund S. Muskie will get the most votes in the March 7 balloting . . . It puts the news media in the position of arbiters. It is they who are asked to decide, in advance, what percentage would constitute a real win for Mr. Muskie.[30]

Who "asked" the news media to decide is not clear, but it is at least doubtful that there was any genuinely clamorous public demand for the press's interpretation. Just why an almost 10 percent plurality and approximately half of the vote in the 1972 New Hampshire primary is not a "real win," while a 6 percent plurality and only slightly over one-quarter of the vote in 1976 is a victory capable of releasing an explosion of favorable publicity is, of course, an unanswered question.

From a practical perspective, the serial nature of presidential primaries, strung out as they are for over three months, tends to build into the process *an interpretive pressure*, because so little of the entire campaign for delegates is actually decided in any one primary. In 1976 the press made a major effort to avoid some of the excessive interpretive intrusions it had injected into the campaign only four years earlier. But even then, and again in the 1980 campaign, the press indulged its own journalistic needs to clearly define "winners" and "losers," at times in opposition to the intended political framework of the primaries themselves. As an example, despite the fact that the

---

[29] Arterton, "Campaign Organization," pp. 10–11.
[30] *New York Times*, February 14, 1972, p. 1.

initial reforms had restructured the rules to reduce the winner-take-all aspect of delegate selection—eliminating the unit rule (for Democrats) at the state level and making major efforts to increase proportionate representation at various sublevels—the new reporting of the primaries still mainly stressed the winner-take-all aspects by overwhelming attention to the "winner."[31]

On another level, the press, particularly television, tends to make a national pattern out of primary results that are often local and discrete, and thus further distorts the federal or decentralized nature of the nomination rules. Network television, specifically, tends to down-play the diversity of the decisions in fifty separate states, deemphasizing variation in political cultures, rules, and political structure among the states so as to present its network audience with a national homogeneous pattern. Thus the networks' processing of political communications opposes intended political values because of their own journalistic imperatives. As F. Christopher Arterton puts it: "If historically diversity is a political value in the presidential nomination process, continuity is a dominant theme in reporters' interpretations which assume that one state's result is indicative of the national trend."[32]

The actual impact of interpretive reporting in the nomination process depends, of course, on a variety of elements, most difficult to measure. These may include the candidate's personal qualities, his stand on issues, and other specific situational factors. Before the dramatic escalation of presidential primaries in the television era, the political interpretation of events was largely, if not solely, in the hands of established party organizational leaders. They assessed trends, evaluated the candidates' qualities and appeal, and negotiated a decision on the ultimate nominee. Since primary elections have become the dominant factor in gaining nomination, however, the function of assessing candidates and of interpreting events has shifted

---

[31] Patterson, "Press Coverage," pp. 3–7; also Arterton, "Campaign Organization," p. 23.

[32] Arterton, "Campaign Organization," p. 23.

heavily in favor of the press. The combination of the press, candidate-entrepreneurs, and rank-and-file participants has formed a new and volatile intraparty dynamic.

Certainly the increased role in internal party politics of the press in general, and television in particular, has shifted influence to media elites at the expense of established party leaders. What is less clear is the impact of these changes at the elite level on "the people," i.e., the rank and file, the party in the electorate. Has the combination of party reform and increased media attention actually broadened and encouraged mass participation in the nomination process—or has there only been more sound and fury, and little, if any, increased interest on the part of the rank and file in critical party decisions? How individuals respond to a major transformation in the nominating process is a critical political question. It bears directly on the organizational future of the party as an institution, on presidential choices, and on the operation of the American two-party system.

Press, Primaries, and Mass Mobilization

Whether the mass electorate has shared in the resurgent activity of presidential primaries bears heavily on the issue of whether there is continuity or change in our election system. If presidential primaries do not attract increased participation by the rank and file in the nominating process, if they fail to become a broad-based popular arena of decision-making, then it is probable that, like primary politics in the Progressive era, they will collapse because of their loss of representativeness, legitimacy, and popular effectiveness. Recent reforms will not have produced a popularly based nomination system after all, but will only have replaced influential party elites with an influential press.

So far the evidence points to increased popular interest and turnout in its presidential primaries, particularly in heated and highly contested nomination races.[33] But long-term prospects for the primary system remain obscure, and the question is the subject of serious disagreement. For example, a prominent analyst of presidential primaries, Austin Ranney, has noted that turnout remains very low, "a small brook" of participation, and his analysis of the 1976 primary campaign sees the turnout in terms of an old and continuing pattern defined largely by an unresponsive and uninterested "primary" electorate. He notes:

While in 1976 the nation had far more presidential primaries—and far more closely contested ones—than ever before, there was a sharp drop-off in turnout. That drop, moreover, was larger than the much discussed drop-off in turnout in presidential general elections.[34]

His judgment that constancy rather than change character-izes existing levels of voter interest and participation in the primaries obscures the magnitude and significance of what has been, in reality, a major alteration of the pattern of electoral participation. The new pattern of primaries does not, as recent evidence shows, merely repeat the old Pro-gressive pattern. Not a continuation of past forms, it is, rather a major change suited to, and shaped by, a new era of mass communications—with durable effects on present and future party structure.

In any fast-changing system, the political variables of change may not be easy to distinguish. Consequently, it is difficult to isolate durable trends. For example, the level of turnout is indeed low after a state first shifts from other, less popular methods to a primary election system, since unaccustomed local electorates have not been "socialized" to primary voting. Therefore, the averaging of turnout from many states that have recently converted to primaries can give the appearance that participation rates are static even

---

[33] William D. Morris and Otto A. Davis, "The Sport of Kings: Presi-dential Preference Primaries," a paper delivered at the American Polit-ical Science Association annual meeting, 1975, pp. 14–18.

[34] Austin Ranney, *Participation in American Presidential Nominations, 1976* (Washington, D.C.: American Enterprise Institute, 1977), p. 22.

though they are not. By accounting for the "socialization" factor that affects the new states—examining, for example, only those states that have continuously held presidential preference primaries since 1948—recent analysis gives a much more accurate picture of actual trends in mass participation in primaries.

Evidence of primary turnout in the last three decades clearly shows a major increase in rank-and-file participation that is particularly strong among Democrats.[35] Until 1964, Republicans turned out at higher rates than Democrats, a not unexpected finding given the traditional relatively high socioeconomic status of Republicans and the correlation of such status with higher rates of electoral participation. Turnout of registered Republicans[36] averaged between 40 and 45 percent from 1948 to 1964, except for the Taft-Eisenhower primaries in 1952 when 54 percent of registered Republicans voted. A new peak (58 percent) was reached in the close and exciting 1976 Ford-Reagan contest, a level almost equated in 1980 despite the far less competitive Reagan-Bush race.

Democrats, conversely, turned out at substantially lower rates historically, with usually between 25 to 35 percent of registered voters going to the primary polls. After 1964, however, Democratic turnout made major successive leaps over preceding levels, reaching a post–World War II high of 49 percent in the anti-Vietnam insurgency in 1968 (up from only 37 percent in Kennedy's spirited 1960 campaign). Major candidate competition within the Democratic party was a clear factor in the initial escalation of

---

[35] See Richard L. Rubin, "Presidential Primaries: Continuities, Dimensions of Change, and Political Implications," in *The Party Symbol: Readings on Political Parties*, ed. William Crotty (San Francisco: W. H. Freeman, 1980), pp. 126–47.

[36] Turnout in primaries is measured in relationship to registered (and therefore eligible) party voters. The pool of potential voters is, of course, larger than the pool of registered voters since only about 70 percent of all eligible voters are registered to vote in presidential elections. While not fully comparable to general election turnout percentages, the upward trend of primary participation is in marked contrast to the downward trend of general election voting.

turnout,[37] and after the conflict of the 1968 campaign laid the groundwork, Democratic turnout reached historically high levels in 1972 after intense primary competition (62 percent in traditional primary states)—a level of voter participation that was unequaled in over half a century of primaries. But when one further considers that in 1976 the Democrats had no close challenger to Carter in the competition for delegates after the Pennsylvania primary (only the ninth out of thirty primaries), and that the intensity of competition was markedly decreased by the less divisive issues and personalities in that year, then the *sustained* high level of primary turnout (also 62 percent) becomes even more impressive.

The primaries of 1980 show a more uneven pattern of voting, principally because the races in both parties were considered close only through the early primaries before Carter and Reagan took virtually insurmountable leads. As a result, whereas the early primaries showed substantial increases in participation in both parties—in New Hampshire and Massachusetts, for example, where voting was up—the apparent weakness of Kennedy in the first stage of the campaign and Bush's lack of appeal outside the Northeast reduced competition, decreased the subsequent importance of voting in later primaries, and, consequently, lowered turnout *moderately* in the later phase of the campaign.[38] As will be seen shortly, the drop-off in turnout in states with a tradition of primaries was relatively small despite the lack of close competition, levels of participation similar to the post-1968 pattern were maintained, and over thirty-two million primary voters went to the polls.

What seems to be happening, particularly among traditionally relatively inactive rank-and-file Democrats, is the institutionalization of high levels of primary turnout. Many potential voters have been socialized to participate more actively in primaries than in the past, reaching levels of activity perhaps no longer directly dependent on the fac-

---

[37] Morris and Davis, "The Sport of Kings."

[38] See *Congressional Quarterly*, Weekly Report (April 19, 1980), pp. 1003–10; and *Congressional Quarterly* Weekly Report (June 14, 1980).

tors that precipitated the initial increases in participation during the 1960s and the early 1970s. Proficient candidate-entrepreneurs, a newfound interest in the primary process itself, and, most importantly, the impact of television coverage, and press coverage in general, have all contributed to the formation of a new and substantial base of mass participation.[39]

Not only the actual events but also the amount and nature of increased political coverage, by television particularly, must be accorded a key role in provoking and sustaining rank-and-file interest in the nomination process. A major increase in national political communications did in fact occur during the past two decades when, as mentioned earlier, the networks doubled their evening network news time from fifteen minutes to half an hour. In addition, the number of primary election stories on the evening news alone increased *fourfold* just between the initial Democratic insurgency in 1968 and the primary campaigns in 1976.[40] Although a full analysis of the 1980 campaign news is not yet available, the substantial increase in the numbers of primaries over 1976 makes it likely that television news coverage at least maintained, if it did not increase, its primary coverage.

The amount of "special election" coverage of individual primaries by network television has also far outstripped the increase in new primaries alone. One leading network, CBS, increased its special election coverage of primaries fivefold between 1968 and 1976 alone; both NBC and CBS gave half-hour late-evening special election reports on most primary elections in 1976, and all three major networks did special reports on almost all primary elections in 1980.[41] Certainly the increase in consumption of primary

[39] See Michael J. Robinson, "Television and American Politics: 1956–1976," in *The Public Interest*, Spring 1977, pp. 23–25.

[40] A comparison of primary election news stories on the *CBS Evening News* between 1968 and 1976 was made by the author with assistance from Charles Skop.

[41] The author thanks Warren J. Mitofsky, director of the CBS News Election and Survey Unit, for making available the 1968 and 1976 comparative information. For the 1976 data see William Bicker, "Network

stories, the excitement generated by the electronic media in the "horse race," and television's legitimation of the primary process itself has contributed to the awareness and active interest of the rank-and-file electorate. Recent analysis by Rubin and Rivers has demonstrated that causal connections cannot only be made from primary participation to increases in media use, but in the other direction as well, i.e., increased media use prompts more primary participation.[42]

Several other considerations indicate the firm links between the major escalations of both primary turnout and television journalism in this same period. The television news audience, for example, is drawn disproportionately from the lower and lower-middle segments of the socioeconomic spectrum;[43] the most dramatic increases in primary turnout are found, correspondingly, in the party (Democratic) that disproportionately houses this population in its coalition. Had this stable but passive body of Americans—traditional supporters of strong urban "machines"—been sharply aroused by a combination of the events of the period and television coverage of them, as we may well expect it was, then we might also expect its reaction to have been reflected by the greater increase in turnout in Democratic primaries.

It must be remembered that strong state and local party organizations have sought (since the Progressive reforms) to keep turnout in the primaries at a relatively low level. Keeping the turnout of rank and file low permitted party leaders to produce a winning slate of delegates (controlled by local organizations) by getting out a relatively small contingent of faithful supporters. Weak party states, on the

Television News and the 1976 Presidential Primaries," in *Race for the Presidency,* ed. Barber, p. 94.

[42] See "Addendum" to Richard L. Rubin and Douglas Rivers, "Mass Media and Critical Elections: A First Report."

[43] This point is stressed by Robinson, "Television and American Politics," as being very important in changes that have occurred in the 1960s and 1970s. But in *The Mass Media Election,* Patterson disagrees with the Robinson thesis, pp. 58–59.

other hand, were less able to contain the level of turnout, as primaries became highly visible media contests where contending candidates fought for delegates by mobilizing voters—with the help of the mass media—rather than by negotiations with established party leaders. Examining primary turnout in two typically strong party "organization" states compared against two traditionally weak party "Progressive" states over the last nine presidential election campaigns underscores both the past strength of party organizations in the nomination process and their present weakness.

Figure 6 below demonstrates with clarity the changing trend in rank-and-file participation. The "organization" states, Pennsylvania and Massachusetts, show considerably lower turnout than the weak party "Progressive" states, California and Oregon, averaging 20 to 30 percent less turnout in both parties until 1968. In response to the series of party reforms, insurgent challenges, and an increased media coverage, turnout, particularly among traditionally inactive urban Democrats, escalates rapidly. While turnout edged downward in some of the 1980 primaries, mainly because of a lack of decisive candidate competition, primary turnout in those states accustomed to primary elections remained at continued high levels. The results show clearly the accelerating decline of party organizational strength by the growing similarity in voter response between organization states and Progressive states, indicating the inability of established party organizations to contain the extent of primary turnout and control the states convention delegates. All primary states now resemble—at least in presidential nomination politics—the weak organization pattern of the Progressive states.

Media coverage of the primaries has thus contributed to a profound change in the structure of the political party as an institution, rearranging the relative influence of competing political elites to each other and to groups of rank-and-file partisans. The impact of television, on top of other factors also furthering the erosion of party organizational control over the presidential nomination, has significantly

Figure 6 Turnout in Democratic Presidential Primaries[a]
Turnout in Republican Presidential Primaries

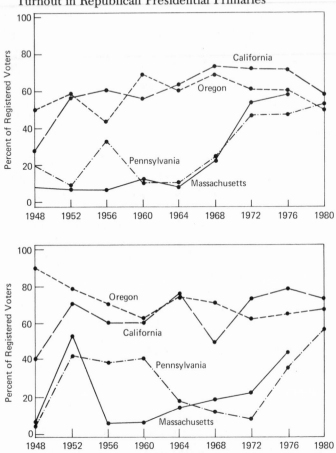

SOURCE: Abstract and update from Richard L. Rubin, "Presidential Primaries: Continuities, Dimensions of Change, and Political Implications," in *The Party Symbol*, ed. William Crotty.

[a] Figured on closed preference primaries only. Massachusetts' results in 1980 are not included because Independents were permitted to vote in either primary and consequently the turnout figures are not comparative.

changed the ability of the party to "manage" intraparty conflict—undoubtedly related to management failures in the
1960s—by encouraging plebiscitary tendencies in electoral
politics. The legitimation of primaries by a press which has
regarded them as the expected, democratic route to the
presidency, together with enormous increases in the
media's primary election coverage, has firmly focused popular attention on nomination politics, produced relatively
high levels of mass voter mobilization within the party, and
largely eliminated the role of established party leaders as
filters of internal party conflict. Thus, though the "proven"
direct, micro-effects of television on the individual may
appear relatively small and obscure—results requiring the
development of better research questions and techniques
rather than acceptance of existing findings as conclusion-
ary—the macro- or institutional effects of the new mass
media on the political party are presently both substantial
and definable.

Television journalism has vastly increased the influence
of the press as a whole in the nomination process by
becoming the most important connecting link between a
variety of competing candidates and an unsettled party
electorate. As a result, the press has arrogated to itself
many of the linkage functions between the party's candidates and rank-and-file partisans that had been historically
mediated by professional party leaders. Whether by setting
criteria for media coverage of candidates or issues, or by
establishing benchmarks for candidates' success or failure
in actual primary elections, the press has assumed much of
the recruitment and evaluative role that was once reserved
for practicing politicians. The collective impact of the press
on the formative and deliberative processes of the parties
has, therefore, markedly changed their former role as an
institution serving to simplify, organize, and structure
political conflict for the ordinary voter.

The impact of the press on the shape and intensity of
internal party conflict has serious and as yet unexplored
ramifications for coalition-building in a two-party system
and, as will become apparent, for presidential leadership.

The two-party system and its patterns of presidential elections have been markedly altered by the expansion of the
full-blown intraparty electoral system of the primaries.
Together with the press's prominent new role in centralizing the focus of mass communications, the primaries have
redirected the flow of political information, restructured
the candidate strategies, and redefined the choices of political alternatives for the mass public. How these changes
have affected the presidency itself becomes, then, the final
link between a changing mass communications environment and American political institutions.

9

The New Electoral Circuitry

Dramatic changes in mass communications over the past three decades have given the press an increasingly central position in the process that links political leadership to mass opinion. Major sociopolitical changes, among them the growth of the welfare state, increased educational levels, and a rise in individual expectations, have combined with major technological developments affecting the mass media to produce greatly accelerated popular pressures on old, established political institutions. The heightening of both the volume and the velocity of mass information, and of public expectations associated with such changes, has altered the environment in which political elites compete, changing the nature of the electoral connection between the leadership and the electorate.

The growth in presidential primaries and plebiscitarian nomination politics has expanded the press's role as a political force. In large part, the press has assumed the evaluative role once held by established party leaders and decisively influences the vital and sensitive connection between competing primary candidates and a volatile rank and file. Simultaneously, the increased range and intensity of the mass media, particularly of television, have accentuated the growing 20th-century separation of presidential candidates from their own parties. The primaries and media have drastically devalued the role and importance of established organizational leaders in choosing a party's candidates, and enhanced the significance of the candidate-entrepreneurs' personal campaign organizations and of the party's rank and file. As nomination success becomes based increasingly on the independent personal resources and campaigning skills of candidates and their ability to attract the notice of the mass media rather than on support from party leaders, candidates are drawn away from links with established party activists toward their own personal followings.

The new mass media environment created largely by television, as noted earlier, has strongly influenced the very expansion of the primaries by popularizing (or democratizing) the nomination processes. It has also shaped the kinds of personal attributes a candidate needs to meet the demands of two distinct campaign arenas, making the path to the presidency an extraordinary test of campaigning skills and coalition-building. A candidate must now satisfy the demands of an intraparty election arena without destroying his chances in the later interparty struggle. He must first fight groups within his own party and, if victorious, then seek to make the losers his allies in the subsequent struggle between the two parties—all under the scrutiny of the press. It is not by chance that in each of the last five campaigns the presidential nominee of the party with the most divisive nomination competition has lost the general election.[1]

Two major questions arise from the situation here briefly sketched. First, how have various media and nonmedia factors affected important operating patterns of the presidential election system? Second, and most important, how have changes in the relationship of mass communications and electoral institutions—i.e., the changed electoral circuitry—affected the operations of the presidency itself?

---

[1] James I. Lengle, "Divisive Presidential Primaries and Party Electoral Prospects, 1932–1976," *American Politics Quarterly* 8 (1980): 261–77. Lengle demonstrates that divisive primaries clearly hurt the individual party's chances of winning the same states in the following general election. This effect is true for both parties but it is more pronounced for Democrats.

That is, how does running *for* the presidency affect the running *of* the presidency?

Changing Electoral Patterns

The New Deal realignment was particularly important in electoral terms because it significantly politicized an economic system that had long been relatively free of major governmental restraint. As a result of New Deal politics, the electoral system became far more "sensitized" than it had been to economic and social tensions. Important issues previously considered outside the national election arena—such as Social Security and unemployment insurance—became competitive political issues between the two major parties.[2] Thus, the New Deal and the developing welfare state that emerged from it heightened the responsiveness of the political system as a whole, overcoming resistance to active intervention by the national government in economic matters. The successful politicization of socioeconomic problems gave the electoral system both new meaning and greater expressiveness.

The direct economic effects of recession on unemployed individuals are clearly much less severe today than sixty years ago. But increased media attention to economic indicators, as well as the New Deal itself, may have helped sensitize the public to relatively small changes in economic conditions. A 1 percent change in unemployment or inflation rates probably receives more coverage today than more serious economic fluctuations merited at the turn of the century.[3] Because the mass media report public reactions to such problems in much wider and more penetrating fashion than formerly, political and press pressure on

[2] See Everett Carll Ladd, Jr., with Charles Hadley, *Transformations of the American Party System*, 2nd ed. (New York: W. W. Norton, 1975), pp. 31–41; and James L. Sundquist, *Dynamics of the Party System* (Washington, D.C.: Brookings Institution, 1973), pp. 183–244.

[3] See Richard L. Rubin and R. D. Rivers, "The Mass Media and Critical Elections: A First Report," Tables 6 and 8.

institutional elites to respond to public dissatisfaction is consequently greater. Thus we find a major escalation in political sensitivity to economic "management" problems.

Presidents of both parties since the New Deal realignment have made politically effective short-term responses to problems of unemployment or declining income both by executive action and by legislation—especially at election time.[4] Though short-term responses do not necessarily resolve fundamental economic problems, and may well be inadequate to meet future long-term economic tensions, they do make the political system more responsive to certain types of economic demands that, in the past, might have gone unaddressed by political leaders and, in time, generated a major electoral realignment.

The rapid escalation of presidential primaries also affects the way in which socioeconomic tension builds within the election system and has significantly affected traditional electoral patterns. Conflict that, in the past, would have been suppressed by the internal structure of basically non-primary parties can no longer be effectively contained. For example, the anti–Vietnam War insurgency and the racially based George Wallace movement, both stressing issues initially unaddressed by competition between the two parties, made their way into internal party battles via the presidential primaries. As the parties have become more responsive to economic and social disturbances, and as the mass media have furthered this responsiveness, ideas, issues, and the personal impact of contenders representing a wide range of political expression can easily spread throughout the electorate.

The rapid increase in both the number of primaries and the levels of rank-and-file participation in them clearly indicates a significant increase in popular opportunities to challenge a party's agenda. This situation undoubtedly allows for increased amounts of conflict to enter a party's internal deliberations, and thus may help dissipate the

---

[4] See Edward R. Tufte, *Political Control of the Economy* (Princeton, N.J.: Princeton University Press, 1978), pp. 28–64.

buildup of tensions by permitting their expression. The increased articulation of conflict within the individual party tends to alter traditional two-party patterns of realignment.

The relationship of the two-party system to the movement led by George C. Wallace in the 1960s and 1970s is an example of the greater "permeability"' or openness of a party's structure and the access it now provides. Wallace first tested himself in the Democratic primaries in 1964 and then posed a third-party challenge by way of the American Independent party in 1968. After the Democrats expanded the role of the primaries in nomination politics he returned to make his claim in 1972 and 1976. The new "openness" provided by primary reforms after 1968 apparently enticed political protest back into the two-party system by offering a potential third-party insurgency a substantial opportunity to make an electoral bid without abandoning the two major parties.[5] Some of the sources of popular support identified by Wallace were, in fact, "borrowed," or absorbed in one form or another, by other candidates. The Republican Nixon, for example, based his "southern strategy" on Wallace's example, and later Democratic candidates, such as Jimmy Carter, borrowed heavily from parts of Wallace's antiestablishment, anti-Washington strategy.[6] What has happened, in effect, is that a primary candidate's uncovering of a dissatisfied segment of the rank and file has produced swift reactions by subsequent candidates. Such adaptation to the political marketplace by major party candidates tends, of course, to keep parties more pliable than in the past, and has undercut the incentives for movements to organize into third parties.

Paradoxically, the enormous media attention given an

---

[5] For an interesting analysis of this process see Benjamin Ginsberg and Peter F. Galderesi, "Irresponsible Parties, Responsible Party Systems," a paper delivered at the American Political Science Association annual meeting, 1977, pp. 18–20.

[6] See Kevin P. Phillips, *Mediacracy: American Parties and Politics in the Communications Age* (Garden City, N.Y.: Doubleday, 1975), pp. 142–45. See also Martin Schramm, *Running for President: The Carter Campaign* (New York: Stein & Day, 1977), pp. 51–91.

attractive primary candidate seems to support the development of third-*candidate* (rather than third-*party*) races.
Candidates' ability to build a substantial personal following
without a serious commitment to form a durable party—in
the manner of John B. Anderson in 1980—is itself testi-
mony to recent changes in the mass communications environment. Anderson's media-based campaign was founded
on his own personality. He repeatedly assured the public
that he believed in the two-party system and that he did
not want voters to abandon their traditional party loyalties—*except* that, "when we come to the very top of the
ticket, let us put country ahead of party."[7]

Overall, the fluidity or openness provided by new intraparty structures has permitted increasing expression of
conflict within the individual party and reduced the
buildup of compression necessary in the past to produce a
realignment in a two-party system. Whether this new level
of primary election activity and the consequent permeability of the individual parties serve merely to deflect rather
than resolve important issues is, of course, an important
systemic question that will be addressed shortly. In any
case, the new structures of intraparty activities play an
important, though not the sole role in changing the operations of a two-party system.

It seems probable that the basic structural properties of
the individual party have undergone such a major transformation that it is now extremely difficult, though not impossible, to build up the kind of unarticulated, broad-based
pressure necessary to trigger a durable realignemnt. The
combination of short-term economic "buy-offs" that the
electoral system has become adept at providing and the
development of intraparty safety valves (the primaries) has
permitted the system to function—at least up to now—
without a major realignment.

To the extent that major party realignments have been
the principal vehicles by which the mass electorate makes
a major impact on public policy, this movement away from
realignments may have important consequences for the

---

[7] Quoted in the *New York Times*, June 12, 1980, section B, p. 13.

role of the voting public in affecting political change. Historically, it has been in response to major shifts in mass party coalitions—realignment—that officeholders have become more sensitive than usual to voter demands and more policy oriented. Past major realignments, such as occurred during the Civil War and New Deal periods, have brought, among other things, a president and Congress not only of the same party but also responsive to the same broad-based political forces—and thus capable of sustained policy action.[8] If the durable realignment of coalitions of the two parties is a crucial means by which voters can register their approval or disapproval of political response to important public problems, what happens to the influence of elections on public policy when realignments become unlikely?

Such a change in electoral patterns poses at least two clear possibilities within the existing political framework. First, were an economic or political crisis of great enough proportions to develop—a severe energy shortage or runaway inflation, for example—that could not be alleviated by various short-term, pressure-reducing responses, then the electorate might realign along new lines of cleavage and produce a long term redirection of public policy. Second, in the absence of any such crisis, the electoral system may gyrate with wide swings between one party and the other (i.e., "dealignment") but without producing *sustained* and *electorally directed* policy legislation. Under these circumstances, other institutions—the bureaucracy, powerful issue or interest groups, or the mass media, for example— would be free to play a relatively larger role than voters in the political process.[9]

Many questions are raised by the development of these

---

[8] See Walter Dean Burnham, Jerome M. Clubb, and William H. Flanigan, "Partisan Realignment: A Systemic Perspective," in *The History of American Electoral Behavior*, ed. Joel H. Silbey, Allan G. Bogue, and William H. Flanigan (Princeton, N.J.: Princeton University Press, 1978), pp. 64–70.

[9] For an interesting exploration of the future relationship between the mass media and the executive bureaucracy see Samuel P. Huntington, "Postindustrial Politics: How Benign Will It Be?" *Comparative Politics* 6 (1974): 163–91.

new electoral patterns that cannot adequately be explored here. Already, however, sufficient evidence exists to permit investigation of at least one set of critical questions about the impact of this new electoral circuitry on presidential relationships. Specifically, what effect has the new circuitry had on the linkage between the president and the political party? How have the new patterns of elections and the enlarged role of the press in the process affected the exercise of presidential power? And finally, in what way has the new system of running for the presidency in the new media environment transformed the exercise of presidential leadership itself?

Presidential Prestige in a New Electoral Environment

The presidency, in contrast to the political party, has grown rather than declined in its importance because of—among other factors—its ability to adapt to major changes in the communications environment. The flexibility of the office, placed in the hands of a single individual and uniquely symbolizing the collective judgment of its nation's population, has enabled certain 20th-century presidents—those with the will and the political ability to utilize the enlarged channels of mass communications—to vastly increase its centrality. Major changes in the flow of political information have challenged the primacy of the parties as cue-givers for electoral decision-making and increasingly weakened their ability to structure political conflict. But the president's ability to exploit new channels of political communications has substantially enlarged his potential influence on the political system as a whole.

The symbiotic president-party relationship established in the Jacksonian era is largely a thing of the past. In fact, the modern presidency has developed at the very expense of the political party. The persistent trend in the 20th century toward a presidency more personally than party-oriented can be clearly linked, though certainly not exclusively, to presidential assertiveness in using the mass media to reach the public directly. Presidents' increasing ability to reach mass constituencies and penetrate an individual's life space outside the traditional party informational channels has furthered the institutional separation of the presidency from the political party and encouraged presidents to draw organizational benefits and other political resources away from the parties to themselves. No longer dependent on the party for certain functions they once performed, such as the organization and dissemination of political information, presidents are increasingly free of reciprocal obligations to the party. The major expansion of presidential primaries has simultaneously removed the nomination bond between party leaders and presidential candidates, further encouraging institutional separation between presidents and their party's apparatus.

The weakening of linkages between the political party and the presidency is one of a number of media-related developments that has affected the stability of public confidence in the president's leadership.[10] The weakening of such key political institutions as the parties and the strengthening of the press have, together, contributed to the *unmooring* of presidential popularity from its traditional anchorages. A new volatility of presidential popularity has only recently developed—with increasingly rapid swings up and down in public confidence—that has weakened, consequently, the president's staying power in office and his ability to govern. With the exception of John Kennedy, who was assassinated, none of the presidents since 1960 could gain and complete the two full terms despite their desire to remain in office. One-term presidencies may be a major effect of the growing volatility of public confidence in the president, since the new electoral circuitry permits sharp declines in the public's confidence to produce challenges from within as well as from without his own party.

The major change in the stability of the public's confi-

---

[10] For an analysis of presidential popularity and presidential leadership see Richard E. Neustadt, *Presidential Power: The Politics of Leadership* (New York: John Wiley, 1960).

dence in presidential leadership can be clearly identified as occurring in the early 1970s. The author's recent examination of monthly changes (Gallup) in popular support over the last thirty years shows a rapid increase in the volatility of the president's prestige as a leader after 1972.

Figure 7 charts the major change in the stability of public confidence in presidential leadership. From 1950 to 1972, for example, the variability of public confidence in presidential leadership within each year—the rapidity of monthly changes up or down—shows a similar pattern and range (a mean standard deviation of 4.2).[11]

The measures of variability from 1972 through 1979 were patently much higher than those of the earlier period (averaging 7.3 and reaching a peak of 12 in the later years of the Nixon presidency). Even ignoring the Watergate resignation year, the volatility of presidential prestige after 1972 is 43 percent higher than the average over the preceding twenty-two years. (One might argue that a genuine comparison must include the Watergate period, because the wide dissemination of information about the events collectively termed Watergate was dependent not only on the instigating events themselves but on the intensity and adversary nature of press coverage.) Even Harry Truman's declining popularity during the Korean War and Lyndon Johnson's drop during the Vietnam War were significantly slower than the declines in the later 1970s.[12]

The post-Watergate presidencies of Ford and Carter both reflected the trend toward heightening volatility of presidential prestige. Carter's presidency particularly resembled an increasingly rapid roller coaster of ups and downs of public confidence in his leadership. Carter's rapid

[11] The volatility of public approval of presidential performance has been measured by using a series of Gallup polls. However, since Gallup has not normally polled through the last six months of presidential election years, election years themselves have not been included in the figures. Because of this circumstance, the increasing volatility of public opinion is probably *underplayed*. In addition, figures for 1974 are omitted because of the midterm resignation of Richard Nixon.

[12] See John E. Mueller, *War, Presidents, and Public Opinion* (New York: John Wiley, 1973), pp. 196–231.

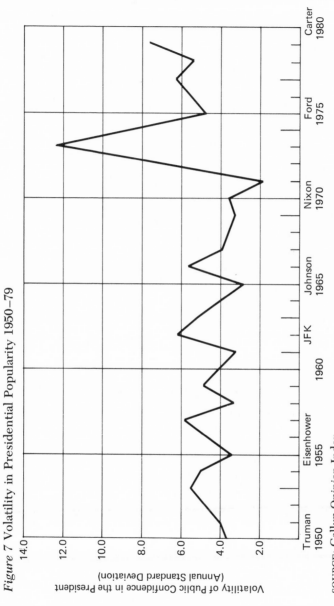

Figure 7 Volatility in Presidential Popularity 1950–79

SOURCE: Gallup Opinion Index

drop in the fall of 1979 to approval by approximately one-quarter of the American population—in the absence of a major political scandal, war, or sharp recession—indicates not only the deeply erosive force of inflation on political popularity, but also—and very clearly—the extreme volatility of public esteem for the president. For perspective, at the lowest point of Lyndon Johnson's popularity during the worst period of the Vietnam War, approval of his leadership ran between 10 to 15 percent higher than Carter's. Carter's unprecedented one-month rise in approval to 61 percent after the taking of American hostages by Iran in November 1979, his fall by June 1980 to 23 percent, and his moderate (but insufficient) rise by the time of the general election in November 1980 offer striking evidence of an accentuation of a broad political trend begun in the early 1970s.

This heightened volatility of presidential prestige, featuring more rapid swings in public feeling for and against the president, appears related in part to the growth of both presidential and press influence over the "presidential image." On the one hand, the president can command public attention by creating news-making events of interest to the mass media. He is, therefore, more able than past presidents to manipulate or coordinate news for his own political advantage through his unparalleled ability to get substantial amounts of free network television time. In addition, the president controls a large cluster of communications resources, from press conferences to "reports" to the nation. These resources can maximize his advantages during political crises or, in noncrisis periods, promote his standing with the public.[13]

On the other hand, the press, collectively, is far more powerful, both in its range and depth of political penetration, than it was only a few decades ago. Particularly since the experiences of Vietnam and, more particularly, Watergate, which involved a major confrontation between the

---

[13] See Newton N. Minow, John Bartlow Martin, and Lee M. Mitchell, *Presidential Television* (New York: Basic Books, 1973), pp. 17–68.

national media and the national administration, the press
has cultivated a less trustful, more autonomous, and more
critical posture than it had previously adopted toward the
presidency. This lack of reverence for the presidency, combined with the enormously increased reach of the mass
media, has offset most, if not all, of the president's mass
communications assets. In any case, the powerful position
of the press, on one side, and the president's own communications resources, on the other, have jointly expanded
the means for more rapidly enlarging or decreasing public
confidence in the president's leadership than in the past.
Certainly, with respect to its focus on the president, the
traditional sluggishness of public opinion has been markedly changed.[14]

But neither presidential influence over the flow of mass
communications nor the press's posture vis-á-vis the president is sufficient by itself to explain the increasingly rapid
changes in public confidence that have characterized
recent presidencies. Certain other factors, some circum-
stantial, some directly related to mass media changes, others only indirectly, need to be considered in order to
understand better both the growing volatility of presidential prestige and the relationship of this volatility to the
quality and durability of presidential leadership. Rather
than emphasizing the impact of specific events on a president, concern shall be focused on the *susceptibility* of the
contemporary presidency to changes in public confidence,
that is, on other institutional changes that have collectively
unmoored the president's popularity from its stabilizing
underpinnings. For example, the increasing separation of
a presidential candidate from his party's organization—i.e.,

---

[14] For an earlier view of the viscosity of public opinion see V. O. Key,
Jr., *Public Opinion and American Democracy* (New York: Knopf, 1961),
pp. 235–236. For findings of increasingly rapid shifts of opinion about
national governmental leadership elsewhere see Walter Dean Burnham,
"Great Britain: The Death of the Collectivist Censensus?" in *Political
Parties: Development and Decay*, ed. Louis Maisel and Joseph Cooper,
Sage Electoral Studies Yearbook, vol. 4 (Beverly Hills, California: Sage
Publications, 1978), pp. 290–92.

a politician's increased ability to gain the presidency by
independent, nonorganizational appeals—has weakened
the obligations of party elites to support an incumbent
president when he is in trouble, particularly if he won the
nomination without their support. For instance, after the
1976 election, which he won as an "independent" Democrat, Carter received little support from party elites whom
he had run against.

Even more important, the weakening of party *loyalty*
among rank-and-file voters, accentuated by the lack of
strong realigning issues between the two parties, has
removed a significant counterweight to rapid drops in presidential popularity. Firm party identification held by
masses of individuals, for example, has been an important
factor in stabilizing popular support for a president even
when events worked against him. Both in adverse foreign
and domestic policy situations, strong partisan identification "shielded" losses for the president in the public's confidence in his leadership.[15]

The weakening of allegiance to a political party—a loyalty built by accumulated knowledge, or "memory," from
a combination of party positions, presidential candidates,
local values, and personal experiences—has left presidential popularity relatively isolated and unsupplemented by
traditional institutional loyalties. Encouraged by their
increased opportunities to use the new mass media to go
into business for themselves, presidential candidates and
presidents have simultaneously accelerated their own separation from their parties. They have thus left themselves
relatively more "free floating" than ever before in the
quickly shifting streams of public approval and disapproval.

Another factor affecting the volatility of presidential popularity, partly related to changes in party loyalty, is the
increasing fragmentation of socioeconomic and political
classes. Scholars link past electoral realignments in American politics with the ascent or decline of major economic-
political groups or classes. The decline of agrarian groups
after 1896 and the rise of industrial labor after the New

---

[15] See Mueller, *War, Presidents, and Public Opinion*, p. 250.

Deal realignment are clear instances.[16] But if, as evidence suggests, definable political classes—such as, for example, Irish Catholics were only several decades ago—are becoming increasingly divided into smaller political subsets, and if the "middle class" consists, in fact, of only a wide variety of competing, socioeconomically diverse occupational and income groups, then the newly fragmented socioeconomic structure beneath electoral politics will only have increased the opportunity for candidates to emphasize personal-image politics. Without definable socioeconomic groups underpinning the parties in the system, and without party loyalty underpinning public confidence in the president, an institutionally and structurally unconnected president must depend on his personal image (and thus on "media politics") to sustain himself.

Further unmooring presidential popularity from its traditional anchorages is the growing sensitivity and aggressiveness of opposing political elites. Among the sources of their increasingly assertive posture are the improved availability of hard statistical information and the technology, such as polling, which can tighten the link between leaders and the popular mood, make "facts" politically convertible, and reduce the "insulating space" for incumbent presidents against potential competitors.[17] For instance, in recent decades our ability to monitor closely various types of social, economic, and political change has increased remarkably, making more available than ever before the statistical raw materials facilitating surveillance by competing elites of various conditions and problems, and the public appreciation of presidential response to them. Whether with respect to small increases or decreases in rates of inflation or unemployment, housing starts, or, for that matter, presidential popularity, a vast series of statistical indicators now assist political and media elites in projecting trends. The new fast-moving flow of mass communications means

---

[16] For an interesting analysis of the breakdown of solid political groups see Ladd and Hadley, *Transformations of the American Party System*, pp. 182–267.

[17] See Daniel Bell, "Notes on the Post-Industrial Society," *Public Interest*, 7 (Spring 1967), pp. 108–10.

that shifts in indicators need not be drastic to encourage potential challengers of the president. Political leaders now very much believe that the new media environment can easily exploit and magnify small shifts in various indicators to create vast shifts in public opinion.

Several other factors fuel the willingness and ability of political leaders to oppose the president with both words and acts, particularly when the crest of his popularity has receded after his first year or two in office. To a certain extent, the severe political problems of the Johnson and Nixon administrations, though different in nature, opened the presidency to increasingly frequent and successful critical attacks by both political and media elites. As a result, intense criticism of the president has become relatively acceptable. It seems probable that, regardless of actual presidential performance, the comparatively soft treatment of Presidents Eisenhower and Kennedy will not be duplicated in the near future.[18]

These isolating features collectively tend to quicken the erosion of public confidence in the president. But by far the most important systemic effect of recent institutional changes is the potential magnification of weaknesses in presidential prestige, which the new fluid electoral circuitry accentuates. The presidential primaries, an open intraparty electoral arena, permit the ready conversion of drops in presidential approval ratings into powerful intraparty challenges. Presidents thus face possible political rejection even before they face the electorate as a whole. Even if a president is able to successfully overcome internal challenges in the primaries, a defensive posture adopted for a prolonged period may weaken his chances in the following general election—as both Ford in 1976 and Carter in 1980 learned. In fact, a CBS election-day survey of actual voters in the 1980 election has shown that fully one-third of all Democrats supporting Kennedy in the primaries did not support Carter in the subsequent general election.[19]

In effect, the president's electoral "leash" has been sig-

---

[18] See Tom Wicker, *On Press* (New York: Viking, 1978), pp. 90–106.
[19] New York Times/CBS News Poll, *New York Times*, Nov. 9, 1980, p. 28.

nificantly shortened by a new electoral relationship between the president, the party, and the press incorporating: (1) a new aggressiveness and increased range and depth of penetration of the press; (2) the decline of stabilizing presidential supports; and (3) growing presidential vulnerability to a new set of intraparty challengers via the presidential primaries. As a result, a president today has significantly less political leeway than he had only a decade or so ago, for the combination of a new two-step popular election process and increasingly influential mass media institutions tends to work against sustained presidential leadership.

Scholars consistently find that presidential popularity declines after a relatively brief "honeymoon," although there is much disagreement as to which factors may be more important in causing the drop.[20] What is new in the present situation, however, is that, first, the downward pitch of public confidence in the president is much more rapid than in the past, and, second, a popular slide by the incumbent can now be more easily converted into either a debilitating internal challenge or the actual loss of the nomination itself. Before the extraordinary expansion of the presidential primaries, for example, even a president with a relatively low level of popular approval, such as Truman in 1948, was virtually immune from popular attack from *within* his own party. In fact, challenges from both the left and right in the Democratic party in 1948 were forced into external challenges—Henry Wallace and the Progressive party, on the left, and Strom Thurmond and the Dixiecrat party, on the right. Similarly, President Hoover easily turned aside popular challenges for the nomination in 1932, despite the tensions built by three-and-a-half years of depression.[21]

When a contemporary president rides high in public

---

[20] See the arguments made by Samuel Kernell, "Explaining Presidential Popularity," *American Political Science Review* 72 (1978): 506–22; and James A. Stimson, "Public Support for American Presidents: A Cyclical Model," mimeo, 1974.

[21] See James A. Davis, *Presidential Primaries: The Road to the White House* (New York: Thomas Y. Crowell, 1967), pp. 72–73.

confidence, some new and significant policies can be initiated, particularly when the direction of intense waves of
public opinion and presidential purpose coincide. He
nevertheless commands no *new* weapons that might better
enable him to convert such favorable popular esteem into
bargaining advantages beyond the short-run. He still lacks
institutional means to persuade other governmental leaders to act favorably on his proposed programs for a sustained period, his program being heavily dependent on
waves of popularity—that have been proven to be of short
duration—and on producing quick results. Particularly in
domestic politics, where the president does not enjoy a
substantial array of constitutional prerogatives, his lack of
partisan tools to induce cohesion between the executive
and the legislative branches usually seriously constrains
him, oftentimes even when he has the benefit of the public's favor and confidence. Thus, to the extent that Richard
Neustadt's model of "influence conversion" holds—i.e.,
that the level of the president's public popularity or prestige can be converted under certain circumstances into
"persuasion" in terms of public policy—the new electoral
circuitry has added little, if anything, durable to help the
offensive side of the presidency while substantially weakening the defensive side.

Another major result of the combination of mass communications strength and party organizational weakness
has been to make it more difficult for a president to take a
long view as a political leader. This combination *raises the
costs* of taking positions that, though unpopular in the short
run, might enable a president to lead or transform public
opinion in the long run.[22] The new, shorter electoral leash
provides less rather than more time for a president to satisfy his increasingly diverse, short-tempered opposition.
This, in turn, restricts his ability to develop long-term solutions to problems by limiting the time he has to educate
the electorate before he is dispatched.

---

[22] For an illuminating discussion of different kinds of political leadership see James MacGregor Burns, *Leadership* (New York: Harper, Row,
1978).

There are, of course, strategies that wise presidents might pursue to improve their increasingly difficult lot. They might, for example, use existing presidential patronage forcefully and astutely to "convince" party members in Congress to help the president's program; use the mass media imaginatively to arouse the public on specific policies; or bring important congressional leaders actively into the administration's policy planning procedures for purposes of advancing executive-legislative cohesion. Nonetheless, the major political problem of short-run politics will persist in the absence of substantial intra- and inter-institutional changes to increase the speed and centralizing thrust of domestic policy-making processes. Particularly as long-run domestic problems—such as energy, inflation, and race—dominate American politics, the weaknesses, not the strength, of the presidency in the domestic policy process will become increasingly apparent.

What has apparently occurred is a major expansion in the ability of the electoral system to express or articulate a variety of political demands—but with little or no change in the government's ability to *translate* such electoral expression into cohesive policy legislation. Though the two electoral arenas, primaries and general elections, provide a basis for an open and sensitive electoral system, the institutional linkages connecting elections to *public policy* have, if anything, weakened rather than strengthened. An already existing disjunction in the political system has been enlarged, for, while knowledge of public wants has increased and the various electoral systems offer greater opportunity for expression of them, the policy-making system—except for brief bursts—has not kept pace.

Only in foreign affairs does the president have a powerful base of resources, both constitutional and situational, with which he can develop national policy—and these have been recently trimmed.[23] But with respect to domestic policy, both the public's demands on and expectations of a

---

[23] See Arthur M. Schlesinger, Jr., *The Imperial Presidency* (Boston: Houghton Mifflin, 1973). See also Richard M. Pious, *The American Presidency* (New York: Basic Books, 1979), pp. 332–70.

president have increased substantially, the ability of voters to express dissatisfaction has also increased markedly, but the new electoral circuitry provides the executive office with short-run tools to do a long-run job. The apparent alienation of Americans from established political institutions may in part result from this growing gap between increased opportunities for electoral articulation—unsynthesized by weak parties—and the limited production of cohesive and durable public policy.

A Perspective: Linking the Past and Future

The structure and mode of operation of instutitions, such as the parties and the presidency, are intimately tied to the scope, velocity, and centralization of mass communications. When the focus, range, and velocity of mass communications change, pressure is exerted on these same electoral institutions to adapt to the new environment. By adapting, or failing to adapt, these institutions then change their relationships with other institutional sources of power and reignite mass-elite dynamics in the political system as a whole.

The weakening of the political parties is clearly related to major changes in the level and intensity of mass communications and the inability of the parties to respond adequately to the new communications environment. In addition to the loss of material incentives that have clearly weakened parties organizationally, the American parties have declined more rapidly because their decentralized structure has seemingly required the existence of only limited amounts of political information outside of party channels and a far less centralized mass communications structure than now exists. The centralizing thrust of direct electronic media may well be incompatible with the decentralized political parties that traditionally functioned primarily to manage a large number of elections and only secondarily—largely during major realignments—to produce cohesive national public policy. The parties' failure to develop into focused policy-shaping mechanisms may have left them, in the light of new communications developments that rob them of their informational significance, as only vestigial campaign organizations needing a new purpose.[24]

The presidency, in contrast, provides a more complex problem of analysis, for its nimble adaptability to the modernizing and centralizing trends of the 20th-century media environment has enabled it to thrive, at least initially. However, recent presidential difficulties in sustaining political leadership—Carter and Ford both defeated seeking reelection, Nixon forced to resign, Johnson pressured into foregoing a run for a second elected term—should give warning that powerful mass media institutions and "open" or porous party institutions have changed the electoral circuitry, making presidents far more vulnerable than in the past. Less attached than formerly to other institutional supports, the unmoored presidency has become at the same time the isolated focus of unrealistic public expectations.

While the mass media increasingly direct public expectations at the president, as the hub of national government, the tools available to the president for dealing with such pressing domestic problems as energy, inflation, race, and the environment are more limited than ever. The president is generally on weak political ground in directing the flow of domestic policy, and recent electoral restructuring has made his negotiating position still weaker. Not only has his public prestige become increasingly susceptible to rapid deflation (providing, consequently, a weakened bargaining position), but also any significant weakening of the public's confidence in his leadership can now be more easily converted—as both our last two incumbents, Ford and Carter found out—into a contest for the presidential nomination itself. Even if these primary challenges are not successful, open primary conflict, magnified by intense and influential press coverage, creates deep divisions among

---

[24] For a different but related perspective on American political institutions see Samuel P. Huntington, *Political Order in Changing Societies* (New Haven: Yale University Press, 1968), pp. 93–139.

key groups in the party's coalition that are not easily healed before or after the general election. "Building coalitions in the United States today," Anthony King noted, "is like trying to build coalitions out of sand," and the job of governing is clearly made more difficult by the present primary system.[25] As a result, while the new electoral circuitry has produced an additional measure of electoral sensitivity to perceived public needs, it has simultaneously lost a measure of presidential persuasion that can integrate electoral and governing coalitions over time.

The impact of the press on the new political configuration reflects the special role of mass communications in present-day American politics. In a much enlarged and centrally focused political information process, a greatly strengthened press today serves, without conscious motive, to weaken traditional political institutions. In fact, its relative influence on politics is increased by virtue of the very instability it has induced. The historical analysis of the New Deal realignment showed that when political institutions were strong the press's independent influence upon American politics was relatively limited. But the major increase in the velocity, intensity, and depth of penetration of the new electronic media has changed a key variable in the political equation and, as a result, accelerated the weakening of the political parties and ultimately destabilized the operations of the presidency.

What is particularly different about the press today is not its motives or intentions, but the new speed and centralizing thrust of political information that the communications revolution has encouraged. Its role in American life has grown with its heightened ability to alter the environment in which political leaders operate and the mass public responds. Pursuing its own organizational and journalistic ends, it transmits a vastly increased quantity of information about personalities, images, and issues to the public. The

---

[25] Anthony King, "The American Polity in the Late 1970s: Building Coalitions in the Sand," in *The New American Political System*, ed. Anthony King (Washington, D.C.: American Enterprise Institute, 1978), p. 391.

substantial centralization of mass communications brought about by the development of electronic media has thus apparently tipped a critical balance between the flow of information and the political institutions that process and respond to those communications.

Before television expanded the impact of the press as a whole, a rough balance existed between the print mass media and the political system. Both were strongly localistic, primarily focused on narrow or segmented audiences, and there was little if any direct, unmediated contact between national leaders and local audiences. But the rise of the electronic media has exacerbated tensions in the relationships between now centralized mass media institutions and still decentralized, fragmented, political and governmental institutions, established in an entirely different environment of informational and political expectation. These new tensions have destabilized the relationships that underpinned traditional electoral structures, and they show themselves in the widening gap between our electoral system's ability, on the one hand, to provide increased expression of nationally directed demands and the national government's apparent inability, on the other hand, to effectively translate and organize these jumbled demands into cohesive, long-term legislative policy. The presidency itself gained initially from the increased focus of both public demands and mass communications on the national government, being better equipped than other institutions to provide political and symbolic direction to the activation of the national government. But the present environment of increasingly rapid, centrally focused mass communications, and the disjunction between the public's electoral demands on the president and his ability to develop and sustain cohesive public policy, has now made the presidency the focus of unfulfillable expectations.[26]

Despite occasional short periods of major presidential

---

[26] See Thomas E. Cronin, *The State of the Presidency*, 2nd ed. (Boston: Little, Brown, 1980), p. 375. Also Stephen J. Wayne, "Expectations of the President," a paper delivered at the American Political Science Association annual meeting, August 1980.

policy initiatives—Johnson from 1964 to 1966 and Reagan early in his administration—the dominant mode of American governance has been one of policy fragmentation rather than cohesion. Recent presidents have had great difficulty in confronting important policy choices. When they benefit from a strong wave of popular mood and capitalize on it with the expert use of the mass media, they can, as Reagan did in his first year, produce the initial legislation for their programs. But the promises of early results that are necessary to swing such legislation almost assuredly raise the public's expectations of the president still further, and it is unlikely that such expectations can be met quickly enough in the new media environment to appease an increasingly short-tempered electorate. While there may be bursts of presidential popularity and legislative accomplishments, a one-term presidency is likely to predominate until and unless *institutionalized supports*, rather than occasional and unsustainable "image highs," can restabilize an unmoored presidency.

The rapid growth of a full-blown primary election system has—unintentionally—compounded the problem by weakening rather than strengthening a valuable political institution—the parties—that could be used to build crucial coalitions to bridge the distance between the *substance of elections* and the *substance of governance*. Many critics of party reform respond to the growing dissatisfaction with the present primary process by presenting a variety of "reforms of the reforms" to reduce some of the unanticipated results that have diminished the role of the parties in politics and consequently enlarged the role of the press. A number of proffered suggestions, such as shortening the length of the primary season, clustering the primaries on a smaller number of election dates, or encouraging states to hold fewer primaries, deserve close and careful consideration. But no modifications are likely to be of much value unless they take into account the broad context of governance as a whole.

The excitement of an almost weekly series of elections, changes in strategies, ups and downs, and winners and losers, obscures the extent to which the new nomination system has widened an already existing separation between the presidency and his party in the legislature and worked against efforts to coordinate public policy between these two institutions. The new primary election system almost fully devalues the influence congressional party leaders have over their party's presidential nomination, largely excluding from nomination decision-making these political leaders who hold political power when the primaries and general election are over. As now structured, the primaries make the presidential nomination a game played almost exclusively by ad hoc election experts, media and election specialists with few connections to pre- or post-election governing leaders. Carter's single term in office clearly reflects the problems of gaining the presidency without support from existing leaders with whom one must later deal as an incumbent.

The primary election system that produced Carter severely weakens operational links between the nomination process and later governing processes. Thus it serves to deepen the constitutional distance that already separates the president from other governmental leaders. Presidential difficulties in forming solid and sustained operating ties with congressional leaders and in maintaining public approval of his performance are related to the general isolation of on-going political leadership from the process of choosing the president.

However, the suggestion offered by some critics that we return to "old style" nomination politics by shifting substantial power back into the hands of state and local party *organizational* leaders—away from the existing combination of candidate entrepreneurs, press, and rank-and-file primary voters—is not at all realistic. Neither public nor elite opinion is likely to tolerate an effort to return the nomination to a process controlled by local organizational leaders—the "bosses"—particularly in the contemporary media environment. One cannot easily envisage either an increasingly independent electorate or the press yielding a controlling influence over the selection of a presidential nominee to some nonpopularly selected and little-known local party officials. At the same time, it is clear that some kind of on-going professional leadership is needed to counterbalance a volatile and distorting primary system. The present system clearly overvalues early contests, undervalues later ones, and leaves no margin for assessing important but late-developing events, shifts of rank-and-file sentiment, or developing candidate flaws. It provides no means by which experienced party leaders can make deliberative or evaluative contribution to the nomination process.

If we cannot return to the old type of party decision-making, and since the present system of primaries weakens the parties and decreases the operating effectiveness of the national government at a time when we need more cohesive and sustainable policy responses than in the past, then what alternatives have we? Specifically, we can inject into the nomination process a new, influential, but not controlling, role for on-going party leadership—not by returning power to local party organizational leaders, but, rather, by yielding some prestructured influence to *elected party members in the national government*. Suppose, for example, that all U.S. senators and members of the House automatically became delegates to their party's convention and would represent approximately 20 percent of each convention's votes. In districts or states where a party has no incumbent sitting, the party's successful congressional *nominee* for the subsequent general election would be sent to the convention—tightening the necessary link between congressional and presidential fortunes—to join in the selection process. A small percentage of statewide elected or organizational leaders should also be sent as delegates.

Such a modification would produce at least two results. First, it would tend to restabilize the primary process by returning some professional party judgment to the presidential nomination process without eliminating the major influence of party rank-and-file voters. Elected national party representatives would leaven the nomination process, though they would not control it, by bringing legislative leaders in government into the choice of the presidential nominee. The convention power delegated to these representatives would tend, for example, to keep the primaries from being decided prematurely, and would thus enable states holding late primaries to maintain their proportionate influence and importance. In addition, having approximately 20 to 25 percent of the convention vote in the hands of party leaders also adds a degree of political protection should a candidate who wins early primaries and knocks out various contenders then reveal serious personal or political liabilities late in his campaign. A convention with slightly over a fifth of its delegates drawn largely, but not exclusively, from *elected* governmental leaders would provide flexibility, balance, and experience, while still continuing to allow for substantial public and media participation in a broad-based primary system. A party leadership role is thus reinjected into the presidential nomination—a reform restabilizing the electoral circuitry—that would reconstitute coalition-building influences without yielding major delegate influence to local party leaders who have no popular political base.

The second and most important result of such a modification is that it would help to recast the political parties in a new mold, one that could produce political parties more capable of creating and implementing public policy than parties at present seem able to do. The problem of governmental fragmentation—when even a Congress controlled by the same party as the president cannot produce coordinated and sustained sets of legislation on pressing issues—has always existed. But no longer does the luxury of abundant resources permit us to avoid hard policy decisions. Real choices, not just log-rolling decisions, or no decisions at all, must be made, and these will require not only stronger but also more policy oriented parties than were necessary in the past. Even if expert use of the mass media can build a president's image and produce policy initiatives in the short-run, image and style wear thin in a few years if workable policy legislation is not sustained by a party apparatus.

Reinvigoration of the governing apparatus will be difficult at best and no proposal or set of proposals for reform can make more than just a beginning in what will be a long and difficult process. But it is a process that must be attempted. The present primary structure has made governing increasingly difficult, for it has isolated nomination politics almost totally from the subsequent legislative process—as Congress can remind a successful primary nominee should he subsequently take presidential office. Congressional party members, with little influence in the selection of the presidential nominee, have, in turn, few durable obligations to the promises and platforms produced at the convention, or to the successful nominee. This modification of the nomination process would tend to increase rather than decrease *shared political responsibility* and increasingly obligate and hold accountable a congressional party—both sitting members of Congress and successful party nominees—that has shared in the choice of the presidential candidate to back up its choice with legislative action. Conversely, a president with some obligation for his nomination (and, perhaps, his renomination) to his fellow party members in Congress is reasonably likely to develop the necessary long-term working relationship with Congress that will yield coalition-building and cohesive policy rather than confrontation, stalemate, or ineffectiveness.

The link between electoral demands and national governmental policy—between expression in elections and production of legislation by government—has not been a tight relationship historically. National legislative outputs produced by an intentionally fragmented system generally lagged behind electorally articulated dissatisfaction, the gap being narrowed by major realignments or short bursts of legislation. But the expectations of the electorate for national governmental action were, during much of our history, low, while the flow of political information, which tends to increase expectations and widen the gap, was limited in scope, volume, and depth of penetration. The apparently unlimited resources of a young nation, its limited need for hard redistributive governmental decisions, and the decentralized nature of mass communications all tended to reinforce the strength of political institutions by keeping the gap between public demand and government output from widening excessively.

In contemporary America, the gap between electorally expressed demands and the national government's production of effective and durable political responses has increased substantially. Our institutions and leaders have failed to respond to our new political and communications environment. If they do not respond with alacrity, the disjunction between the increasingly rapid and fluid *electoral circuitry* and government's laborious and disjointed *policy circuitry* will eventually undermine American politics, turning presidential elections into mere sound and fury signifying nothing. Major developments in mass communications, an example of the country's capacity for productive innovation, have markedly—and permanently—changed our political environment. They have thus forcefully indicated the need for further redevelopment of traditional political institutions. The demonstrated flexibility of America's past political institutions offers some hope that our present leaders can adapt to the new political-communications environment, for the political system has enjoyed luxuries that it can no longer afford.

Index

Index

Collins, Charles, 69*n*
Comstock, George, 171*n*
Congress, U.S., 22, 70–74, 85, 100–101
Congressional Caucus, 24, 27
conventions, 106, 109, 149–50, 184, 186, 187, 188
Converse, Phillip E., 105*n*, 186*n*
Cooper, Joseph, 107*n*, 223*n*
Cornwell, Elmer E., Jr., 86*n*, 129*n*
correspondents:
    television, 161, 163–64
    Washington, 85, 87, 127–29, 138, 162, 163
corruption:
    "machines" and, 73–74, 106–8
    as news, 60, 99–102
Cosmopolitan, 99, 100
Crawford, William H., 24–25
credibility, 130, 150
Croly, Herbert, 98*n*
Cronin, Thomas E., 233*n*
Crotty, William, 110*n*, 203*n*, 208*n*
Crouse, Timothy, 168*n*
Crump, Ed, 142
Cunningham, Noble, Jr., 21*n*, 24*n*, 51*n*

Davis, Allen F., 140*n*
Davis, Dennis, 171*n*
Davis, James W., 109*n*, 187*n*, 227*n*
Davis, Otto A., 202*n*, 204*n*
Davison, W. Phillips, 171*n*
Dean, Morton, 194*n*
decentralization, 30–31, 67–68, 70–74
Degler, Carl N., 95*n*
demobilization:
    of party organization, 104–13
    of presidency, 65–70
Democratic party, 74, 106, 187–90, 192–93, 203–4, 206, 215, 227
    Franklin D. Roosevelt and, 142–45
    Populism and, 90, 93–94
denationalization, *see* decentralization
Depression, 117–18, 121
Diamond, William, 95*n*
differentiation, 76–83
Dorsett, Lyle W., 142*n*
Dreyer, Edward C., 172*n*
Duverger, Maurice, 10

economy, American, 78, 115–24
Edelman, Murray, 117*n*
Eisenhower, Dwight D., 150
Elder, C. D., 117*n*, 176*n*
elections:
    1800, 48*n*
    1824, 24–28, 33, 35, 42
    1828, 29–37, 42, 48–49

1832, 30, 42
1840, 42
1872, 59
1884, 59–60
1896, 82, 90, 93–95, 106, 137
1904, 109
1912, 109–10, 188
1924, 132, 137, 140
1928, 132, 140
1932, 126, 132, 142, 227
1936, 126, 127, 138
1948, 227
1952, 203
1960, 150, 203
1964, 149–50, 203
1968, 188, 190, 192–93, 204, 215
1972, 174, 175, 188–89, 190, 192–93, 199, 204, 215
1976, 169, 174, 189, 190, 198, 199, 202, 203, 204, 215, 224, 226
1980, 178–79, 199, 203, 204, 216, 226
    see also primaries
electoral circuitry, 5–6, 52, 211–39
    analysis of, 230–39
    presidency and, 218–30
    realignment and, 213–18
electoral college, 29–30
Emery, Edwin, 11*n*, 57*n*, 60*n*, 126*n*, 136*n*, 138*n*
Epstein, Edward Jay, 161*n*, 163*n*, 164
Epstein, Leon D., 185*n*
Erbring, Lutz, 173*n*
Examiner, 21

Farley, James A., 142
FCC (Federal Communications Commission), 161, 162, 166
Federalist Papers, 6, 26–27, 52–53
Federalist party, 11–17, 27
Fenno, John, 11–14
Filler, Louis, 99*n*, 100*n*, 101*n*
Fireside Chats, 132–33, 139
Fish, Carl Russell, 38–39
Flanigan, William H., 116*n*, 217*n*
Flynn, Ed, 142
Forcey, Charles, 98*n*
Frazier, P. J., 117*n*
freedom of the press, 7, 14–17, 18–19, 35
Freneau, Philip, 13–14

Galderesi, Peter F., 215*n*
Galloway, George B., 71*n*, 72*n*
Gallup polls, 220, 221
Gannett chain, 126*n*
Gans, Herbert, 165*n*
Garraty, John Arthur, 67*n*
Garrow, David J., 155*n*